W9-BKV-302

★ THE HUMAN FACTOR

★ THE HUMAN FACTOR

Inside the CIA's Dysfunctional Intelligence Culture

Ishmael Jones

ENCOUNTER BOOKS
New York and London

Copyright © 2008 by Ishmael Jones

All rights reserved. No part of this publication may be reproduced, stored in a retrieval system, or transmitted, in any form or by any means, electronic, mechanical, photocopying, recording, or otherwise, without the prior written permission of Encounter Books, 900 Broadway Suite 601, New York, New York, 10003.

First edition published in 2008 by Encounter Books, an activity of Encounter for Culture and Education, Inc., a nonprofit, tax exempt corporation.

Encounter Books website address: www.encounterbooks.com

Book design and composition by Wesley B. Tanner / Passim Editions, Ann Arbor. Manufactured in the United States and printed on acid-free paper.

♾ The paper used in this publication meets the minimum requirements of ANSI/ NISO Z39.48-1992 (R 1997) (Permanence of Paper).

FIRST EDITION

Library of Congress Cataloging-in-Publication Data

Jones, Ishmael.
     The human factor : inside the CIA's dysfunctional intelligence culture / by Ishmael Jones.
          p. cm.
     Includes bibliographical references and index.
     ISBN-13: 978-1-59403-223-3 (hardcover : alk. paper)
     ISBN-10: 1-59403-223-8 (hardcover : alk. paper) 1. Jones, Ishmael. 2. United States. Central Intelligence Agency. 3. Intelligence officers—United States. 4. Intelligence service—United States. I. Title.
     JK468.I6J68 2008
     327.1273—dc22   2008001921

"One good spy is worth 10,000 soldiers."

Sun Tzu

"I would trade every satellite in the sky for
one reliable informant."

Army Lieutenant Colonel Ross Brown,
Cavalry Squadron Commander,
3rd Armored Cavalry Regiment,
South of Baghdad

Author's Note

All individuals, unless they are public figures, are obscured in order to make it impossible to identify any CIA employee or agent. Dates and places of non-public events have been obscured or changed. No classified information, sources, or methods are revealed. As a former CIA employee, I was required to submit the book to CIA censors for their approval. I initially sent a copy of the manuscript to the CIA's Publications Review Board, asking them to identify any classified information, which I would then take out. I am an expert on what portions of intelligence operations constitute classified information and already knew there were none. Without reviewing the book, the CIA disapproved the publication of every word. During the course of a year, I repeated my request to the CIA that it identify any classified information in the book. The CIA eventually returned it to me with all but a few paragraphs wiped out. Words deemed appropriate for public viewing by the CIA were reduced to less than one percent throughout the book.

Before writing this book, I exhausted all avenues open to me to improve human intelligence programs. I repeatedly confronted all levels of my chain of command without result. I met with the Inspector General's office, but found it a broken system—the IG was not up to the task and was under investigation by the FBI for leaks.

The Director at the time was sympathetic and cleared the way for my final foreign assignment, but he was soon removed and replaced by managers who represent the status quo. No anti-corruption or whistleblower systems exist in the organization, possibly because the CIA's official secrecy makes such checks and balances dead-ends. Only open, public debate will lead to reform.

I worked with the CIA's censors in good faith. During telephone conversations, CIA censors seemed to recognize the manuscript contained no classified information and at one point suggested it might be approved with minor revisions. During each of my many communications with the censors, I repeated: Show me the classified information in this book and I will take it out. In each case they replied, after months of delay, with evasive letters, from anonymous P.O. boxes, signed by people using fictitious names.

I believe the CIA sought to block publication of this book solely because it is critical of the organization. All of the dozens of books written by ex-CIA officers and approved by the CIA demonstrate that censorship standards are lax and inconsistent. Some of the books, especially the recent Tenet and Drumheller books, reveal what I consider to be a startling amount of classified information. These books criticize the President, however, and not the organization.

Funds allocated to protect Americans are being stolen or wasted on phony or nonexistent intelligence programs. By attempting to censor this manuscript, the CIA puts Americans at risk. The purpose of the book is to add to the criticism and debate about reform of the organization. Criticism and debate is how we solve things in America and I consider it my duty to publish this manuscript.

Contents

Introduction

Human sources are those individuals who provide information about terrorist organizations and hostile governments. Gathering intelligence from human sources is the fundamental purpose of the Central Intelligence Agency's clandestine service. Some of the most important foreign policy decisions made by United States Presidents require this intelligence.

Lack of good human sources can be a President's downfall.

George W. Bush's presidency was poisoned by a lack of human source intelligence on the 9/11 terrorist attacks, the Iraq war, and the issue of Iraqi weapons of mass destruction (WMD). President Clinton's legacy was tarnished by the 9/11 attacks, and he was taken by surprise by the arms race on the Asian subcontinent. Presidents Reagan and Carter were humiliated by hostage crises. Lack of reliable information about the Soviet Union nearly led to war on several occasions. The 1973 Arab/Israeli war took President Nixon by surprise. The war in Vietnam ended the Johnson presidency. The Korean War ended the Truman presidency. The handling of the U-2 incident was President Eisenhower's greatest regret. The Bay of Pigs was President Kennedy's greatest failure. In each of these cases a lack of good human sources was largely to blame.

CIA officers are, of course, skilled and well-trained, but the structure of the organization discourages human source operations. In the darkness of secrecy, with unlimited billions of tax dollars, and with little or no accountability, the CIA bureaucracy has mutated into a living, breathing leviathan that serves its own aims. It has grown some very unruly tentacles: layers of unnecessary managers, lucrative pay and benefits packages for current and former employees, obscene contracts for companies run by former employees, and massive expansion of the CIA's operations within the continental United States. Very few of the CIA's top managers have ever recruited a good human source.

I joined the CIA in the late 1980's with one purpose in mind: to serve my country. My service, except for initial training, was in continuous field assignments overseas, in the Middle East, Eastern Europe, and Western Europe while working on WMD targets, and in Iraq while working on terrorist targets during the war. Few have equaled my record of consecutive, successful foreign assignments. My service was unblemished.

I resigned when I decided further service was pointless and that my best contribution to our nation's defense would be to enter the debate on the reform of the CIA. This book is the story of a deep cover case officer, the day-to-day obstacles to survival during dangerous operations—and without the benefit of diplomatic immunity—and the challenges of pushing intelligence operations through an unwilling and dysfunctional bureaucracy.

The CIA, a corrupt, Soviet-style organization, is not serving the purpose for which it was created, and the result is that our lives and the lives of our allies are in jeopardy. The Agency must either be restructured as an American organization—which encourages achievement, creativity, and accountability—or it must be dismantled. I have offered suggestions and solutions informed by the wisdom of experience.

My profits from the sale of this book will go to the children of American soldiers killed in action.

 THE HUMAN FACTOR

Prologue

The CIA bureaucracy was doing everything in its power to stop me, but I had vowed that morning to find myself at least one good human source of intelligence on enemy nuclear weapons.

During the winter of 2005, I boarded the No. 1 Metro line at the Louvre and traveled west, getting off at Porte Maillot and walking through underground passages to a scientific conference at the Hotel Concorde Lafayette. I'd seen it advertised on the Internet that morning, and it looked promising. Scientists network with their peers at such conferences, to exchange ideas, learn about the latest developments, and advance their careers.

In other words, it would be a perfect watering hole for visiting rogue state weapons scientists, who might make for good human intelligence targets.

Most of the attendees were middle-aged professionals, some dressed in inexpensive suits, others in collared shirts, with a smattering of neckties here and there: Scientists focus on their specialties and ideas, not on dressing up. I paid an entrance fee, pinned on a nametag, and entered the part of the room where people were conversing in scattered small groups.

I also surveyed the room for anyone who might pose a danger. Any venue that attracts weapons specialists might also attract other intelligence officers. Some might be keeping an eye on their own government's scientists or looking for intelligence sources, just as I was. If I correctly played my cover, other intelligence services wouldn't present any threat—at least, not near-term.

Of even more concern to me were my colleagues from the CIA. We tended to flood events like these with intelligence officers and access agents, i.e., informants. This causes turf friction between different parts of the organization, but I hadn't had time to tell anyone I'd be there. We wrote up voluminous reports to Headquarters (HQs) back in Langley, Virginia, describing moods, impressions, and observations of events. If I'd crossed one of these guys in the past, or if any of them wasn't happy with me invading his territory, he might note, "I saw Ishmael there and thought he looked like a spy," or, "Ishmael was too aggressive and he was attracting attention to himself." The last thing I wanted was to show up in a colleague's after-action report.

A warning signal ran through me like an electrical charge. Across the room and deep in conversation were the Twins— American professors who taught science at an American university and worked for the Agency as access agents. A couple of months before, at a conference in Istanbul, they'd marked my colleague Loman as a spy. "Something didn't seem right" about Loman, they wrote; his cover "didn't seem believable in that venue." The Twins had met Loman before and knew he was an Agency officer. HQs scolded Loman. A month later he was given a one-way ticket home from his assignment in Eastern Europe to a cubicle at Langley. There were other factors involved, but the Twins had undeniably played a major role.

Keeping out of the Twins' line of sight as best I could, I methodically covered the room, like a farmer plowing a field, eyeballing each nametag, on the lookout for people who might make good sources. A target from North Korea, Iran, Libya, Russia, or China would be ideal. If I couldn't see a nametag clearly, I'd get as close as I had to. Finding no one of special interest, I strolled over to the conference's poster area, where scientists display their latest papers. During evening sessions, the authors stand next to their posters and discuss and defend their ideas.

I glanced over the papers until I came to one belonging to a nuclear scientist from a rogue state—Dr. B—.

I returned to the main hall, inspecting the attendees' nametags closely again for Dr. B—. No Dr. B— anywhere. At the reception table they said he'd been unable to attend. That was perfectly normal. Scientists often had funding or scheduling problems that forced them to cancel their plans. Scientists from rogue states had to obtain government approval for all travel, which made their plans doubly uncertain. By signing up for the conference, though, they could get their papers posted on the board even if they didn't show up.

Dr. B—'s telephone number was listed on his paper, so I pulled out my cell phone and gave him a call.

"Hello, Dr. B—, my name is Ishmael Jones from Acme Software Solutions. I'm calling from the conference in Paris."

"Yes, I had hoped to attend, but I had trouble scheduling it at the last minute."

"I saw your paper at the poster session. I had been hoping to meet you here. My company has a technical problem with one of our products, and reading your paper, I realized you may be the one to help us with a solution."

We exchanged email addresses and, soon thereafter, emails. I invited him to visit me, at my expense, and we set an appointment to meet in Warsaw. Dr. B— could be an excellent source of intelligence—information that might prevent the advancement of his nation's nuclear weapons programs. If my relationship with Dr. B— went well, the effects might alter the world for the better, perhaps even save lives.

But first I had to cover my tracks.

HQs didn't know I'd be attending the conference. I had, however, been cleared to be in Paris that morning. I'd tell HQs I just happened to walk by the conference because I'd had a cover business meeting nearby. HQs would rather hear that my attendance was serendipitous than that I'd specifically targeted it. There should be no fallout from having dropped by. I'd done a good job of avoiding the Twins and hadn't recognized any other CIA people, so I didn't expect my name to come up in anyone's after-action report.

I wouldn't tell HQs how I'd closely eyeballed everyone's nametag. That broke an unwritten Agency rule from back when many spies were embassy diplomats. Diplomats don't charge into scientific conferences and scrutinize nametags. They're expected to sidle up casually to people at cocktail parties, make small talk, and set a date for tennis.

Few at HQs had ever met a rogue state weapons scientist. HQs didn't even realize how approachable they were. The scientists' occupations—creating weapons of mass destruction for use by tyrants—made them intimidating, but I knew they sat next to a phone just like anyone else. They liked to communicate with people, indeed *had* to, if they wanted to keep informed within the scientific community. Most had relatives in the United States, and all of them wanted to come to the States to study. Nearly all spoke English and enjoyed speaking with Americans.

As for me, I was merely a businessman. I wasn't at the conference for fun—I was working, and attendees fully expected strangers to read their nametags. No reason to be shy about it.

The biggest problem would be explaining to HQs how I'd managed to arrange the meeting in Warsaw. By telephoning Dr. B— as he sat at his desk in his office, I'd broken an ironclad rule. No officer may ever contact anyone in a rogue state without prior approval.

Approvals from dozens of bureaucratic turfs and layers of Agency managers were needed before I was allowed to make a telephone call to anyone, let alone a rogue state scientist. Protocol required that I first write a memorandum with the proposed content of the telephone conversation, then get the go-ahead from several tiers of managers at my home station, several in Paris, several in Warsaw, several at the European Division at HQs, several at the Eastern European Division at HQs, several representing Dr. B—'s home country, and several others for the HQs division of Dr. B—'s home country. As a weapons scientist, Dr. B—'s activities also came under the rubric of Counterproliferation Division, meaning several layers of management from that division, too, would have to review and approve the request. Within all of these layers were offshoots responsible for counterintelligence and security. There was yet another set of layers just for dealing with my own office. If anyone, anywhere along the way, considered my request a bad idea, the operation wouldn't go forward.

I solved this problem by claiming that Dr. B— called me. Dr. B— didn't need approval from the Agency to call me, of course, since we had no control over him. I told HQs that I'd seen his paper and left my card with the conference organizers, who had passed it to Dr. B—. I described all communication with Dr. B— as having been initiated by him: He called me and told me he planned to visit Warsaw. He emailed me his travel details.

And he invited me to visit him in his country. This was an impossibility. HQs was afraid even of making phone calls there. A CIA officer visiting a nasty rogue state to conduct an intelligence operation was out of the question.

Having established contact with Dr. B—, my request to meet him in Warsaw now had to be approved through all the above-mentioned layers. I wrote my request to make it seem completely devoid of risk. In truth, I planned to start prying secrets from Dr. B—as soon as I could, in the interests of American national security. In my request to HQs, I made it sound as though he and I would just exchange pleasantries.

Layers of management above me weakened my proposal even more in their edits emphasizing how *incredibly* light my contact with

Dr. B— would be. In the end, it sounded like we'd be two ships passing in the night. That way, HQs would perceive the proposed meeting to be absolutely harmless.

The request to meet Dr. B— percolated through the layers at HQs. It didn't seem to be meeting any resistance, but the sheer number of layers and hurdles meant the pace was slow. I had several weeks before Dr. B—'s arrival in Warsaw, but still the approval hadn't come in by the time he left his home country. I decided to get on an airplane and fly to Warsaw, approval be damned.

At the airport in Warsaw I met the portly Dr. B—.

"Hello, my friend," he said, "it is a pleasure to meet you."

We dropped off our suitcases at the hotel and strolled through Warsaw. The old town center, obliterated during the war, had been completely rebuilt. We sat at an outdoor café and ordered large glasses of beer.

After making polite introductory conversation, we discussed the scientific problem I needed to solve, a commercial application in Dr. B—'s specialty, then adjourned to my hotel room to work on the problem. This was a key step, as it placed us in a businesslike setting. I asked questions and took notes.

In discussing the technical problem, I learned much about Dr. B—'s background and education. While describing his past work experience, he unwittingly furnished interesting information of clear intelligence value.

His field was nuclear weapons. I had wanted to give him a technical problem that would not arouse his suspicions, then allow him to steer the conversation to the areas he best understood. Dr. B—'s ability to help with the problem I had described was limited because it wasn't his specific field. But scientists like to talk about their areas of expertise, and the conversation drifted to his work. As he went on about it, I told him I didn't know much about his specialty, and asked him to teach me a bit about it.

We met for several meetings of two hours each. Between

meetings, I reviewed my notes and listed questions for the next, which would later form intelligence reports.

At the end of the meetings, I reimbursed Dr. B— for his travel expenses, gave him some walking-around money, and supplied an advance on expenses for his next trip out of my own pocket. I knew it was too early to expect HQs to commit money to the operation. We drove to Warsaw's airport together and boarded our separate planes.

A few days after I returned home, a message from HQs arrived approving my plans to meet Dr. B— in Warsaw. The operation was on and I was simply a few steps ahead. I had learned after years in the organization that this was the only way to accomplish anything, and accomplishing something was the reason I had joined the CIA. God willing, if all went well, Dr. B— might provide information that could prevent a nuclear war—information that could save millions of lives.

 THE HUMAN FACTOR

PART ONE

★ 1 ★

Daring Greatly, Perhaps

> Far better it is to dare mighty things,
> to win glorious triumphs, even though
> checkered by failure, than to take rank
> with those poor spirits who neither enjoy
> much nor suffer much, because they live
> in the gray twilight that knows not vic-
> tory nor defeat.
>
> *Theodore Roosevelt*

When I was a boy, my family lived in different countries in eastern Asia, Eastern Africa and the Middle East. As I grew up in these dictatorships and tribal kingdoms, I was acutely aware of being different, as an American, and of the special status and privileges conferred by my nationality. My family's household wealth, ordinary by American standards, was enormous by the standards of our host countries. During upheavals in these unstable places, my family needed only to board the next plane home, while the country's native inhabitants had to stay and suffer. The United States was a refuge we could always seek in times of trouble.

During our rare visits to the US, I felt a weight lift, knowing that I could think or speak as I chose. Prosperity, openness, creativity, and freedom surrounded me in a great roaring tumult. In Africa and eastern Asia, I'd never seen a road larger than two lanes, usually potholed or unpaved. The Los Angeles freeway system, with its six and sometimes eight lanes, astonished my young eyes. Even then, I foresaw the immigration of coming decades, when getting to the United States became the goal of people everywhere in the world. I understood that a person could earn more in the US in a few hours as an unskilled laborer than he could in a month in most of the rest of the world. Everything functioned in America. The tap water flowed, the electricity worked, and the police were honest.

Despite the disillusionment of the 1970s, I thought an American living in America must be in heaven, going about daily life in a state of elation. I also felt a bit out of place in the US, and as if I had something to prove, to show that I genuinely belonged there.

The most visible Americans in our African city were the Marines who guarded the US embassy. They lived in the Marine House, just a block away from our own residence. Before sunrise each day, the Marines ran in formation through the neighborhood. The tropical climate and open drainage systems kept the city awash in powerful smells. As they ran, they chanted in time with the pace, in restrained voices so as not to awaken the neighborhood. At that early hour, Africans walking to work or setting up outdoor stands selling fruit and bread softly sang out greetings in English and Swahili upon first seeing the Marines, contributing a sort of accompaniment to their chants.

The Marines raised the American flag in front of their house each morning after their formation run. *That's my flag,* I said to myself. The Marines were my connection to my home country. I often ran the same route they did on my way to school in the morning.

I came back to the US to go to college and the Marine Corps boot camp for officer candidates—that head-shaving and hollering introduction to the Marine Corps's unique culture. It took two summers. Most of the candidates from the first summer never returned for the second. I was proud to be one of the few who stuck it out. It was truly difficult to go back for a second summer and endure boot camp all over again.

It was particularly unstylish on college campuses of that era to join the Marine Corps. Fashion dictated that long hair was chic, while shaved heads signified some deep emotional disturbance. It was the path less traveled—not the path of conformism. I was an infantry officer for three years and I thoroughly enjoyed the Marines' camaraderie and sense of mission. Although most Marines leave the Corps after their first three- to six-year commitment, we all behaved as if we were there for a lifetime career, because the Marines gave us a sense of ownership. The Marine Corps was not a faceless bureaucracy but a living institution, and it belonged to us as our personal property.

The Marine Corps has an effective and winning culture that inspires a powerful motivation to succeed. When the Corps fails, Marines die. When something goes wrong, as in Vietnam, the Marine Corps studies and improves its weaknesses. Adherence to traditional rank structure actually helps keep management layers flat, and prevents the creation of new management layers.

While in the Marine Corps, I spent a lot of time traveling with my infantry company, and some time alone on special assignments. One night, sitting on the top of a hill on an island in the Indian Ocean, I realized what I wanted to do next: get married and start a family. I had a vision of my ideal wife. I'd saved most of my pay during my service, so had plenty of money to take time off. I went to graduate school, met the woman I had imagined, and before long we were married.

After graduate school, I took a job on Wall Street. I went to work early each day and made telephone calls to people who didn't particularly want to talk to me. Money drives business, and in order to make money it's necessary to make contact with people. I learned to "make the call," to make contact even though the outcome might be rejection and humiliation. It's tough work, and not something one puts up with unless he truly cares about getting what he's after.

In the competitive American economy, the rewards go to people who can make contact. I'd learned from talking to military recruiters and to retail stockbrokers. They had to make cold call after cold call, facing rejection hundreds of times a day. As time went on, their personalities seemed to harden and they became emotionally distant, but their hard work made them successful.

Contact is what drives human progress. Bill Clinton and George Bush have made thousands of contacts to gather money and political support. All businesses are built and sustained by people who get out and meet others. This, the importance of "making the call," was the most valuable lesson I learned on Wall Street.

Money, however, had never been much of a motivator for me, so after a few years I found myself feeling a familiar pull to service and adventure, the same pull that had drawn me to the Marine Corps. As Aristotle asked, how should a human being lead his life? I did a lot of pondering about the important things, so to speak— about deeds and destiny. I resolved to send my résumé to the CIA. Weapons of mass destruction had always concerned me. With the proliferation of nuclear and other gruesome weapons technology, I knew it was only a matter of time before an American city was targeted and possibly destroyed. Would the CIA be a path to great things, to preventing a nuclear war or giving advance warning of the next Pearl Harbor?

A CIA REPRESENTATIVE responded to my résumé and sent me to a local college where Agency recruiters had scheduled a series of written tests.

I waited with the other applicants outside a lecture hall, all of us wondering how we ought to behave. What if the "testing" had begun already?

An elderly man called us into the room and administered a battery of tests, some designed to judge intelligence, but many of them personality-oriented or psychological, with questions like, "Would you rather write a poem or watch a movie?" Some of the "yes or no" questions were phrased a bit archaically: "Do you like to cut up at a party?" Others were downright creepy: "Do you wake up sweating at night," "Do other people talk about you when you are not around," "Are you being followed," or, "Do you sometimes just want to hurt others?" I never saw any of the other applicants again.

Shortly after the tests, my telephone rang at work. "Be at your residence at 1900 and we'll talk," said the caller. I made sure to be home well before 1900 and sat next to the phone. It didn't ring. I made sure to be at home at 1900 for the next several days.

A few months later, I finally heard from the caller again. "I see what happened," he fibbed. "The person who called you last time handed me your phone number, and this 3 looked like an 8, so I wasn't able to reach you." He scheduled me for the next series of tests, the Agency's polygraph examinations.

The polygraph device comes in a small suitcase, nicknamed the "Box." My "Box" exam took place in a hotel room near Washington, D.C. The curtains were drawn. My examiner was a massive and intimidating man with a head that must have weighed fifty pounds. He hooked me up to the "Box" with wires to the fingertips, a belt around the chest, and a pressure band around my upper arm. Later he switched the pressure band to my calf, saying that it would give a better reading. The examiner went through about ten questions, from simple ones like "Are you applying for a job with the Agency?" and "Do you come from Casper, Wyoming?" to more significant ones like "Do you use drugs?" and "Are you currently working for a foreign intelligence service?" My test took most of the day. The examiner peered at the charts. He seemed troubled by some of my reactions. He repeated certain questions and created new ones.

Evidently I answered these to the Box's satisfaction, because the Agency proceeded with my security investigation. It sent an investigator to interview several of my friends and acquaintances as to my trustworthiness and reliability. Running into them years later, they'd give me sideways looks and ask, "Do you remember when that guy came to interview me, the guy with the dark suit and the white socks, who asked whether you could be trusted with important US government secrets? What did he want? What was that all about?"

THE NEXT PHASE of the application process was a series of interviews in Washington, D.C. These were held in hotel rooms, always with the television set on in the background. Our first interview was with the man in charge of the training program. He was missing the fingers on his left hand, but in his mind they must still have been there, because he pointed and gestured with the phantom digits.

My wife had come to the interview with me. Roger asked my wife whether she knew what organization was conducting my interview. He'd recently interviewed an applicant who had not informed his wife of the purpose of the interview, and, to his question, "What do you think about a career in the CIA," she'd screeched, "A career in the *what*?"

Roger said he'd rejected that applicant because he thought he should have been honest with his wife. I sympathized with the applicant, who must have only been trying to do the right thing by his wife. Nearly twenty years later, a CIA memoir tells a similar story[1], but I suspect that the story was apocryphal, a bit of Agency folklore. Roger had followed it with: "In any case, don't worry, we don't really 'terminate' people!"

Prior to the interviews, I had assumed that all Agency officers were members of the State Department under diplomatic cover in embassies, but Roger asked if I would consider working in a non-State Department program.[2] I'd lived in foreign countries and had also had a business career, so he thought I'd be a good candidate. I agreed to it.

He explained that the purpose of the non-State Department program was to get at potential human intelligence sources who were inaccessible to diplomats. Terrorists and nuclear weapons scientists, naturally, do not talk to them. Iranian diplomats were expressly forbidden by their government to speak to American diplomats. Indeed, Agency managers during our interviews said flat-out that the State Department's embassy system wasn't effective any more. The non-State Department program would be the future of the CIA.

After my interview with Roger, several groups of three or four heavy-set women arrived to discuss various more mundane personnel topics, such as salary and insurance. Typically only one woman actually spoke during a meeting, while the others listened and nodded.

More interviews followed, and I was in full interview mode, perched on the edge of my chair and ready to give eager and energetic answers. But the questions never came. The interviewers just introduced themselves, sat down, and talked about themselves. I sat upright and nodded attentively at appropriate moments, wondering if it was all a test. Did they want me to interrupt, to show aggressiveness? No, I decided. They just wanted to talk about themselves. None of the interviewers had prepared any questions because none of them had any interest in questioning me.

When the last interviewer and the last herd of administrators had gone, a corpulent man who identified himself as a chief of the non-State Department program blustered his way into the hotel room. Omitting the usual chitchat, he fixed us with a steely glare and was silent for what felt like a very long time.

At last he said, "You're seeing me now for the first time. Tell me what you perceive about me. Tell me what you know about me. What makes me tick."

My mind raced at this unexpected challenge of my spy's perceptiveness and intuition. I opened my senses to draw in and analyze the situation and the man, and what it all meant. His personal appearance was awful, but I was sure he knew it, and that was part of the test. I'd fail unless I gave him a straightforward analysis.

"You're morbidly obese," I said, "and it's a 'hard' sort of obesity caused by stress and a bad diet. Bags under the eyes and yellowish skin. You have a darker aura about you as opposed to the pink, jolly glow that some heavy folks have. This suggests—"

"I own a stake in a business in Portland," he snapped, gathering the direction I was heading in and having heard quite enough, "and I've been doing this job for thirty-five years. I can retire any damn time I want to. I can take my retirement check, plus I can go to Portland to work in my business any time I damn well choose." He slipped into the conversational style similar to the other interviewers and talked about himself, describing his past CIA assignments by location and length of time spent in each.

He had been closely involved in planning the failed attempt to rescue the American hostages held in the American embassy in Tehran. He had figured out how the vehicles to be used in the rescue attempt, otherwise too tall to fit in the helicopters, could be made lower to the ground by having their tire pressure reduced. He told us this as if the hostage rescue mission had been a success, rather than a disaster for the ages that had helped take down a President and made America impotent in the eyes of its enemies.

While in Vietnam, he said, he had paid a gang of elephant drivers to report intelligence to him. The men traveled with their elephants and heard and saw things, so he devised a bamboo stick with a radio in it that they could use to send messages. When he first gave the bamboo stick to the elephant drivers, they looked concerned. They explained that the type of bamboo he'd brought grew only in South Vietnam and would look suspicious to people in North Vietnam. He'd had to scramble to get them the right kind of bamboo. Correct bamboo notwithstanding, the Viet Cong eventually became suspicious and killed all of the elephant drivers and all of their elephants as well.

"The point of these stories," he said, "is to show that case officers have to be ready to do a lot of different things."

After talking without pause for nearly two hours, during which my wife and I were completely silent, he finally checked his watch, excused himself, and left.

The interviews were over. Despite my near miss with the chief, I received instructions several days later to report to the Washington, D.C. area for the start of the training course.

★ 2 ★

Training Days

Two months of training
crammed into a year.
Anonymous

We were assigned fictitious names to use during training. Although they were throwaway aliases meant only for the course, they stuck and we tended to use them throughout our careers among our friends and colleagues in the Agency. I was called Ishmael. My enthusiastic new class began its great adventure by gathering in a set of offices in a low-rise office building in the Washington, D.C. area. This was a training "safe house," specifically chosen not to be connected in any way with the State Department, and thus presumably better cover for the training of non-State Department officers.

A psychologist visited during the first few days of our training and discussed the psychological and personality tests we'd taken before joining. He said that we'd been selected because those tests had showed in us a mixture of extrovert and introvert. We could work well with others but were also capable of spending extended periods alone. I asked him about some of the tests' more bizarre questions, like, "Are you being followed?" and "Do you sometimes just want to hurt others?" They'd seemed too obviously designed to weed out crazy people; surely no one would be so foolish as to answer "yes." He replied that some people really do believe they're being followed, and some really want to hurt others. Such people don't find anything unusual about the questions, so they do, believe it or not, answer "yes."

The psychologist also explained that the Agency sought to weed out anyone who had a strong belief in unquestioning obedience, because our work would require us to break many foreign laws. We'd have to guide ourselves by our mission and our judgment, not a foreign country's rules. "We want people who question," he said, "people who would have made poor concentration camp guards."

Roger welcomed us on this, our first official day, by saying, "This is the best class we've ever had." I assumed there must have been an assassin's bomb, or a knife fight with a terrorist, behind those missing fingers of his. "Nah," said Max, one of my new classmates. "He lost those to a lawnmower."

Our chief instructor, Harry, welcomed us to the course, also saying, "This class is vastly superior to previous classes, much more highly qualified." Most of the speakers who followed him also congratulated us on how much more qualified we were than previous training groups. All the speakers emphasized the Agency's push to move away from embassies, and how we represented the future of the Agency.

The first week was a "Hell Week" of cruelty far worse than the mere push-ups and abuse of a Marine boot camp. For ten straight hours each day, with rare breaks, we sat in an airless conference room—shades drawn, of course—as a procession of Agency employees talked about themselves, their day to day lives, their opinions and feelings, and their past assignments. Each speaker arrived late, which was of no consequence, since the previous speaker usually hadn't finished talking yet. None of the speakers used notes or had organized their talks in any way. They arrived, got a cup of coffee, sat down, and spoke in a monotone. I penciled a note to my classmate Max, asking for an explanation. He replied, "Welcome to the Agency speaking style. The highest-ranking guy in the room gets to

talk for as long as he wants. The lower-ranking guys sit and listen."
It was excruciating.

Getting to know my new classmates, I learned that my hiring path into the Agency was unusual. Most of the new hires had come in through personal connections—or through "blind ads," newspaper ads for employment at unnamed companies geared to people with experience with international business, foreign languages, and foreign travel. I'd sought out the Agency as a patriotic duty, so I was wary of that hiring method. Blind ads respondents hadn't come to the CIA out of a feeling of obligation; they were mostly unemployed people looking for jobs. My classmate Jonah, a tall, red-haired man, had answered a blind ad and described the process. "Just imagine how I felt when I found out who it was behind that blind ad!" he said. After being hired, Jonah had first worked as a desk officer at HQs.

Max, however, had been recruited from the paramilitary branch of the Agency and called himself a "knuckle dragger." He had a hard, military look, complete with a flattop haircut. He didn't fit the typical profile of someone who traveled a lot and spoke foreign languages, but he was confident and had a lot of Agency experience. We had similar military backgrounds and soon became friends.

Given their prior employment within the Agency, Max and Jonah knew their way around. I asked them for an insider's view of the polygraph. My own exam had taken almost a whole day. Max said, "That's nothing." He explained that when he'd first joined, they used the Box to filter out homosexuals. His Box operator didn't like his reactions to that set of questions and thought he was concealing something. The operator put him through a new test based only on questions about homosexuality, among which was the question, "Have you ever held another man's penis in your hand?" After the test, the operator still didn't believe him, but let him into the Agency anyway provided that he sign a special form confirming that he was not a homosexual and promising not to engage in homosexual behavior. "I think you got off easy," Max said.

For me, the Box had been a grueling all-day affair. It had taken Max two days to complete. Jonah's experience was different. He boasted, "From the moment I saw the operator until the time I left, I took twenty-five minutes."

Our instructors were retired case officers, mostly with careers in Western Europe. Harry had spent time in East Asia and the Middle East, and had been the chief of station in a country during its revolution. I'd been there as a child at the same time. We even realized that we had a few acquaintances in common.

The night of the revolution, my family could hear the small arms fire. The shooting went on all night, rifles and pistols being shot into the air. For all the noise, it was considered a bloodless coup, and few people were hurt. Because my family had just arrived, we lived in a temporary apartment in the city center. My father snuck out the next day to find the family some food. He returned in one piece, and when it felt safe to go outside, we went tentatively into the streets. They were covered with spent shells and, here and there, a ricocheted bullet. In an odd twist on boyhood beachcombing, I filled a box with these mementos. I still have it in my basement somewhere.

THE AGENCY TRADITIONALLY had deployed spies through the State Department, so our training course was still designed to teach us how to work as diplomats. The course, which set our spy activities in the fictitious country of Slobovia, is still the basic foundation of Agency training.

The instructors took delight in inventing and discussing obscure facts about Slobovia: the personality traits of Slobovian leaders, Slobovian historical anecdotes, and so on. The Slobovia scenario had been designed in the 1950s and edited only lightly since then. We paged through a thick binder of information about this fanciful nation. "The best trainees are method actors, people who convince themselves that they really are in Slobovia," one instructor told us. My classmate Jonah made an intensive study of his Slobovia book, and, later, an ostentatious show of his Slobovian mastery.

The fundamental work of the clandestine service was to find people with access to secret information of interest to the US government and to recruit them to provide human intelligence, or "humint." The traditional means of meeting new contacts overseas was on the diplomatic cocktail party circuit. Our exercises began by attending a faux embassy cocktail party to meet instructors who role-played as potential human sources.

Moe, a hulking youth, was in charge of our safe-house apartments. The afternoon of our first faux cocktail party, he arrived at our safe house to stock the refrigerator and cabinets with a collection of alcoholic beverages, which Max dubbed "Moe's Private Reserve." Moe lined up sample beverage selections on a conference room table and set himself up as bartender.

Max and I arrived at the party, asked Moe for two bottles of beer, and went to work, mingling with our Slobovian "guests." We'd been assigned specific people with whom to try to build a personal connection, in hopes of making a more private future appointment. I made my way around the gathering, met my target, and got his phone number for a lunch meeting. Max did the same thing with his target. It seemed like a fairly simple introduction to spycraft.

At the safe-house office the next day, Max and I sensed that something was amiss. When Harry spotted us, he barked, "You two, Max and Ishmael, get into the conference room." There, we found a panel of instructors.

"What the hell were you guys thinking at the party last night?" Harry demanded. The others scowled and grumbled. They were genuinely upset.

"Well, I thought the exercise went well," I said. "We found our targets, struck up good conversations, and then prepared to set follow-up meetings. I thought everything went fine."

The instructors' grumbling increased. When Harry saw that Max and I had no idea what we'd done wrong, he patiently explained that diplomats never drink directly from beer bottles at diplomatic cocktail parties. "I tried to help you out," said Harry. "Don't you remember me asking if you'd like a glass?" I did remember: I'd thought Harry was just trying to be nice. Max and I acknowledged our mistake, but the instructors never let us live down our faux pas.

THE INSTRUCTORS LED US in classroom work and exercises on tradecraft and agent recruitment. The classroom portion was most difficult for me, because it meant long hours sitting in a closed, curtained, airless room, listening to Agency veterans drone on. At least they were paid a reasonable hourly rate, nothing like the free-for-all that erupted years later, after 9/11. They were restricted to a thirty-nine-hour work week, without overtime. This meant our training day was usually held between 8 and 5, and night work was rare. Of course, if an instructor hadn't booked his 39 hours in a given week, he could extend Friday evening by speaking on any topic that tickled his fancy until he hit the mark. As is true of many older men, the instructors loved to talk and to be listened to. It was a blowhard's dream.

The classroom was a hard slog, and after many months of it I built up an aversion to long talks. To this day, I have trouble accepting dinner invitations for fear of being trapped with a bore.

The instructors had videotaped themselves talking during previous training courses, so if they had an appointment and couldn't deliver the lecture in person, they'd pop in a video of themselves and torment us from the VCR. We watched Roger present a three-hour lecture on "international finance," much of which consisted of him holding up foreign currency and saying, "This is a German mark. This is a British pound. . . ."

I considered the training a necessary evil, an obstacle that had to be overcome to get out to an overseas field assignment and protect our nation—anything to make me feel like a genuine case officer. Jonah did a better job of handling the frustration, keeping a look of engagement on his face and asking questions designed to show interest and enthusiasm. Yet every day that I sat in that classroom, I felt weaker. Every day Charlie spent conducting espionage, he got stronger. Time is all we have on this earth, and I knew that I wanted to spend my time battling America's enemies. I also knew that my instructors were sensitive to "attitude," so what I needed to do first and foremost was wipe that bored scowl off my face.

I came up with a solution. My foreign language skills were lacking, so each day before work, during breaks and lunchtime, and after work, I drew up lists of foreign words and phrases to memorize. While seated in the classroom, I kept the list in my lap so I could glance down at it surreptitiously. While the instructors prattled on, I memorized. Listening to the lectures and memorizing at the same time, I felt challenged and productive. The bored scowl gradually disappeared.

I also rose early each day to exercise, running in parks near my home or working out on a weight set I kept in the basement. I saw the poor physical condition in the faces and bodies of colleagues, especially graduates of mid- and late-1980s training classes, and I wanted to keep myself in top shape. I did exercises I could measure, like distance running, pull-ups, and resistance training, to keep track. If the numbers stayed the same or increased, at least I knew that I wasn't falling apart.

Training outside the classroom involved meetings with instructors role-playing as agents or potential agents. We'd perform surveillance detection by car, public transportation, walking, or some combination, until we arrived at the meeting, usually held in safe houses, hotel rooms, our houses, instructors' houses, restaurants, or parks. Afterwards we'd write it all up in proper Agency format. The

Agency had strict writing standards. Spelling and grammar were always to be flawless.

On exercise days, when there was less classroom work, I often wound up with free time to study languages and to be with my family. I did my best to complete exercises in three hours. Some of my classmates, particularly Jonah, claimed to be putting in twenty-hour days. Concerned that I was missing something, I studied their written after-action reports and was relieved to see that they were the same quality and length as mine.

The instructors urged us to create highly detailed written reports about our meetings. After a role-playing rendezvous with an instructor at the instructor's house, Max described the interior: The instructor was "a pack rat"; his house was "filthy, with stacks of papers and piles of refuse all over the place. A real pigsty. Can we rely on an agent who keeps his house in such a mess?" The instructors read Max's write-up, passed it around, enjoyed it immensely, and teased the messy instructor mercilessly. They'd all been to the house at one time or another and agreed with the "pigsty" verdict. When the pig's wife found out about the incident, she made him throw out all his hoarded piles of stuff, then made him pay for expensive remodeling.

OUR INSTRUCTORS LED US in candid discussions of the harsh realities of human source operations. Ever since "the Lord commanded Moses to send spies to report on the land of Canaan,"[3] good leaders have recognized the value of human intelligence. My experience in the CIA was limited to human intelligence collection within the clandestine service, or Directorate of Operations.

The skeleton in the clandestine service's closet was that the CIA's primary mission since its founding had been to recruit Soviet spies—and that the Agency had never succeeded. The methods used during our recruitment exercises seemed valid, the instructors dedicated and intelligent, but Soviets were immensely difficult, even impossible, to recruit. Our instructors admitted this. They told us that the only Soviet spies with whom the CIA had worked were volunteers.[4]

Our case officers had encountered Soviets at social and diplomatic functions and had documented those meetings in writing. "After each social contact with a Soviet," a veteran instructor said, "we just kept making those files thicker and thicker." Knowing that our instructors had never really mastered the skills they taught added a slight but inescapable friction to the classes in which we studied our new trade.

The act of volunteering was a challenge. "In two of the most important Cold War cases involving Soviet volunteers, Popov and Penkovsky, these two Russian GRU officers literally had to throw themselves at Western officials before their offers to spy were taken up."[5]

Information provided to the KGB by CIA case officers Edward Howard, Aldrich Ames, Harold Nicholson, and by FBI agent Robert Hanssen later led to the execution or imprisonment of most of the later volunteers. In April and June 1985, Ames gave the KGB information on *all* Soviet cases run by the Agency.[6] (The KGB morphed into the SVR and the FSB during the 1990s, but for simplicity's sake I continue to call it the KGB. The GRU is the Soviet military intelligence service, a counterpart to the KGB.)

In the 1950s, the Agency sought intelligence about the Soviet Union by digging a tunnel from Berlin into East Germany, and by tapping into Soviet communications cables. Harry was proud of the work he had done on the Berlin Tunnel.

"I cut my teeth—" He paused, relishing his audience's rapt attention, "—on the Berlin Tunnel."

Max asked, "Wasn't the Berlin Tunnel a failure?"

Harry explained that although the Soviets had learned of the tunnel from George Blake, their own human source within the British SIS, well before the tunnel was even built, the Soviets chose to let us continue the project in order to protect Blake's identity. Some information gained from the tunnel operation had been useful, but it had also been given up willingly. (Several CIA memoirs, including those by Hitz and Helms, rate the operation as a strong success. I would rate it more soberly as an expensive, low-risk, and people-intensive operation.)

The Soviets eventually staged an accidental discovery of the tunnel, at a point when they felt that they could shut it down without blowing Blake's cover.

Our instructors' experiences varied by the locations of their assignments. An old hand with a lifetime of service in Third World countries had made countless recruitments, or "scalps"—a sign of achievement and prowess, or so we thought. He didn't agree that they were good measure of anything. "Shake a tree and the President's cabinet would fall out," he told us. "Get all the scalps you want. Or go find the President of the country and pay him and he'll tell you everything he knows."

WE LEARNED TO CREATE disguises suitable to our various features. Max's appearance changed dramatically when his flattop haircut was hidden with a wig and his clean-shaven appearance masked with mustache and glasses. Jonah was harder to disguise because he already had bushy red hair, large glasses, and a mustache: He employed hair colorings and gels.

We practiced impersonal communications, such as dead drops, brush passes, and secret writing. I constructed concealment devices from small branches found in the park, which, when hollowed out with a knife, could hold tiny rolled-up messages. Max and Jonah scoffed at my little branches and built huge, sloppy devices, complete with glued-on pine needles and leaves. They mocked the "laziness and ineptitude" of my humble devices; I rejoined that their elaborate messes revealed simple minds.

Our secret writing materials didn't work. The instructor figured they must have been "on the shelf" too long. In any case, I never ended up conducting much "impersonal communication." Those techniques always seemed to be geared to agents operating in Soviet states, rather than in the conditions that prevailed around the world today. It was always more important to me to meet informants, or "agents," in person and to receive their information in a businesslike situation, such as in an office or a hotel room. This was especially important because the agents and I usually spoke different native languages; there wasn't a lot that could have been communicated well using impersonal methods.

We didn't practice breaking-and-entering. The Agency's breaking-and-entering operations were done by technicians who had undergone extensive specialized training. Max had met one of these specialists. During a period of financial strain combined with feelings of idleness and boredom, the specialist had started breaking into banks during his spare time. Max said he'd actually robbed a few before he was caught and sent to prison.

In the entryways of our safe houses, in an attempt to look like an ordinary business office, Moe had placed IN/OUT boards with fictitious names. Max rearranged the letters in the names to form new names that he found amusing. The instructors were enraged. Jonah didn't think it was too funny, but kept Max's identity secret. The instructors sought to deal with the name-changing by mocking the immaturity and childishness of the anonymous perpetrator. This had little effect; the names continued to change. Then the instructors threatened mass punishments; finally, they surrendered and endured it, until Max just lost interest.

JONAH OFTEN BROUGHT HIS COMPUTER in to the training safe house on weekends to work. The safe house had a burglar alarm. One Sunday, Jonah arrived, set his computer down, opened the door, set off the alarm, then realized he'd left the alarm system's disarm code in his car. He ran to his car to get it, but when he returned the police had already responded to the alarm.

The police saw the computer outside the door, which made the situation look like a theft in progress. They tried to arrest Jonah.

"It's okay, officers," Jonah said. "I'm authorized to use this office. This computer belongs to me. I just forgot the alarm code and had to run back to my car to get it."

"Can you show us some ID, sir?"

Jonah showed the policemen his identification.

"Can you show us anything that proves you have legal access to this office? Can you show us your desk?"

The policemen looked inside. Each desk was bare and the office was empty of any personal objects. There was nothing in the office that could be connected to Jonah.

"Which one are you?" The policemen pointed to the IN/OUT board that listed the names Ben Dover, I. P. Lowe, etc.

The police put Jonah in their squad car and drove him to the precinct. Fortunately, he had a phone number for Moe, who rushed down to the station and convinced the police that Jonah did have legal access to the office.

A rumor spread through HQs that Jonah had been caught trying to steal a computer. Max and I pointedly squashed the rumor whenever we heard it repeated.

SINCE WE WERE ALWAYS TO DENY that we were diplomats working for the US Department of State, my classmates and I were given details of a light cover company for use during our time in the US, prior to overseas deployments. The cover company consisted of a mailing address in a high-rise office building, plus telephone and fax numbers. When a couple of friends asked for my business contact information, I gave them these numbers. Later, a friend called one of the numbers and reached something called "Acme Office Solutions." He asked for me.

Long pause. "Please hold." Another pause. "No Ishmael here."

"Well, Ishmael gave me this number. Are you sure he's not available?"

"Sorry, no Ishmael working here."

When I heard about this, I resolved that in the future I would test and evaluate cover company numbers before handing them out.

We prepared and practiced cover stories. If we were meeting an agent, we always had to have an excuse ready to explain *why*. The instructors said we had better beware, though. We might have a great cover story, but a KGB officer observing us might not even bother to ask for it. He might just see us with the agent together and figure it out.

This point was based on the apocryphal story of an American case officer working for the State Department as a diplomat who was having lunch with a Soviet weapons scientist. Their children went to the same school; his cover story was that they were discussing the school's sports program. A KGB officer happened to walk by the restaurant, saw the American diplomat and the Soviet scientist having lunch together, and didn't bother to look at the sports and school brochures the case officer had arrayed on the table. He saw an American diplomat meeting a Soviet scientist. It was all the information he needed to reach the correct conclusion. The KGB bundled the Soviet scientist off to Siberia.

The instructors taught us the Agency's history with Cuban agents, a case study in bad tradecraft. The Agency had run dozens of Cuban agents over the years and in the end nearly all turned out to be double agents. Those who were real agents had been captured and imprisoned or executed by the Cuban government.[7]

Our case officers handled Cuban agents by connecting them in networks. This meant that bad agents had access to the identities of legitimate agents. Some legitimate Cuban agents were infiltrated on missions into Cuba straight into the arms of double agents, where they were immediately arrested. The Cuban double agents then used the communications gear of the legitimate agents to communicate false intelligence back to the Agency. The legitimate agents had been instructed to include signals within their communications to indicate they were not under duress. The signals, appearing in the communications, would mean that all was well. When communications from these agents did not contain the duress signals, thus indicating something had gone wrong, the Agency figured the Cuban agents had just forgotten them. Refusing to believe that there might be a problem, the Agency continued to send agents to their imprisonments or deaths in Cuba. When the double agents realized the Agency had figured out at last that they all worked for Cuba, their last messages to their case officers were words to the effect of "Die, capitalist pigs."

In the aftermath of the Cuban debacle, the Cuban government produced a TV documentary. We watched it during our training class. It showed our case officers, as members of the State Department, driving around Cuba servicing dead drops, doing surveillance detection routes, and leaving signals. The Cubans had rigged cameras in trees and bushes at the places where these clandestine acts were to occur. Our people looked around furtively as they picked up or dropped off items. The documentary was narrated in a lighthearted style: "Here is John Smith from the US interests section! He is taking a walk in the woods. Why is he looking around nervously? Lo! What did he just pick up?"

The Cuban programs were among the most important that the Agency ran during the Cold War. Many case officers earned promotions and awards based on their handling of Cuban agents. As time went on, many of these officers became Agency mandarins. No promotion or award was ever rescinded, no accountability ever enforced.

Vast amounts of false intelligence were fed into the system by the Cubans. Although a scrub of the system should have erased a lot of it, our instructors felt that because there had been so many Cuban doubles and such a large volume of production over a long period, a great deal of the false intelligence remained in our databases. All of the Cuban double agents had passed polygraph examinations.

Criticism of the operations was open and refreshing. Our instructors didn't pull any punches on the Cuban program and felt it was important to analyze the past to learn how to avoid repeating mistakes.

In this analysis, HQs looked back on the cases and tried to find clues that could have shown these agents were bad. If an agent took a long time to respond to instructions, or was late for a meeting, it might mean that he had to check in first with his real handlers. In meetings, agents were scrutinized with an eye toward whether they were trying to control or manipulate the proceedings. Some speculated that the Cuban government prohibited its double agents from reporting to the Agency on certain restricted areas of information, even if the information they intended to report was false.

FOR TRAINING IN RECRUITMENTS, we studied the motivations of a human source and the rewards necessary to gain his cooperation. Usually the motivator was money, but it could also be the desire for praise, or the dictates of personal ideology. Playing to the natural human weakness for praise and attention, the KGB was reputed to take its agents, dress them in Soviet military uniform, promote them to general, and pin medals on them. Then, for "security purposes," the uniform and medals would be taken away for safekeeping. Kim Philby, an infamous British spy for the KGB, was told that he was an official KGB officer. When he fled to Moscow, however, his uniform and full access to KGB headquarters were denied.[8]

A parade of speakers visited our safe house throughout the course to give valuable tips picked up during their careers. Later, we had the opportunity to meet informally with them. I enjoyed meeting one veteran officer in particular—a gregarious and charismatic man with the personality of James Brown, the Godfather of Soul. The Godfather was one of the Agency's best recruiters.

"Aim at getting overseas," the Godfather said. "Take any assignment you can get, just get overseas. Don't be picky about location.

Don't be picky about the mission you're assigned, either. Once you're overseas, you'll be able to figure out ways to work on the important targets, regardless of the initial intent of the assignment."

That evening, following his visit to our safe house, the Godfather gave me some tips privately, over drinks, on working the system. The Godfather, for example, often married and divorced women who were not US citizens. Marrying a foreigner could get an officer sent to a cubicle at HQs for five years or more, while the Agency pondered what to do or just waited until the wife could get US citizenship. The Godfather's solution was simple: Just don't tell anyone. He'd never told his wives or ex-wives about his Agency job, and he'd never told the Agency about his wives and ex-wives. As a result he'd been able to remain overseas for many years.

A retired officer named Two Dog Dave dropped by our class periodically, always to give us the same disturbing prescription for life in a foreign country: Get two dogs. "This way," he explained, "if a burglar tries to feed poisoned meat to your dog, one dog will eat the poison, but the other will still be ready to bark and bite."

A visiting speaker described a recent breakdown in an overseas station. The station chief accused the deputy chief of being a wife-beater. The deputy in turn accused the chief, a woman, of sexual harassment and sexual misbehavior. The Agency charged the chief with sexual misbehavior, removed her from her position, and sent her back to HQs to an unimportant job. She sued the Agency, which settled out of court and paid her $410,000. She later became a lawyer specializing in litigation against government agencies.[9]

In the past, most of the Agency's employees had been men. The case officers had all been men, and the wife's role had been to support her husband and the family. Our instructors' wives had never worked for the Agency. But by the early 1990s the Agency was about 40 percent female and by 2007 the gender ratio was about one to one. An increasing number of HQs employees were married to each other and were called "tandem couples."

Jonah envied these tandem couples and called them *One For the Price of Two*s or OFTPOTs. He wanted to put his wife on the payroll, too, but she'd refused. Equality of men and women in the workplace became a tool used by many Agency employees to double their household income. In most American workplaces, it's an enormous challenge for both parents to work full-time jobs while raising their children. In the government, with a relaxed eight-hour day of chatting and coffee, it's not a problem. OFTPOTs could use "flex" time, in which one of them might work from 0700 to 1500 and the other from 0900 to 1700, so that one of them could be there to see the kids off to school and the other could be home when the kids returned. Both would have plenty of energy left over to play with the kids and help with their homework.

In theory, there were rules meant to prevent conflicts of interest—that is, rules prohibiting wives and husbands from working in the same office. But the OFTPOTs were often the same age, grade, and specialty, and given the Agency's love of bureaucracy, it wasn't unusual for a husband and wife to end up as two distinct layers of management within a single office.

DURING THE TRAINING COURSE, one of our children was born. Babies have a way of arriving at inconvenient hours, and this one came at about 0300. Later, at about 0800, I made a series of phone calls to family members to give them the happy news, and to my instructors to say that I wouldn't be in that day. At noon I got a call from Harry.

"Where the hell are you?"

"My wife had a baby early this morning," I said. "I called and left a message."

"You get in here now," he said. He was not impressed. "This is a demanding course and we can't afford to be falling behind like this."

The baby and my wife were resting and I wasn't needed at the hospital, so I obeyed the order. Harry was waiting for me with a document.

"Sign the document," he said.

"What's it about?"

"By signing this document, you acknowledge your failure to report for training this morning. We'll keep this document in your training file."

I signed the document. Harry filed it in his briefcase, then assigned me an exercise that took a couple of hours to finish. I shrugged it off. It would have been nice to be with my family, but a couple of hours of training exercises before returning to the hospital wasn't so terrible.

THE NEXT WEEK, Max had a car pickup meeting with a role-playing instructor. He picked up the instructor and they drove around, talking. Max noticed the instructor looked a little gray, and as the meeting wore on the instructor started to make choking, gurgling sounds. Max stopped the car and the instructor opened the door and made more gasping noises, then vomited a bit, mostly spitting and noise. The instructor said he'd been out too late the night before.

After Max's exercise, we all met up in a local bar, and his instructor, feeling better, told stories about his past operations. The stories were windy and incoherent. I signaled the others to join me in another bar, the Vienna Inn, a place in Northern Virginia popular with Agency employees. The instructor didn't seem to notice us slip away, one by one, until only Jonah remained, listening attentively to his stories.

At the Vienna Inn, a friend of Max's joined our group. Max had known the man in the Agency's paramilitary program. The man assumed Max had left the Agency and that none of us worked for it. After downing half a dozen glasses of beer, the man whispered that he had something to show me. He pulled out his wallet and showed me his CIA identification card.

"That's who I really work for," he said. He gave me a proud, boozy smile.

"Wow, you're a secret agent? That's really something."

"You got that right."

THE INSTRUCTORS, all of whom were retired, had had solid careers. Some of them had been high-ranking managers. Our active duty HQs managers, though, were more of a mixed bag. Some of them were officers who'd gotten in trouble overseas and, after receiving their one-way tickets home, had been assigned to managerial positions at HQs.

One morning, a chief from HQs came to speak to us—a chief whom a previous class had nicknamed "the Worst Spy in the World."

The Worst Spy in the World had been assigned to a US ally. After meeting with an agent, he sat in his hotel room typing up the results on a computer. He heard a knock on the door of his hotel room, so he shut down his computer and got up to answer. A cleaning lady had come to deliver clean towels to the room. He took the stack of towels, thanked the cleaning lady, and went back to work.

A few minutes later there was another knock at the door. Figuring it was the cleaning lady again, he left his computer on with his notes visible on the screen, and went to answer the door. This time a squad of policemen surged in, pinned him down, took his computer and notes, and hauled him down to the police station for questioning. The country, though a US ally, was not an ally of Israel. The Worst Spy had used an Israeli-sounding alias, so the police thought he might be a Mossad spy. They spoke to him in harsh tones. After a few minutes he responded by breaking down and confessing to his CIA affiliation.

"Well, why didn't you just say so!" the police said, relieved.

Everyone was all smiles, and the police gave him a ride to

the American embassy. The embassy gave him his one-way ticket back to the US.

The Worst Spy, true to his moniker, was a whiner: "After all I'd been through, as soon as I got back to HQs, the first people who came to see me were from Accounting. They demanded that I account for the missing $100,000 in cash I'd been given for my revolving fund!" The Worst Spy's personal finances and Agency accountings were in disarray when he returned to the US, so he picked up a paper route to help make ends meet. He arose early each morning to deliver newspapers before reporting to his job at HQs.

We later learned that the Worst Spy had first come to the attention of the police because, while riding a bus to a meeting, he'd discussed his religion with his fellow passengers. They were drug smugglers. Feigning interest in his nattering, they distracted him while filling his suitcase with cocaine. This would make their border crossing less risky. Since the police at the border knew that his traveling companions were drug smugglers, they followed him to his hotel.

As the Worst Spy finished his sorry tale, another manager came by to tell his story. He'd been on a foreign assignment for a few months when he began to suspect that he was under surveillance. He hadn't been able to confirm it, but he'd spotted furtive movements by people on the street. He begged HQs for help and advice.

HQs thought he was seeing "ghosts"—incidents that look like surveillance but aren't. But his persistence convinced them, and they spirited him back to the US. Later, the Agency learned that he had indeed been under surveillance and that his host country had been on the verge of arresting him for espionage.

"Bet you don't have any plans to go back to that country on vacation," Max said. "Probably don't want to get on any airplanes that plan to make a fuel stop there, either."

MY TRAINING CLASS enjoyed hearing that we were the best and most qualified they'd ever had, but there was a definite edge to the praise, a hint that there was more to the story. We eventually learned why.

The Agency had been promising to separate itself from the Department of State for years. Today, intelligence targets, human sources in WMD programs, or members of terrorist groups are all inaccessible to American diplomats. Everyone admitted that our Department of State diplomats weren't getting the job done and that the Agency needed to find new ways of doing business. But it was hard for a bureaucracy to change.

During the early 1980s, Director William Casey ordered the Agency to increase its non-State Department capabilities. In response to his orders, the Agency hired and trained large classes during the mid- and late-1980s. My class entered shortly after this, and we had front-row seats for the aftermath.

The individuals in these classes encountered strong bureaucratic resistance, with a failure rate of nearly 100 percent. Within a few years, only a few of these non-State Department officers were operating successfully overseas, and most had left the Agency. A few continued to work at HQs in other jobs, and a few switched over to become diplomats with the State Department. The official explanation within the Agency was that Casey had pushed the Agency too hard and too fast, so that it had had insufficient time to properly evaluate the new people before hiring them.

We saw these forlorn individuals wandering our safe-house apartments, and we listened to their sad tales. They looked like they'd been through a rough time physically: out of shape, unsmiling, bags under their eyes. Andy, a member of a class of about twenty recruits during the mid 1980s, said that most of his fellow trainees were qualified but a few were indeed a bit strange. Several of them barely spoke English. One man made loud snorting noises and occasionally grabbed his crotch.

Another had an odd habit of repeating the last few words he heard spoken in a sentence. If the instructor said, "Today we will talk about surveillance," this fellow would mutter, "About surveillance." During a break, the man went outside, lit a cigarette, and then put the entire cigarette in his mouth and chewed. Then he pulled his trousers down to his knees and fell to the ground in a trance. When he awoke a few moments later, he didn't remember anything about what he'd done. It turned out that he had a medical condition which had led to a fit and seizure. The instructors transferred him into an HQs job.

Andy said a fellow classmate had approached him and said that she planned to have a little plastic surgery done, and would he be so kind as to pick her up at the doctor's office afterward, as she might be feeling a bit woozy. When Andy arrived at the hospital, the minor work turned out to have been a major facial reconstruction. The woman was bloody and semi-conscious. The doctor said, "So, you're the boyfriend," and showed him how to insert the anal suppositories that she would need to control her pain. She was bedridden for a week, and he nursed her back to health.

Bad luck haunted this class. Once, while filing out of a safe-house training site, the class was photographed as a group by a man who passed by in a car. The class noted the car's license number and traced it. The plate had been stolen from an elderly woman in Iowa. A few days later it happened again, with a different car, and this time traces revealed that that license number did not even exist.

A rumor circulated at HQs that some of these trainees' IQ scores were quite low. Another had it that one of them was an ex-convict.

Day after day in the airless and artificially-lit classrooms, tension mounted between the mid-1980s classes and their instructors. The trainees spiked their instructors' coffee with Ex-Lax and let air out of their tires. The instructors fought back by flunking several trainees. A lawyer in an office below the safe-house apartment noticed the odd comings and goings and began telling clients that the CIA lived upstairs. When the office's location became widely known in the neighborhood, the Agency closed the office and moved the training class to a different location.

Two decades later, the Agency was still pointing to the debacle of these training classes as a reason not to push the Agency to separate from the State Department. Officers who'd entered before or after this period were careful to point out that they weren't part of that big hiring wave.

I'd met a lot of the people from the mid-1980s classes, and thought that most of them could have been successful if properly led. None of them had joined thinking, "I'd like to be a failure." Bureaucracy thrives in office environments, and Casey had pushed upon the bureaucracy a whole bunch of case officers who would be operating in a freewheeling way. I figured the mid-1980's classes had been eviscerated by the bureaucracy because they presented a threat to them.

The way these people were abused by the bureaucracy was tough on their families as well. They'd go to a domestic office for six months and then get sent back to HQs. Those few who got an overseas assignment were usually given a one-way ticket home within a few months, only to remain indefinitely in temporary housing. Some spent years with their families in the Oakwood, a popular temporary housing complex in the Washington, D.C. area. There's nothing wrong with the Oakwood, a clean and efficient housing service, but to be in limbo there was to be in a kind of hell. I swore to my wife that we'd never do time there.

One man had returned to the US after deciding, he said, that the intelligence service in his country of assignment was on to him. (I doubted this story: The country in question was a terrible place to live, and I suspected he'd just done it for his family's sake.) When he left the country with his family, he didn't bother to let HQs know where he was or what he was doing. He took a ship, a train, and a plane on a circuitous route out of the country, so it took him several days to get back to the US. HQs was panic-stricken. The man and his family got themselves stuck in the Oakwood for a year and a half. Surely its use as an instrument of punishment says something about the desirability of a long visit there.

IN THE WANING DAYS of our training course, a manager at HQs belatedly realized that Max had once been a paramilitary "knuckle dragger" with the Agency and suggested that this made him unfit to be a non-State Department officer. The manager wanted him removed and sent back to the paramilitary group. Max wanted to stay, and he put up a fight.

While he negotiated with the bureaucracy, he continued his training. In the "building inspector" exercise, a trainee meets with a role-player acting as a Slobovian agent. During the meeting, a knock comes at the door. It is another role-player acting as a Slobovian building inspector. It's an easy exercise. The correct thing to do is to stay relaxed and ask what you can do to help the inspector, to prevent him from developing suspicions and potentially calling the police.

Max felt that he'd put up with enough play-acting foolishness. He said, "Go away. I don't have time for you."

The building inspector went berserk and tried to force his way in. Max placed his hand on the instructor's face and pressed him out of the room, screaming, "Get out of here, you geezer."

Max earned a failing grade, but the violence of his response so frightened the instructors that their criticism of his conduct was surprisingly subdued.

Perhaps by coincidence, he convinced HQs to let him stay in the program.

TOWARD THE END OF the training course, Max was convinced that there would be a climactic final exercise involving days and nights of challenges—something to push us to our limits and beyond. He was eager for it. I didn't see why the course, having flowed like a lazy river so far, should suddenly get any more difficult. As graduation loomed, I taunted him: "Three days left, Max, how tough do you think it's going to be?" Finally the course ended with a big *blah*.

At our graduation ceremony, Roger said, "You know, you guys were a good bunch, but you ought to see the next training class. Those guys have some amazing qualifications. They'll be the best we've ever had." Thanks, Roger. We all could have seen that one coming.

The director of the CIA and some other HQs mandarins attended our ceremony as well. The entire class graduated. We didn't have a final ranking as far as I knew, but at a celebration that evening at a nearby bar, a classmate took me aside and said, "The instructors ranked me first in the class."

Another classmate confided, "Harry told me I was the top graduate in the class."

A late-arriving classmate: "Just got done talking to Roger. He says I was ranked number one in our class."

Coming out of the restroom, still zipping up his fly, Jonah said, "Hey, Ishmael, you know I was ranked at the top of the class?"

I decided that if so many people were at the top, surely I must be at the bottom. "I learned today that I was ranked last in the class," I said.

Word spread to Max that I'd been ranked last. Confronting me in front of a group of our classmates, he jabbed me in the chest and said, "Sir, you are a liar. I was ranked last in the class."

"My friend, I am sorry, but you are mistaken. None other than the director of clandestine operations told me that *I* was ranked last in the class."

"Ishmael, stop the lies. I have been personally informed by the Director of the Central Intelligence Agency that *I* was ranked last."

The next day, we said goodbye to our instructors. They'd taught us everything they knew. I thought the training course could have been quite a bit shorter, but the instructors meant well. My training class was assigned to stations located within the US for "on the job" training (OJT). I left immediately for my assignment, eager to pursue better living through espionage, but my classmates hung around the area for a few more days.

Jonah, finding himself alone in the empty safe house with our only female classmate, backed her into a corner and said, "You know you want it!" He'd sensed her signals of desire throughout the training course; now was their opportunity. It turned out she hadn't sent any signals. Shoving him away, she fled the office. She was engaged to be married. We'd all met her fiancé.

At the end of the course, I took a State Department language test in German and on the scale of one to five, in which three is fluent and five is native, I scored a four-plus in reading. (Sometimes I'd challenge my wife to open up the German dictionary and try to find a word I didn't know.) My understanding score was three, my speaking score a two, but I hadn't had anyone with whom to practice. Encouraged by these test results, I turned immediately to the study of Arabic.

The training year hadn't been too bad. I'd made good progress in two foreign languages, completed the case officer course, made some good friends, and had a new baby in my family. Still, all I could think about was getting to my new assignment and doing real case officer work.

★ 3 ★

American Apprenticeship

> Must I not serve a long apprenticehood
> To foreign passages, and in the end,
> Having my freedom, boast of nothing else
> But that I was a journeyman to grief?
> *Shakespeare*

The next phase was an on-the-job training tour at an Agency post within the United States. We were now certified case officers, so we'd be able to work on espionage cases, but only under close observation by our domestic offices' management.

Before I joined the Agency, I'd read that the CIA and the FBI essentially split their operations, with the CIA operating in foreign countries and the FBI operating within the United States. Americans didn't want a domestic spy agency that could become a threat to liberty, a potential Gestapo or KGB.

In fact, most of the Agency's offices and people were located in the United States, at HQs and countless stations, bases, and other offices throughout the country. Some employees located in US offices made occasional and brief trips to foreign countries, but most spent the bulk of their careers operating within the US. Eighty-five percent of Agency employees are located domestically at HQs at 24 unmarked offices within the United States, according to one author.[10] I suspect the percentage of Agency employees in the US is higher—more than 90 percent. Years later, after 9/11, the number of US offices grew dramatically. Today it is certainly much higher than 24.

My family flew to our new city and I drove our car, stuffed with household odds and ends. In making a move, bank accounts have to be changed, a rental lease signed, the car put in good shape, the home furnished. The mundane chore of moving from one US city to another is the same for a spy as for anyone else, involving a series of small tasks requiring measured amounts of self-discipline. Before 9/11, the Agency treated its employees located in the US the same as any other federal employees. It paid some moving expenses, but the bulk of the move was on the employee's dime.

Making a move is relatively simple, but some case officers have trouble getting their families settled properly. If the family is unhappy or insecure at home, it is hard for a case officer to deal with the challenges presented by espionage cases.

After a year of training, I was full of restrained energy. Early in the morning I left my family at our temporary home, a motel, and got to my new domestic post. I stood outside the office, the same kind of nondescript complex as back in D.C., waiting for someone to arrive. The first person came in at 0800, a woman named Sylvia, big and blonde. She was in charge of communications and various administrative tasks in the office. "Who the flock are you?" she said.

She showed me to my office, a cluttered jumble of mismatched furniture and office equipment. I'd have to share it with several other trainees who'd been at the post for several months already. They arrived an hour later and briefed me on their operations.

My fellow trainees showed me the office's safe room. Each safe contained a drawer stuffed with files on foreigners living in the US: nationality, address, phone number, and occupation. These files were the Holy Grail, the real Glengarry leads. Sitting down at a table in the safe room, I sorted them into piles to explore further (Chinese diplomats, Iranians studying nuclear science) and piles to re-file or shred (Swedish ballerinas and Nicaraguan gardeners).

By mid-morning I was ready to grab the phone. In the Marine

Corps I'd learned a sense of urgency and on Wall Street I'd learned how to "make the call." Success depended on it. I believed that in the Agency it meant this: *Make contact with intel targets or Americans will die.* After a year of sitting in dimly-lit conference rooms, listening to the droning voices of instructors, I was well beyond ready. I leapt for the phone and began making calls.

My calling created a commotion in the office. My fellow trainees enjoyed the commotion, which unsettled the older employees. The deputy chief was out of the office running an errand, so someone sent the word for the chief. But the chief remained behind his closed door.

"Have you done traces on these leads before calling them?" a woman asked.

"Have you run these leads by the referents? Do you have HQs approval?" asked her husband.

"Ishmael is 'cold calling' in there," said one employee to another.

The hubbub surrounding the door to my office increased, but I kept on smiling, dialing, and setting appointments with potential human sources. Sylvia laughed. "You're a crazy flocker," she said.

Finally the deputy chief returned from his errand and the older employees ran to him.

In a calm and gentle way, he took the phone from my hand and hung it up. He asked me to come to his office, where he explained the process for approaching intel targets. It required a written plan and then approval to make the call, both well in advance. Obtaining the approval was a complicated task involving the coordination of many layers of management.

To make a call to a person from China, he explained, I'd first have to go to a "referent," the man in charge of all things Chinese. Then I'd need to go to that man's wife, who handled liaison with the FBI, in order to clear it with the Bureau. Then on to the deputy of our office, and then to the boss. The boss would send it to

HQs, which would reply within a few weeks. If everything went smoothly it usually took at least a month to get approval to make that first contact.

The deputy studied the appointments I'd made and allowed me to call my contacts back to postpone—except in the case of an Israeli military officer. I had to cancel that meeting. Israel was theoretically an intel target, but in practice we didn't target Israelis. The deputy explained that the complexities of US/Israeli politics precluded any realistic operations. (Close liaison with Israeli contacts produced one of the Agency's clearest strategic intelligence successes. An Agency team under the direction of expert CIA officer Waldo Dubberstein[11] had provided an uncannily accurate prediction of the starting date, length, and outcome of the Arab/Israeli Six Day War in 1967[12].)

I went back to the OJT office where the other trainees showed me how to use the office's computer system. Then I spent several weeks drafting messages seeking approval to contact my targets.

OUR OFFICE WAS staffed both by trainees and by case officers ineligible for foreign assignments. Sylvia said she wasn't eligible for overseas service because of her weight, but the way she back-talked Agency managers may have had something to do with it, too. I found her attitude refreshing, but I wasn't her boss. The managers in the office, for their part, seemed almost frightened of her. Believing the word "flock" to be technically innocent, she used it liberally, bellowing flock this, flock you, you flockhead.

There were several pairs of married couples in the office. When I'd encountered these OFTPOTs during training, I'd assumed it was just a clever way for an employee to double his or her family income. Later, I realized it was a more complex and often difficult situation. It was harder for OFTPOTs to get overseas assignments because a station had to agree to take both of them. If one had a bad reputation, both suffered. Spouses worked closely with each other.

In any working environment there are opportunities to make mistakes and look foolish; OFTPOTs had to look foolish in front of their spouses, as well. Worst of all, there was no respite from the Agency's dysfunctional bureaucracy: You took it home with you every night. Needless to say, OFTPOTs tended to be bitter.

In later years, whenever I ran into an internal conflict, there always seemed to be an OFTPOT involved.

The deputy and several other employees had health problems which prevented them from further foreign assignments. The chief had done a few tours in the Middle East, but since then his wife had refused to live abroad. He expected to be in the US until he retired. He was so reserved and reclusive that I imagined he'd been through something terrible in the course of his service. Later I learned that he was just naturally shy. What seemed to bother him most about his US assignment was that he made less money than when he was stationed in the Middle East.

AS THE WEEKS PASSED, management's confidence in me grew as they realized I'd be less likely to cause a flap than they'd first thought. I settled into a routine. I'd create proposals for contact, get approvals from the office and from HQs, and then, armed with a plethora of commercial aliases, plus a beautifully made CIA badge, make appointments with foreign targets at their consular posts, universities, or businesses. I'd meet them to see if they had access to any secrets of interest to the US and if they did, advance the relationship and then recruit them.

I worked from lists of foreign diplomats assigned to consulates in the US, lists of military officers in the US (usually in training courses), and lists of foreign students studying at US universities. Since I was in the Midwest, the quality of foreign diplomats was poor—mostly consular or visa processing personnel. We rarely contacted military officers, as most were in the US for only a few months. The approval process was slow; if we hurried it up, we could possibly get a go-ahead to call a target within a few weeks, but then to recruit him would take more approvals that could drag on for months. Anyone who was in the US for fewer than four to six months just couldn't be worked through the system.

Typically I sought out graduate students from rogue states whose educations were being paid for by their governments and were studying something useful to the rogue state—such as nuclear science. I marveled at the fact that we allowed these people to come to the US to learn to create the weapons they could turn against us.

Some leads came from other government agencies. At the airport, which I visited often, the INS holding pens were always full of arrivals from Asia. An INS officer explained that illegal immigrants would flush their passports down the toilet on the plane, then arrive with no documents and claim that they'd be killed if they were forced to return. Sometimes they'd cut their wrists, though never deeply enough to endanger their lives. Once, a group of men chained themselves together. The INS would have to release them and tell them to come back again to the office for an interview. Of course none ever did.

Hats in all shapes, colors, and sizes hung from a wall at the airport office. A customs officer saw me looking at them and explained, "Drug dealers always wear funny hats. Whenever we see a guy with a funny hat, we send him to secondary inspection. It often turns out they're concealing drugs, so when we arrest them, a lot of the hats tend to get left behind. We pin them up on the wall."

Each day I went to the office in the morning to complete paperwork, then usually headed out for a lunch meeting, then back to the office, then sometimes to an evening or dinner meeting. I kept up my rigorous exercise routine, usually taking a break in the day for a workout or a run.

The word processors in the office were linked, so messages could be passed from computer to computer. Messages which were to be sent to HQs were revised as they went through the layers of management in the office, each manager making changes as the message came through. After a while, I had a large number of proposals and requests in the system still waiting for forward motion. I began to feel the same frustration I'd felt during the training course. Several layers of management, I saw, did nothing but process and edit the cables created by the OJT trainees.

As my operational proposals and requests for approval to meet foreigners built up, the system seemed to freeze up. I filled the time—and vented my frustration—by turning once more to language study, this time Arabic. As with the German I'd practiced during training, I could memorize Arabic unobtrusively by occasionally glancing at lists of words.

The cable, having passed through many layers of management, rarely read as it had going in. It was like a game of Telephone. Many "editors" seemed to make changes to suit their personal agendas. My cables often mutated into something shapeless, flaccid, and always risk-free.

DURING MY DOMESTIC ASSIGNMENT I worked with a professional group of FBI agents. The FBI's work was easier to measure than the Agency's—either they caught criminals or they didn't—and I thought this gave their organization a clearer sense of purpose. They weren't perfect. A key FBI manager I dealt with was suing the Bureau for passing him over for a promotion—due, he believed, to his country of origin. He tended to be brittle and he was especially sensitive to any suggestion that the Agency knew the intelligence business better than he did. For the most part, however, FBI agents struck me as forthright and professional.

An immense tension existed between FBI agents and Agency officers because there was an overlap of mission—both were trying to recruit foreigners in the US. Many Agency officers incorrectly believed that FBI agents were little better than unsophisticated cops, good at catching bank robbers but inept at intel work. FBI agents, for their part, felt snubbed by Agency officers. [13]

At a joint conference of FBI and Agency officers I attended, the Agency speaker talked down to the FBI without realizing it. "You FBI agents don't operate in the intelligence realm a lot, so naturally we know more about these topics that you do. You guys can't concentrate on this stuff because you are out doing bank robbery investigations." In protest, FBI agents began getting up and walking out of the conference. Eventually, only Agency employees remained. The speaker and the other Agency people present seemed oblivious that the FBI agents had just walked out.

Agency officers were supposed to check with the FBI before doing any operation involving the more important targets such as Soviets, Iranians, and Chinese. Anything with a possible criminal angle required coordination with the FBI. Working with the lower-level FBI agents was more effective than having our managers talk to their managers, so I got a badge that enabled me to roam the FBI building at will, and it was very useful in building relationships with my counterparts.

USING FALSE DOCUMENTS and a cover company's address and phone numbers, I contacted a rogue state citizen doing graduate research in nuclear engineering at a local university. I expressed interest in his field. His education was sponsored and paid for by his government. I left him my phone number.

The next time we spoke, he said, "I tried to call you, but your number did not work. They say you are not working there."

"Of course that's my number. It must have been a temporary secretary who answered the phone when you called."

"But she was forceful. She said she worked there a long time, in a very small office, and she knows everyone, but not an Ishmael."

It had taken me two experiences to learn an important lesson:

Never rely on the backstopped phone numbers issued by the Agency. From then on I used my own answering services.

I'd cleared all my routine Agency and FBI approvals to contact the scientist, but the local FBI office in his small university town wanted to be notified personally prior to any meetings on his turf. It was a one-man office. The other OJT trainees had dealt with this agent before and they instructed me in how to deal with him: "He never picks up his phone, so you have to go there in person to talk to him. He's usually asleep at his desk, with the window shutters closed, so you have to knock. Knock softly so as not to startle him, but knock persistently. If he thinks you might go away, he won't answer the door."

Softly but persistently, I repeated to myself. There was something absurd in all this, but at least it turned out that when correct procedures were followed, the agent in question invariably granted his approval.

My scientist was a suspicious fellow, and I had little doubt that he'd been briefed by his government to expect someone like me to give him a call. CIA officers, traditionally working as part of the US Department of State, usually posed as government employees, so I hoped that my approach as a businessman would be more plausible. I planned to ask him to help me solve a technical problem. I'd say that his help might lead to my offering him a job.

I rented a car using my alias identification and credit card, then traveled to the pretty campus where the rogue state scientist studied. We'd planned to meet in the cafeteria. Within fifty paces of it I could feel the heat from the eyes of American graduate students loitering in the area. Several of these scruffy kids followed me as I entered the cafeteria. They affected a studied nonchalance; they were the worst surveillance team I'd ever encountered.

I found my target and greeted him warmly, but he had a smug look that practically sing-songed, "I know something you don't know." Some pouty members of his impromptu surveillance team flopped down at adjacent tables, pretending not to listen, and others lurked nearby exchanging glances and whispers.

I pulled some "litter" out of my briefcase, brochures on Acme Software Solutions products, and launched into a discussion of the products and the technical problem which, if solved, might lead to desired product improvements. I set my voice to a drone, my demeanor suggesting nothing out of the ordinary. After half an hour of this, some of our "neighbors" lost interest and drifted away.

Our meeting concluded, I headed back to my car. The surveillance team had dwindled to one long-haired fellow in a dirty tee-shirt. As slyly as possible, he wrote down the license number of my rental car.

Over the next few months, I continued to meet the scientist on campus. Each time, there were fewer graduate students lurking nearby, until finally there were none. He agreed to move meetings off-campus as we came closer and closer to an intelligence relationship.

IN THE SPIRIT OF COOPERATION, HQs asked our office to maintain better relations with other CIA offices in the city. Our chief followed these instructions with enthusiasm. He visited our colleagues in those offices and invited them to visit ours for meetings and cocktail parties. When HQs required the chief to send a list of our office's achievements each month, half of our list dealt with these efforts to improve good fellowship.

The chief needed more than that, though. He wanted to recruit an agent. Searching our files, he found a former agent who had worked for us in the Middle East for many years. Eventually, things had heated up in the agent's home country, revolution broke out, and the agent had been exposed as an American sympathizer. He'd fled the country with Agency assistance and had taken refuge in the US, where, for the last ten years, he'd lived a quiet life.

Our chief contacted the former agent and asked if he'd be willing to discuss events in his home country, and keep an eye out for any of its citizens visiting the US. The agent readily agreed to help. He'd missed working for the Agency, had all but been waiting by the phone for a call.

The chief handled the paperwork as though the agent were a brand-new contact. Each month, our office's list of achievements contained a lengthy paragraph on this operation. The first month described spotting and locating the target, the next month, assessing his access and willingness to cooperate. Finally, a full paragraph announced that the target had agreed to provide secrets to the Agency. This was the classic recruitment cycle we'd all been taught in training. At each step of the cycle, HQs congratulated the chief on the progress he was making.

THE GODFATHER, the veteran spy and man of many wives, visited our office for a few weeks and used it as a base from which to run an operation. While waiting for his meetings to begin, he amused himself by pulling out a local telephone book and dialing up names he recognized as terrorist tribal names. He'd find a Fadlallah or a Mugniyah, pick up the phone and, without a script, give them a call.

"Hello, this is Hussayn," he said in Arabic, "is this the number for Muhammad? I have not seen him in many years. I am visiting from Lebanon." Whether there was a Muhammad there or not, the calls often developed into lengthy conversations. He was able to find someone in the world that they knew in common—and he might even stumble upon a traveling terrorist.

The Godfather didn't obey many Agency rules, but his charisma and strength of personality kept the bureaucrats at bay. He was a bit like Sylvia in the sense that the bureaucracy didn't smell fear in him and so didn't know what to do with him. An uncommonly skilled linguist, he could go to a country and learn its language in a short time: "I went to Spain," he once said. "I was there studying the language for three months. Then I went to meet a target. Talking to the target, it suddenly occurs to me I'm recruiting him in Spanish after only three months of studying the language."

The Godfather was so effusively outgoing that he almost never had to wait for HQs to give him a go-ahead. He'd just put on a *kaffiyeh*, rent a limousine and driver, tell a target he worked for a Saudi prince, and hand him a fistful of money. Then he'd tell him to go home and think things over, and they'd meet again the next day.

At seminars and conventions, the Godfather sat in the front row and clapped loudly when his target gave a speech. The target would smile broadly at the Godfather. After the speech, the Godfather would approach the target to ask if he could help him with his particular problem. The target was always eager to converse.

Because of his gregariousness and high-octane activity, the Godfather had to be careful. His cover was utterly blown. Numerous foreign intelligence services knew he worked for the Agency. Most officers would be sent back to HQs when their covers were blown, but not the Godfather.

I spent a lot of time with Lebanese immigrants to target terrorists and counterfeiters. Lebanese targets are complex because their country contains so many different factions. The Godfather helped me to better understand this. A Lebanese Christian will be eager to assist against terrorism, but may have no ability to do so. A Lebanese Sunni may also lack access. Lebanese Shi'a have potential, but then their loyalties are so diffuse that they could be bitter enemies or close allies of any other Shi'a. During my OJT tour I spent many midnight dinners getting to know Lebanese contacts.

We had potential Indian chemical and nuclear targets in the area, but they were tough to evaluate because Agency experience showed that Indians rarely returned to their positions of access in India once they made it to the US. Some of our Agency offices in the US abandoned targeting Indians; one could waste a lot of time courting an Indian only to find he had no intention of returning home.

Dinners and lunches were an important feature of agent development. My Chinese targets couldn't stand any kind of food except Chinese. They had a visceral hatred of sushi. I also had trouble moving Chinese targets forward because the OFTPOT in charge of Chinese targeting was a sort of James Jesus Angleton character, one who saw the world of espionage as a wilderness of mirrors. The OFTPOT figured that if I'd met a friendly Chinese citizen, he must surely be a Chinese spy trying to recruit me: Any Chinese student in the US had to have an income from the Chinese government.

Several retired case officers worked in the office as contractors. Agency people usually came back as contractors the day after retirement. Prior to 9/11, contractors were paid a reasonable hourly rate. One spent his day chatting and doing crossword puzzles. Another had once been held hostage by terrorists while serving in a foreign assignment. He carried a concealed pistol and swore he'd fill his captors full of lead the instant he saw them. One of the OFTPOT couples in the office sold products in some Amway-style pyramid scheme.

One day, a local FBI agent called. "Ishmael, what the hell are you guys doing over there?" he asked. "I just met the target we're working jointly with your office, and he told me you guys are trying to sell him consumer goods." I learned that the OFTPOTs had pitched their products to agents and prospective agents, as well as to US government contacts at the FBI and INS.

DURING MY DOMESTIC OJT assignment, I traveled back to HQs a few times to try to push forward the paperwork for my overseas assignment. The HQs offices were strewn with the carnage of the non-State Department training classes: officers in limbo, officers just back on a one-way ticket from some aborted foreign assignment.

While I'd been on my OJT tour, the recruiting trend at HQs had been to hire people reputed to be from wealthy families. The Agency seemed fascinated by wealth. A recent training class had been lousy with the spoiled progeny of *nouveau riche* families. Most of their fathers had connections to the Agency as contractors.

One of these trainees required that the Agency hire his wife, and the Agency complied. The couple confided that they were open to assignment in any foreign city, so long as that city had Concorde service. Once the kids found out that working for the Agency wasn't as much fun as they'd expected, they quit the training course. The husband made it about halfway. His wife stuck it out a bit longer, but the instructors noted that she'd often leave unexpectedly to go fox hunting in Virginia. Nevertheless, come graduation day, both were awarded their certifications as case officers. Other trainees complained, but to no avail. The instructors advised that the train-ees had rated certification for their valuable "life experience," an explanation that satisfied no one. Soon after, the couple quit, mak-ing the complaint moot.

I studied the walking wounded hanging around the HQs office, listening to their stories. I wanted to learn from them and avoid the obstacles they'd faced. A Portuguese speaker had been locked into a triangle of Portuguese-language assignment possi-bilities: Brazil, Portugal, or Angola. He hadn't gotten along with the people in Portugal so he requested he be sent to Angola, but as soon as he received that assignment, the people from Portugal were sent there, too. There was no escape.

Another officer's station had given him a list of targets he was forbidden to contact—including every conceivable target in the region. He was on the first plane back to HQs to seek an overseas assignment somewhere else.

One poor fellow got back from an assignment in Southeast Asia. He was married, but he also had a lot of girlfriends. For counterin-telligence purposes, the Agency requires officers to report the iden-tities of their girlfriends, which he dutifully did, thereby developing a reputation around the Agency as a ladies' man.

Time went by and he continued to report his girlfriends, until he was assigned to a chief who thought their quantity indicated a moral failing. In the officer's annual evaluation, the boss indicated as much, buying the officer his one-way ticket back to HQs. The officer sought to have the dreaded "morals problem" removed from his file. Under pressure from HQs, the boss agreed to remove the comment—but he spitefully replaced it with "this officer cannot be trusted with government funds"—an even more serious charge.

It was around that time that I met Charlton for the first time. Charlton was a no-nonsense officer who didn't have any complaints, and, if he did, he kept them to himself. He was a foreign national with passports from three countries and excellent native language skills. He was never frustrated, because the Agency bureaucracy wasn't much worse than the ones he'd dealt with in his homelands. At the same time, his overseas pay package made him rich by the standards of two of his three home countries, so he wasn't as tempted as some were by opportunities in the business world.

★ 4 ★

Perseverance and Soothing Language

> Let what will be said or done, pre-
> serve your *sangfroid* immovably, and
> to every obstacle oppose patience,
> perseverance, and soothing language
> *Thomas Jefferson*

I spoke to Max on a secure line between our domestic posts.

"I now hold the record," Max said.

"What record?"

"The record for the earliest recorded 'Christmas holidays' excuse. It's June, and a man from HQs just told me he might not be able to get my overseas assignment approved, what with the holiday season coming up."

"June! Not bad, Max. June will be tough to beat."

Max and Jonah had been assigned to domestic OJTs in a part of the country where there weren't many good targets. Still, they were such hard workers that they managed to call just about every target country foreigner in their region and made some decent recruitments.

Max put Jonah on the phone.

"Acute attacks of diarrhea stand between me and service to my country in an overseas assignment," Jonah said. The man responsible for processing Jonah's overseas paperwork suffered from intestinal problems. "A bad attack will keep this guy out of the office for three weeks at a time. I'm trying to figure out ways to get the process moving. Maybe I need to create a crisis. Government employees never act until a crisis forces them to act."

We were eager to get to our overseas assignments. Members of our training class had begun to quit the Agency. All of us sensed that the oft-repeat delay "two more weeks" could go on for years. Most of us were in our late twenties or early thirties, eager to achieve. As we looked over the sad sacks at HQs, we asked: "Is this what I want to be?" To them, time meant nothing; each day was just another one closer to retirement.

Max and I were just as frustrated by this Kafkaesque process of promise and delay, but we also saw the enormous potential for achievement—for America's security—once we finally *did* get overseas. We'd been through plenty of "only the strong survive" courses in the military and figured that this was just another obstacle we'd endure. Not many trainees felt this way, however, and there were numerous resignations.

An OJT trainee came into our office one day to resign. He brought his spy gear to turn in and Sylvia pointed him to our office, where he dumped it off. After the man left, my colleagues and I looked at each other quizzically for a few moments and then blurted out, "Everything in this office is spy gear." So many employees had quit that our office had become a dumping ground for equipment.

A new trainee, Martin, arrived. Soon thereafter, he did a commendable job of recruiting a valuable human source, a visiting government official considered important by HQs. The foreign official was a member of a powerful and wealthy family. Such connections were important in the source's country, and he loved to talk about his ancient and influential line—descended from royalty, naturally. As far as we knew, all that he said was true. Yet the man rolled over for the customary $1,000 per month. I would see this again and again, a source who claimed to be connected to great wealth and influence, yet was willing to sell his country for a song. Martin had built his relationship with the target through scuba diving, bungee jumping, deep sea fishing, and duck hunting.

I'D HELD OUT A LONG TIME against the temptation of resignation. When the cycle continued, I thought about what Jonah had said: Government employees never act until a crisis forces them to act. The next written message I sent to HQs said, "I have completed the training course and compiled a good recruitment record in my domestic post. There are no obstacles to my overseas deployment. Please get organized and do your duty. Do the job you have been assigned to do and approve my overseas assignment."

They fired back, "You should watch the tone of your messages. They're vituperative. Be patient. Your overseas assignment should be all set in about two weeks."

That about did it. I telephoned Roger. "Bullshit," I said. "You people are lying. You'll say 'two more weeks' until the end of time. I'm moving back there to Washington, D.C. right now to sit on top of you until this gets done."

Roger lost his mind over that. "You can't come back here without orders! You have no authorization to come back here! We won't pay for your travel!"

A calmer "good cop" voice got on the line: "Look, Ishmael, we're doing what we can do to get your assignment arranged. There are a multitude of managers who need to sign off on your assignment first. If you come back here, you'll upset a bunch of people, and that won't help you."

"I understand that I'm going to offend people at HQs. I don't care. I won't allow myself to wind up like all the sad sacks waiting around for you to act. You've already caused the resignations of some of the members of my training class, all of them good people. We have missions in this Agency and I want to get them done."

I made good on my threat to HQs.

I MOVED MY FAMILY BACK to the HQs area. Like an Okie headed

for California, I drove a car crammed full of household goods. My wife and children went by plane, and we moved back into a hotel room.

As soon as I reached HQs, I confronted the management about my assignment.

The files they'd supposedly kept on me were empty. They hadn't done a thing during the year I'd been away. Each time they'd told me they were working on it, they'd lied.

The Worst Spy in the World came by the office to see me. "I know you're frustrated about the slow pace. Perhaps we should pause a moment and pray." He leaned over and took my hands in his.

"I don't want to pray," I said. "I want to solve the problem."

"You need to learn to be patient," he said, and then he left.

Roger approached.

"You haven't gone to language school. You need to go to language school."

"I've already got the languages. I learned them on my own during training. I have the test scores to prove it."

"Well, maybe so, but you need to put in the hours."

HQs had created language schools for case officers. The schools taught difficult languages like Chinese and Japanese by way of a single teacher who met the class daily in an apartment. Unfortunately, the schools had been around long enough for everyone to realize that even after a two-year course confined in an apartment, the students weren't learning

A linguist colleague suggested the best way to learn a language was to go to the country where it was spoken and actively use it. He had traveled to Japan after graduating from high school. "After I'd been in Japan for a month," he said, "I was speaking Japanese on a functional level, and I traveled around the country with a group of Japanese friends who spoke no English."

He visited our Japanese school and spoke to the students. "They're not learning the language," he said. "When they do speak, they sound like women. Japanese men and women speak in different tones. Since the teacher is a woman, the students naturally sound like her."

In the Chinese school, the students decided that their instructor wasn't good enough and tried unsuccessfully to get themselves assigned another. Tensions mounted, students weren't getting along with one another, and before long they were at each other's throats. The frustration led to at least one fistfight.

HQs loved to assign people to language school. It was an easy and risk-free way to keep them *looking* busy.

"What's Smith doing," a senior bureaucrat might ask.

"Smith is in Chinese language school," came the reply, and everyone would be pleased that Smith was productively occupied learning such an important language. Chances were that Smith would never put this skill to work.

Jonah was back in the HQs area for some meetings and was hanging around a safe-house apartment with one colleague who spoke Japanese and another who spoke Korean. They were waiting to see Roger, to discuss their overseas assignments. Roger arrived and met privately first with the Korean speaker and then with the Japanese speaker.

After the meetings, the Korean speaker said, "Roger just told me that we don't have any requirements right now for a Korean speaker, and he's set me up for a two-year language school to learn Japanese."

The Japanese speaker said, "Damn that Roger. He just told me that we don't have any requirements right now for a Japanese speaker, and he's set me up to go to a two year language school to learn Korean."

Thankfully, my test scores enabled me to avoid the dead end of language school.

Some colleagues made things harder on themselves by demanding certain locations, usually the nicer cities of Western Europe, which severely narrowed the range of possible assignments. Remembering what the Godfather had told me, I made things as easy on HQs as possible by telling them I'd go *anywhere* overseas. I figured this would mean the Middle East. No one wanted to go to the Middle East. The Middle East wasn't a nice place to live, and it had been a graveyard for non-State Department officers.

"We only have one officer between Burma and the Atlantic Ocean who isn't a State Department diplomat," I said to the Worst Spy. "That's a stretch covering most of Asia through to North Africa. So we should be able to find a vacant spot somewhere."

After I made a nuisance of myself at HQs for several weeks, my assignment was finally approved.

HQS SENT ME to another training course, a sort of prerequisite to overseas assignment. Max and I were the only two in this class, and we found ourselves back in Slobovia, land of make-believe. The Agency devoted incredible resources to our training. Much of the instruction involved advanced surveillance detection, and for those exercises there were as many as 30 instructors working on just the two of us.

During classroom portions, we studied the Agency's problems with a Middle Eastern agent program. Nearly all of the agents had proven to have been doubles or had been exposed and arrested by their own government. As had been the case with Cuba, the Middle Eastern country had fed us massive quantities of false information.[14]

We studied the psychologies of some of our rogue state targets. A favorite of mine was a fascinating paper on the psychology of Iranian men. It argued that negotiating skills were so important in the ancient Persian trading culture that personal communication had become a high art. Iranian men were masters of histrionics, able to act out emotions dramatically, and skilled with facial movements such as the rolling and flashing of eyes. Almost all Iranian men could cry at will. The handout said the men were spoiled by the females in the family and grew up with megalomaniac perceptions of their abilities and talents.

We learned more about the polygraph during this course. The Box measures physical reactions: Normal people will react less perceptibly to a question like, "Were you born in Pennsylvania?" than they will to, "Have you stolen money or goods valued at more than $25?" The examiners can fail applicants whose reactions are simply too strong. But what Box operators really seek is some admission of guilt. At times in the Agency's history, operators have been paid bonuses for each such admission.

Box sessions are essentially interrogations disguised as interviews. The operator's favorite technique is to encourage the examinee to confess a seemingly minor offense so as to "clear up" the exam and allow the applicant to pass. He states outright that most aberrant or criminal behavior is of no consequence: "Look, we don't care if you once stole $20 from someone. We're after big stuff: Did you rob a bank? Have you committed a murder? That's what we're after here." Of course, the examinee probably hasn't murdered anyone, but there was that time he shoplifted a pair of underwear from a department store. He sheepishly confesses, and with that, he's out of a job. If the "minor" admission truly is inconsequential, the operator focuses on persuading the interviewee to make a larger one.

Edward Lee Howard, one of the first of the CIA's turncoats, admitted during a Box that he had stolen $12 from the purse of a woman sitting next to him on an airplane. Howard was fired. The Agency had been preparing him for an assignment to Moscow and he'd been briefed on the identities of several important Russian agents. He sold this information to the KGB.

The Agency suspected Howard of having gone to the other side, so the FBI put him under surveillance. Eluding it, he made his way to Moscow. Years later, Max spotted Howard walking in a park in Budapest. Ideas of capturing him, putting him in a bag, and spiriting him back to the US ran through his mind, but Howard quickly disappeared from view—probably for the best. He was a broken alcoholic by then. He lived in Moscow until he supposedly died by falling down and breaking his neck—the cause was murky—in 2002. He was 50 years old.

Listening to CIA employees talk about their Box sessions can be as boring as listening to people talk about the dream they had last night. Most employees were believers in the machine's quasi-magical infallibility. "Then, finally," they'd say, "I remembered the time I had taken a quarter too much out of the office coffee fund, and I admitted that to the examiner. My reactions cleared up!" There is no scientific evidence that the Box actually works, but it has had so many successes in extracting admissions of guilt—"I have been having sex with dogs for the last twenty years"[15]—from applicants and employees the Agency will probably never get rid of it. It is a great interrogation tool—though, given the power of suggestion, hooking someone up to a photocopier might be just as effective.

MAX AND I alternated exercises, morning and afternoon. If the instructors put me through one in the morning, they'd put him through the same one later in the day. Naturally, we kept in touch about this.

I'd tell him, "The Slobovian agent had information about a planned coup against the regime. Then he got up and went to the bathroom. He left an envelope on the table. I think we're supposed to open the envelope to see what's inside and then put it back as if we hadn't looked at it."

He did as I said. The envelope contained dates, times, names of the leaders of the coup.

The next day he called back. "The agent threw a tantrum. He's worried that his status as an agent may have been exposed. I calmed him down and we reviewed our emergency plans. I think that was the point of the exercise."

A couple of weeks into the course, my phone rang. It was an instructor. I wondered why Max hadn't called. "Go to 23 Washington Street," the instructor said. I'd never been to that address before.

When I arrived, I saw some burly fellows in the parking lot. As I walked through the lot, they angled to intercept me. I slightly altered my direction, and so did they. They were law enforcement officers, without a doubt. At last they threw me to the ground, then hauled me into the building for questioning.

The interrogation lasted for hours, which was evidently why Max hadn't been able to call. After the interrogation, they evaluated my conduct and gave me pointers:

"Con men know to look you square in the eye and give you a firm handshake, so a steely gaze and a firm handshake have no validity as measures of a person's truthfulness.

"A person's curiosity is a good test—if a person is innocent, and knows nothing of the accusation, he'll ask a lot of questions about why he's been arrested.

"The suspect might seem angry, but we can tell when the anger is false. False anger is a good indicator of guilt. Another is falling asleep—sometimes we'll leave the suspect alone in the interrogation room for a while to see if he'll fall asleep. Guilty people have been under a great deal of worry and pressure for some time already, so once arrested and left alone, they tend to go to sleep. They're exhausted and know that a lot lies ahead. The innocent tend to pace back and forth, trying to figure out what's happening.

"If you've been found with an illegal item, and the only course is to deny that it's yours, then do so, but don't suggest that the policeman must have planted it. Never insult them or they'll take a personal interest in getting you.

"Always keep a cool temper. It's hard for an interrogator to get worked up if you stay cool. Talk a lot, but don't give any facts. Don't move backwards, stay where you are even if the interrogator's nose is in your face. Act as if you are not a criminal suspect but an innocent person. You understand that the police have made a mistake. There are no hard feelings, and you will help them find the right person. Remember that the interrogation situation was created to make you feel helpless and to get you to confess."

The Agency had taught us to use the concept of "cover within a cover," in which we were prepared to admit to a lesser crime in order to avert suspicion from the larger crime. For example, if I were picked up by the police while standing on a dark street corner and accused of being a spy, after interrogation I might break down and admit that I was looking for a prostitute.

These officers, however, noted that "most criminals, especially drug dealers, use 'cover within a cover.'" The officers continued: "When a law enforcement officer sees 'cover within a cover,' it really gets his attention and he focuses even harder on the suspect. Better to just stick to your original story."

It was advice like this that made the interrogation exercise the best in the course. I was disappointed to learn, however, that most of my colleagues had not realized it was an exercise until it was over.

NORMALLY, large surveillance teams were available to train us, but today they had been sent to Baltimore to handle an unexpected "requirement" there. Without our teams, Max and I had no exercises.

Our instructors went to HQs and rounded up a bunch of guys who looked like they weren't doing anything. The instructors piled these unfortunates into vans, gave them a few rudimentary instructions, and drove them to Old Town Alexandria to be our surveillance team for the day. The Agency and the FBI both used Old Town Alexandria for this training because there was a great deal of foot traffic in the town.

I set out on my run, beginning at the old Torpedo Factory build-ing in Alexandria. Walking my route, I couldn't detect any surveil-lance. It started to rain. I tried every trick but still couldn't see the surveillants. The fundamental principle of surveillance is to see one's pursuers but not to let them know you do. If the surveillants see you looking, they'll think you are a spy, because ordinary people don't imagine that they're being followed. It's easy to detect surveil-lance by backtracking or looking behind, and it's easy to evade sur-veillance, but if you do any of that, you'll be as good as made.

But I couldn't detect the team. I stood in front of a restaurant on King Street taking shelter from the rain. I eyeballed the area, eye-balling more than I should have. A man standing next to me buying takeout said, "You guys aren't very good, are you?" The Agency and the FBI did so much surveillance training in the neighborhood, even the locals had become sensitized.

That evening the exercise drew to a close and we met our instruc-tors to discuss the day's work. The instructors asked us how we'd done. Max and I said we hadn't seen a single thing all day.

"Neither did we," the instructors said. "After we released that surveillance team on you, we never saw another one of the surveil-lants ever again."

THERE ARE TIMES when it's necessary to look at surveillants—for instance, when they're right in front of your face. A colleague who was under close and continuous surveillance, with surveillants wait-ing outside his door and walking next to him every time he left his apartment building, continued to obey the "look without looking" principle. But this was foolish: If they're right in your face and still you ignore them, they'll know you're a spy. Any sane person would assume he was being stalked, and notify the police.

Our chief instructor told us to surveil any car we saw bearing diplomatic plates with the letters "FC." "FC" meant the car belonged to the Soviet diplomatic mission. Our instructor insisted that the

FBI had chosen FC as short for "f-ing Communist." He wanted us to surveil them just to give them a hard time. I happened upon FC plates twice. On both occasions the FC car was able quickly to recognize me as a surveillant, and evaded aggressively, by doing illegal U-turns and accelerating to high speeds.

The instructors wanted us to go off to our foreign assignments in a proper spirit of awe and respect for the abilities of a good surveillance team, so they gave our team copies of our pre-planned routes. Sometimes we went through an entire route without seeing the surveillants because they weren't there, having not bothered to show themselves that day. But in theory, we'd been under surveillance the whole time. "Wow," we were supposed to think, "we were under surveillance the whole time but didn't see a thing! I sure learned respect for surveillance!"

As a corollary to "look without looking," our instructors taught us to go easy on our shadows. "Remember, surveillants are ordinary people working for a salary. Don't make life difficult for them. If you're under surveillance, make it easy for them to keep up with you. You don't want them to hate you. Surveillance teams will knife your car tires and put dirt in your gas tank if they think you're giving them a hard time."

Teams from the FBI and the Agency followed us during our exercises. The after-action critiques from the FBI teams were methodical and professional, while those from the Agency teams tended to be emotional and accusatory. The Agency instructors wanted to impress us with the capabilities of surveillance, so they never loosened up, badgering me mercilessly for my ineptitude in the exercises, especially a vehicle surveillance exercise that took place in the Leesburg area of Virginia. I'd felt ill that weekend, because I'd tried to repair a sewage backup in our rental house myself instead of hiring a plumber. The problem wasn't easy to solve, and I soon was covered in raw, black sewage.

My wife felt sorry for the ribbing I was taking and sought to help out by interjecting, "Oh, but you don't understand, Ishmael was suffering from a terrible case of diarrhea during that exercise."

The crones on the surveillance team cackled and sneered. "Oh, poor thing, were you unwell? Is that going to be your excuse when you're overseas, too?"

Our chief instructor had trained Edward Lee Howard, and had liked him a good deal more than he liked us. "Eddie did the exercise this way," he'd say, or, "Eddie liked this exercise best."

A fellow officer, William Loman, had gone overseas only to be blown right back after about six months, having lost a briefcase containing sensitive papers. He'd left it on a bus; the Agency never saw it again. Loman and his family moved into the Oakwood and would be going through the lengthy process of securing a new overseas assignment. It would be a rough road for him with many extended delays.

With nothing for Loman to do, HQs assigned him to oversee some of our surveillance training. Suddenly he wasn't our colleague, but our boss, and a most domineering boss he proved to be. His fraught years with the Agency had turned him into a terrible martinet. Max and I served as his personal toadies for weeks. "You guys don't get it," he said. "There's something missing in your thinking process. I can't figure out what it is, but I don't think you two should be allowed to go overseas."

We debated how to solve the Loman problem. I couldn't ask the Worst Spy or Roger for help, having burned both of those bridges. "Let's put a bag over his head and beat him with telephone books," Max said.

"I think Loman's bullying us, so I'm also leaning toward a confrontational solution," I said, playing straight man.

The next day we carried out a series of exercises Loman had invented, then stood around our cars in the parking lot of the Tysons Corner shopping mall, reviewing our performance. "You guys need a lot of work," Loman said. "I'm not sure you'll pass this course.

I'm enjoying my new management role, though. I'm good at it."

Loman's wife drove up and got out of her car. We'd met her before, and said hello. The day's exercises were over, and she asked Loman if he would go into the mall and do some shopping. She tore off a list of things for him to buy. They made plans to meet up in the mall and he walked off. She paused until he was out of hearing and said, "Hey, I just wanted to thank you guys for dealing with Loman these past few weeks. I know he's been a handful. He worked hard to get his overseas assignment and then losing it was really hard on him. He's had a hard time adjusting to being back in the US. It's meant a lot to him to be able to work with you guys all day."

We realized he was in a bad way and deserved our sympathy. "We like him, too," Max said, "but don't let him give us any trouble." Our feelings toward him slightly softened, we buckled down and endured the rest of the course.

Max and I and our wives next attended a "crash and burn" course in rapid escape and how to deal with attackers and terrorists while driving. We used a fleet of battered cars and raced around, ramming them into each other. Everyone enjoyed this course immensely. We did a lot of "nerfing" by hitting a car in one of its rear wheels, causing it to spin off the road. The instructors had just finished teaching a group of highway patrolmen how to do it. Nerfing is an excellent way to get another car off the road, far more effective than ramming it in the side.

One of the points of the course was to learn how to cause damage to cars when necessary. Chauffeurs in particular can freeze up during a terrorist attack, as they've spent years making sure their car doesn't get scratched and aren't prepared for the moment when it's time to let all hell break loose.

AT THE END OF the driving course, HQs invited me to join the Counterterrorism Center (CTC). Combating terrorism sounded like the perfect use of my time, so I went ahead with it. At the CTC I found rows of TV sets tuned to various news stations, with people watching them attentively.

A friend of mine worked in the CTC. He told me privately that just the previous week, a cable had come in saying that a terrorist group in Lebanon was planning to kidnap a US citizen upon his arrival at Khartoum airport that day. "I walked the cable around here, trying to get permission to warn him," he said, "but the managers didn't want to do anything. They said they didn't like the source, and anyway, it was almost 5 o'clock and time to go home. The next day, the US citizen was indeed captured and held hostage by the terrorists. Luckily, he was able to convince the terrorists that he meant them no harm and was on their side, and they let him go, all by himself. But no one in the Center was reprimanded. In fact, no one ever said anything more about it."

CTC was, in fact, an early and innovative attempt to break through the Agency's geographical turf barriers, with the authority to track terrorists through different countries.[16] But CTC couldn't grant overseas assignments because the geographical divisions controlled those.

Max and I graduated from our final training course on the evening the first Gulf War began. Several Agency mandarins attended our graduation cocktail party, including the chief of the Middle East division. They'd been taken aback to hear that the US military had begun the war. Nobody had bothered to let them know.

Max and I were euphoric at having at last finished our training and domestic service. We were sad to have lost so many of our classmates, though. Most had quit. Max, Jonah, a fourth classmate, and I were all that remained of the original group. The people who quit were all well-qualified, and I remember them fondly.

As it happened, I was the first of my class to land approval for an overseas assignment, and my family and I packed up happily to head for the Middle East.

★ 5 ★

Sent to Spy Out the Land

And Moses sent them to spy
out the land of Canaan
Numbers 13:17

Our plane descended in the night and we could see the gas flares
burning in the distant oil fields. We arrived in the Middle East
on a midnight flight and checked in to a hotel by 0200. A wedding celebration in the ballroom turned bellicose and broke out into
the street and parking lot below. Men swirled about, yelling and
fighting. They hiked their robes up around their thighs and slapped
at their opponents with their sandals. At one point, a car swerved
out of the darkness and rammed into a dense hedge in front of the
hotel.

Jetlag woke us up a few hours later. We watched the sunrise, the
sky red with dust and humidity. We took our children for a walk to
a crude playground across the street, with an ancient rotating platform and a big rusty climbing gym—the kind long since judged a
liability hazard in the US. The kids darkened as the playground dirt
stuck to them in the humidity. Competing "Allahu Akbar" prayer
calls bellowed from all directions. We were overjoyed to be on our
first adventure overseas. At last, I was a real case officer on assignment. But goals are a moving target. I'd won my overseas assignment, sure, but now I had to make it a success.

If I received a one-way ticket home because I couldn't get

properly established, it would be the end of my Agency career. I couldn't bear languishing in the Oakwood or at a US post, praying that HQs would approve another overseas assignment. I promised myself never to wander the halls of HQs with the other beaten-down non-State Department officers. I had to make this assignment work.

We quickly set up by renting a house and buying furniture and a car. Our oldest child was ready for school, but there were no slots available in the nearby British school. On a hunch—a hunch informed by the overtly defined racial and class distinctions in the Middle East—my wife took my son for a visit and the school made a space available. They'd just wanted to get a look at the boy first.

I bought a modest, mid-sized car. I only needed one because my wife could not legally drive. I'd already guessed how important my choice of car would be, and as my career progressed I saw the issue arise again and again. Sly colleagues wheedled lots of money out of HQs by convincing them that an expensive car was necessary for the officer's high-powered position. A modest car might draw suspicion. Why, they'd ask, does such an important businessman have such a mediocre car?

Of course the threat came less from what a hostile foreign intelligence service *thought* than from how our colleagues behaved. When a State Department officer—himself issued a modest car—saw another Agency officer driving around in a shiny black Mercedes Benz, his mounting envy could end the officer's tour. During the course of my career I counted at least a dozen situations in which an officer's extravagant car led to a one-way ticket home. Then again, the car may have been merely a symptom of the officer's lack of judgment.

Exploring the region, an American business associate and I headed out over the desert to find an ancient oasis we'd read about. We got some rough directions and eventually saw a spot of green in the distance. The oasis is lush, but it is surrounded by sand and there is not another living thing, not even a blade of grass, as far as the eye can see. About the oasis there were many theories and legends. As we got closer, the car got stuck in the sand. The 120-degree heat bore down on us while I tried various methods to get the car out. "I see death, death," said my friend. Fortunately, another traveler appeared and gave us a ride into town. I left my friend next to a refrigerator full of cold drinks in a "cold store," the Middle Eastern version of a 7-11, and I hired a tow truck.

Setting up overseas was expensive, and the cash from HQs often took a long time to arrive. I'd always been a good money manager and I had plenty of savings and credit cards to tap, so I didn't have any cash flow problems. Throughout my career I was usually at least $100,000 in the hole and was once almost $300,000 in arrears, usually the equivalent of about one to three years' pay. I could have been paid more quickly if I'd complained, but I had limited capital with HQs and wanted to spend it making sure I stayed active and operational. I'd do this job for free, I told myself. HQs always reimbursed me eventually, so what I was buying by letting them take their time was a sterling reputation for not whining and not causing administrative problems.

I always got on the plane as soon as my assignments were approved, without any cash from the Agency, and so I was already in the location before anyone at HQs had a chance to change his or her mind. If I waited several months to get my cash, I ran the risk of losing the assignment.

I'd moved to the Middle East at my earliest opportunity, and one drawback was that I'd arrived without all the necessary residence and visa paperwork. Arab countries monitor their populations strictly. If your residence permits expire, you can be turned away at the airport or forced to board the next plane out. The local immigration authorities might even come looking for you to boot you out.

We lived in a compound, which might suggest that we were

isolated from the local people. As it turned out, though, this enforced privacy isn't atypical for an Arab country. Arabs tend to isolate themselves, with most dwellings surrounded by high walls. There is no socializing with neighbors over the fence as in the suburban US.

A neighboring country provided more recreational opportunities. We took our children to Shaykh's Beach, the king's beachfront home. The king graciously opened this estate for visitors, provided they were of specific ethnicities. Guards at the entrance enforced a strict entry code: whites and East Asians were permitted; Muslims, (including citizens), Hindus, and South Asians were not. Within the estate, the whites, Japanese, and Chinese spread their blankets at one end of the beach and the Filipinos spread theirs at the other. I guessed that the ban on Muslims was because the king didn't want to expose Muslims to a European-style beach setting.

The ban on Hindus was a bit more peculiar and arose, I believe, from the Arabs' strong aversion to Hindu worship. Muslims disagree with Christians and Jews, but theologically understand them. The Hindu worship of multiple gods, and Hindu attitudes toward cattle, both mystified and disgusted the Arabs.

I had an Indian friend who was Christian, and asked him to come to the Shaykh's Beach with us. "No way," he said.

"Really," I said. "It'll be fun."

"You don't understand. The guards at the gate will stop your car and they'll point at me and say, 'Not you, you get out.' I'd enjoy going, but they won't let me in."

I apologized for my naiveté. He was a Christian, but he looked like a Hindu, and that was what counted.

"Tell you what," he said. "Why don't you come by my apartment next week for Ashura? My balcony looks right across an intersection onto the main Shi'a mosque. I've got a great view."

Ashura is the Shi'a commemoration of a seminal event in the history of Shi'a Islam, the martyrdom of Hussayn, grandson of Muhammad.

The next week I went to visit my friend. I drove toward the souk, passing Shi'a villages flying black flags from their rooftops. I parked my car on the outskirts of the souk and walked through the alleyways toward my friend's building. The shops were locked and the alleys deserted.

My friend and I drank beer in brown paper bags and took in the spectacle. Shi'a men spilled out of the mosque across the courtyard from my friend's building. They formed a line, waiting to be hit on the forehead with a straight razor. After receiving these ceremonial cuts, they slapped themselves with the heels of their hands to encourage blood flow. Blood spilled down their faces, turning their white shirts red.

Throughout the 1990s, the country's rulers were concerned about the restive Shi'a population. The Sunni population controlled the government and most business. Young Shi'a men usually dressed in western shirts and trousers, while Sunnis wore the traditional long thobe. The Shi'a acted up now and then, with routine outbreaks of low-level violence—burning tires in the road, or staging a small-scale riot near a suspected location of Christian or Hindu worship. Police disrupted these scenes with tear gas.

The Middle East was a pleasant place to live, however, with plenty of consumer goods, low crime rates, relaxed lifestyles, and cheap household labor. Shi'a antics weren't a threat, because the Shi'a had no power. A well-connected Sunni could have had me thrown out of the country on a whim, if he felt I'd insulted him, or if he thought my business represented a competitive threat. HQs had taught me how to avoid counterintelligence threats, but not how to avoid giving offense to Arabs in business interactions. An Irishman, giving a speech at a trade show, sought to warm up his audience with a joke poking fun at the resemblance of family names like Faqer and Fakhro to a certain expletive. The police gave him a lift to the airport the following day.

I DROVE TO A MEETING with my base chief, Horace. On the way, I listened to a program on Radio Qatar, which broadcasts throughout the Gulf, discussing the Hadith, a collection of the Prophet Muhammad's sayings. "Oh Prophet, I have the choice of a young woman and an old woman; which should I choose?" a voice on the radio asked.

"The young one, of course, that you may better sport with her," replied another voice.

After checking to see that I was clean of surveillance, I parked and met Horace, who picked me up in his own car. The counterintelligence threat was low. We drove around town while we talked.

The bureaucracy at HQs was incredibly slow-moving. No leads or instructions had arrived. It would be up to me to create my own leads, my own missions. Horace was a kindhearted man from Kansas.

"When I first started out in the Agency," he said, "I was sent to language school to learn Romanian. After a year of language training, my Romanian was pretty good and I was sent to our office in Bucharest. I began trolling diplomatic cocktail parties and I met a Romanian intel officer. I invited him to my house for dinner and we hit it off pretty well. Later we played tennis and continued to meet for lunches and dinners. Eventually I assessed that there was a good chance that he would accept a pitch to work for the CIA, so I arranged for the necessary approvals from HQs in order to pitch him.

"HQs gave approval and I set a meeting with the Romanian. Everything seemed in order, so I asked him if he'd provide us with secret intelligence. He didn't say anything, just pulled out a camera and took a picture of me. Then he got up and left. The next day my photo was on the front page of the newspaper, and I was declared *persona non grata* and given 24 hours to leave the country.

"I went back to HQs, where no one seemed to want to talk to

me. I worked on an HQs desk for a few years. Eventually I got an assignment to Rangoon, Burma.

"After I'd been on my new assignment for a while, I ran across a Romanian who had good access to intelligence of interest to us. I used my Romanian language skills to get to know him. We spent a lot of time together, played a lot of tennis, and I assessed that he was ready for a pitch. I got HQs approvals to pitch him.

"When I asked him if he would work for the Agency, he pulled out a camera and took a picture of me. The next day my photo was on the front page of the newspaper. The Burmese government didn't really care, so I wasn't kicked out, but HQs decided to pull me anyway, and I spent another several years working desks at HQs."

We handed each other messages written on water-soluble paper. He dropped me off at my car, and I drove home. I sat in the bathroom of my house reading each message he'd given me, and then I dropped them in the toilet. The paper dissolved, and the little letters swam around like Alphabet Soup.

HORACE WAS A GOOD MAN, and though his story suggested that he'd be risk-averse, he proved to be one of the more aggressive men I worked for. He didn't block many of my operations in that country. He never gave me any instructions, ideas, or leads, but this was typical of the Agency. It was a one way street—I came up with my own operational ideas and proposed them to the station and to HQs.

Horace was under diplomatic cover, which can be effective in the Middle East. All power in the region derives from governments, and Arabs respect American diplomatic power. An American diplomat carries more weight in a small Arab country than he would in a large Western European one. Horace did a lot of liaison work, which entails dealing diplomatically and openly, as a representative of the Agency, with his host country's intelligence service. Liaison work was a risk-free, friendly exchange of information over tea or coffee, and it produced a great deal of the Agency's intelligence reporting.

Some of this reporting was useful, but it's important to bear in mind that most of it was selected by the host country. The Agency assigned encrypted names and file numbers to official liaison contacts, as if these people were real clandestine human sources. Without knowing more about a case, it could be difficult to tell whether an intelligence report had come from a unilateral agent, or from a digest of a friendly government's misinformation.

Liaison work only occurred with friendly or neutral governments, not with enemy rogue nations such as Iran, North Korea, and Libya. If we didn't have an embassy in a country, we didn't have an Agency office there. In other words, we didn't have offices in the countries that mattered most.

A popular way for our overseas stations to generate activity was to recruit American citizens as intelligence sources. Americans are generally patriotic and happy to help the Agency when they can, and they present little risk to the Agency. As with liaison contacts, American citizens were assigned encrypted names and file numbers as if they were real spies. Like those contacts, however, they rarely brought in any valuable information.

An advantage of not being a member of the State Department was that I wouldn't have to do liaison, recruiting of American citizens, walk-ins, or meetings with other embassy officials. I had only one option—intelligence operations—and if I wasn't doing it successfully, it would be readily apparent.

WE SUSPECTED SOME BANKS in the Middle East of handling money for terrorists and rogue states. The Libyan government was under US and United Nations sanctions as punishment for its terrorist activities, for example, so banks handling Libyan currency were always good targets.

In the worst example of Libyan state-sponsored terrorism, an intelligence officer had placed a bomb aboard Pan Am Flight 103. It exploded on December 22, 1988, causing the plane to go down at

Lockerbie, Scotland. Two hundred and fifty-nine passengers died, as did eleven residents of Lockerbie. Also on board the flight was an Agency officer named Matthew Gannon.[17]

Palestinian money was of less interest at the time because the Palestinians had shifted to being more of a government than a terrorist organization. Terrorist organizations such as Hizb'allah and rogue states used banks to purchase weapons and WMA technology. As Islamic banks grew in popularity with Muslim investors, they were also used more actively by terrorists. Islam prohibits the payment or collection of interest, and Islamic banks developed methods of conducting banking in accordance with those principles. A preferred technique used an intermediary to receive the interest payments, who would pay the client without telling him that the money had come from usury.

To investigate the banking issue, I hit the social circuit in several cities in the region, attending cocktail parties and dinners to meet potential human sources—and making sure to drink from the glass and not the bottle. Bank employees were often British, Indian, or Pakistani nationals, and easy to meet. Many Middle Eastern countries had been influenced by the British Empire, particularly in language and legal structure, having once been British protectorates.

One night, as my wife and I prepared for dinner at the home of a key bank executive, we heard a blast in the distance. Young Shi'a men routinely set off propane tanks by lighting fires underneath them. When the heat built to a certain point, the tanks exploded, resulting in noise but not much destruction. Only rarely was anyone hurt.

We heard another explosion, this time accompanied by a shock wave that rumbled through the house. "That one must have been just a few hundred yards away," my wife said. She looked out the second-story window of our house to get a better view. "It doesn't look like anyone's power has gone out."

Traffic was normal and we drove to the executive's house. The scene was always the same: Guests gathered in the living room for several house cocktails before moving into the dining room. The living room would have sofas and chairs around a low table, but no television set; the dining room always featured a large table for eight or more, a china hutch, and a sideboard. Dinner was served by South Asian servants and included countless bottles of wine. Port, cigars, and after-dinner drinks were staples, as well.

Ex-pats liked spirited dinner parties. Accents became more and more upper-class as the evening wore on. That night, after numerous drinks, I was loudest of all, amusing myself by mocking the other guests, their national characteristics, their presidents, dictators, kings, and religions. I cornered a man who was involved in concealing rogue state money and I asked him what the hell was going on at this bank.

I bellowed. I challenged one man to an arm wrestling match. A glass of wine spilled; silverware and a plate fell to the floor.

The next morning, and throughout the weekend as I typed up the results of my "social activities," I felt ill and ashamed.

On Saturday morning, the beginning of the week in the Middle East, I drove our children to school. I knew that some of the diners I'd insulted would be at the school that morning, and I hid as best as I could in a corner of the yard.

From the distance I saw a British woman headed straight for me. She'd been at the party. I looked for ways to escape, but there would be no avoiding the confrontation.

"We'd like to invite you and your wife over to dinner this Thursday," she said. "We're having the directors of our bank come in from London for a visit. We had so much fun with you the other night. We do hope you can make it."

OUR RELATIONSHIP WITH the British government, a close ally, prohibited us from spying on their operatives. Our station in London was the ideal pre-retirement post for Agency mandarins because risk was impossible—in fact, it was specifically forbidden. London station only issued cables with the word "stand-down" in them, advising that we couldn't recruit British nationals, couldn't hold meetings in Britain, couldn't do much of anything.

We couldn't formally recruit British nationals, but we could report anything they said voluntarily, so I met them where I could and engaged them in conversation.

Bankers in rogue states were sloppy, however, and easy targets. They'd heard plenty of threats from the US government and had earned plenty of bad press, but they were rarely confronted. They also may have believed what they were doing wasn't really illegal, and so felt none of the shame that might have made them more prudent. One of our target banks claimed that it had no rogue state money, then, several weeks later, boasted that it had frozen $700 million in rogue state money. The banks used non-US currency whenever possible, but there was no way to avoid keeping large amounts of it.

I traveled to a banking center in the region and invited a banker, a potential human source, to an Indian restaurant. We couldn't understand each other very well during the dinner because of a house band playing ear-splitting music. After dinner we headed out for a crawl of the many bars hidden within small hotels in the souk. Night life in the souk appealed to a variety of tastes: There were Arab bars, Indian bars, bars for Westerners.

We picked an Indian one. "You cannot enter. This is the Indian bar," the doorman said. He hadn't meant to sound hostile: We were welcome to enter if we really wanted to. He'd only meant that we wouldn't like its music and atmosphere.

He directed us to another hotel, accessible through the Indian bar. We crossed to a door at the far end which led to a passageway. Midway through, we heard music coming from the far end. The smells of Indian spices dissipated. We saw chips and dip on the tables and recognized the places as a country-and-western spot.

The country-and-western band was from the Philippines, but

it sounded as good as any Nashville outfit. It was the Muslim holy month of Ramadan, and special rules imposed on bar bands during the month of Ramadan mandated that only two members of the band play at a time. The other members of the band sat around the edges of the stage, waiting to take turns.

After a few pints of stout, the banker, much to my surprise, began to unburden his conscience. He described the methods he used to hide the flow of the rogue state funds—and named some of the entities for whom the money was destined. I pushed him as hard as I could without overplaying my hand. I was unable to write anything down, but the intel was simple and would be easy to remember.

It was a solid breakthrough.

Some mutual acquaintances joined us. The drinking got away from us; an Egyptian friend started nodding off. One man was diabetic, but insisted on keeping up. When he rose from his chair, I saw that it was wet—he'd soiled himself.

We parted company at 0300. A few hours later, I had a breakfast meeting with a Pakistani from the same bank as the previous night's informant. His outline of the movement of rogue state funds was even more detailed. He had more news on the political angle: The ministry of finance knew, but didn't care about, the rogue state money. I had enough information for a report, so I headed home and typed it up on my water-soluble paper.

From a payphone, I scheduled an emergency meeting with the base chief. "I'll see you on Wednesday at 2200," I said. We'd been taught in training to set meetings at different times than they would actually occur: Wednesday at 2200 actually meant Tuesday at 2100. On Tuesday I waited at the meeting site at 2100, but he didn't show. I knew he must not have checked the commo plan. I wondered if he might have subtracted 24 hours instead of 25 hours, so I came back an hour later, but he wasn't there. The next night I would try again.

HQs liked these elaborate procedures, but they weren't very useful if nobody remembered how to use them.

I almost missed the meeting the next night. On the way there, I saw an Arab woman hit by a car. She was completely covered in the traditional black abaiya and veil, and she hit the ground like a bag of coal. Bystanders ran to her and pulled her to her feet, but she collapsed again. With her face covered, it was impossible to evaluate her condition. I called an ambulance—sure that no one else had—and asked the crowd to stop yanking her around, in case she had spinal or neck injuries. I pulled off her veil so I could look at her and communicate better. She was a middle-aged, heavy-set woman, wincing, but breathing and alert. No one seemed to mind that I'd torn off her veil. I told her to be calm, and a few moments later an ambulance arrived.

I left the accident scene as soon as I could and was able to get to the meeting site on time. The chief showed up at 2200. He hadn't checked the commo plan. "I wasn't sure who you were," he said, "but I thought I'd show up anyway." We drove around, avoiding the Sheraton Hotel area because of a convention of Arab intelligence organizations.

The chief read my reports and said that HQs liked my bank cases. My intel was going into the system.

LITTLE INFORMATION on bank targets was forthcoming from HQs. All they ever sent were interoffice memos, the contents of which were invariably useless. The chief of the Middle East division was proud that no flaps had broken out or that no hostages had been taken. The chief of the clandestine service had gone off to London for his cushy pre-retirement tour. Vacation days should henceforth be calculated in such and such a way. Once in a while the monotony would be broken up by a warning about the counterintelligence climate in some irrelevant place like Cameroon.

There were major budget cutbacks at HQs after I went overseas.

Our water-soluble messages suddenly started describing "early outs," in which employees were encouraged to leave, as well as "synergies" and "cooperation" to achieve these organizational goals. There was a letter from an employee who took an "early out." He explained how great the whole early retirement process had been for him. "Better hurry, it won't last," he advised. Another message discussed California Congresswoman Maxine Waters's accusation that the Agency had created the crack cocaine epidemic in the US. Later investigations debunked this preposterous charge.

HQs and my base chief were happy with me. I kept on pouring drinks into drunks and listening to the loose talk that came back up. All the same, I was having a difficult time getting approval to ask my sources to work for the Agency. I couldn't see why HQs should be so shy about operations against rogue states—especially rogue states who were thumbing their noses at US and UN sanctions.

HQs worried that if we shut down a big bank, our host country might *persona non grata* (PNG) the base chief, and he didn't want to get PNG-ed again. The chief admitted to me that he had sat on some of the more incriminating information that I'd given him.

I couldn't empathize—I was always within 24 hours of getting kicked out of the country myself. One advantage I had over the embassy employees, however, was that the host country didn't know about me, so if they got mad at the US government, they wouldn't come looking to punish me for it.

During our next car meeting, I pushed the chief to approve formal recruitment of several bank sources. He became nervous and frustrated, and vented by swerving and cursing at some pedestrians. It was a tense encounter.

I talked about the Godfather in an effort to encourage the chief to be more aggressive. The chief didn't like him. The Godfather's energetic style intimidated some in the Agency. Also, the Godfather was arrogant and had no patience for cowering introverts. Back at HQs, he'd shove a fistful of receipts to anyone nearby, and say,

"Here, do my accounting." He'd done that to the chief once. The chief whined, "I sent a female officer out to work with the Godfather on a case, and he made a pass at her while they were in a hotel room preparing for the operation."

When I felt like I'd pushed him too hard, I sent him messages with nothing of substance in them—messages that seemed official but required no work. These I called "happy letters," and they never failed to do the trick.

As time went on, my intel reporting had a positive effect. The US government was able to locate and freeze rogue state money based on my reporting, hammering one bank's profitability. Another bank was shut down following US pressure on the local authorities. Though a relatively minor player in the rogue state money game, that bank had issued traveller's cheques that had been used to finance aspects of many terrorist attacks.

WINTER IN THE MIDDLE EAST was mostly pleasant and cool. Swarms of flies appeared for a couple of months, making it unpleasant to be outside. Flies in earlier times had laid eggs in the eyes that could lead to blindness. Blindness was very common in old men. Since there was so little rain, there were no storm drains; when it did rain in winter, sometimes for two weeks straight, the country turned into a muddy flood plain.

Things proceeded as usual. I made the rounds of embassies and individual targets. At one point I volunteered to go to Somalia, but my base chief kept me around: He was afraid to let his power be undermined by losing personnel in his command. In addition to the operations I generated myself, my local station assigned me several agents to handle. These fellows had been recruited in the past by other case officers; my duty was to meet to collect and process the intelligence they provided. They were poor quality agents, but I did the best I could to run them properly. I performed extensive surveillance detection before meeting them. It was a benign environment and I never saw anything, but for their safety I kept up the discipline.

I usually met my agents at night. They'd bring takeout meals: lamb burgers, shawarma sandwiches dressed with french fries, or meat porridges with brains and bread soaked in grease. I loved exotic food and looked forward to each evening's surprise. We drank soda, first using Kleenex to wipe the desert grit off the tops of cans. Often my agents all but poisoned our meeting sites with insect repellent. Another spot was cooled with "Iranian air conditioning," a centuries-old method by which hot air would rise up wind towers and cool air would drop into the house.

Within the Agency, I'd heard stories about case officers' inventing false agents, rather than going to the trouble of recruiting them. They'd create plausible intelligence reports and process them into the system. I myself never saw any completely fictitious case. More often I saw weak agents whose production was fluffed up to look more impressive.

I continued to handle my local agents and to work on other targets, including the banks. I was stimulating plenty of activity, but I realized that I'd need to move out into the region to hook some bigger fish.

★ 6 ★

Trying to Hustle the East

> And the end of the fight is a tombstone white
> with the name of the late deceased
> And the epitaph drear: "A fool lies here who
> tried to hustle the East."
> *Rudyard Kipling*

I sent off requests for approval to travel to more distant countries in the region.

I was learning. I knew that if I wrote: "I want to travel to your operational area to find human sources," the response from Agency managers would have been a terrified, "No!"

So I obtained approvals by telling stations that I needed to come onto their turf in order to do my software solutions business. To convince people I was a real software man, I argued, I'd have to travel their region selling our products.

Once on foreign turf, I lulled the Agency managers into complacency by sending studiously boring after-action reports. The managers would come to see me as harmless, and I'd be able to increase the tempo and scope of my operations before they'd even noticed what was happening.

SUNSETS IN THE MIDDLE EAST were beautiful, the dust in the air amplifying the brilliant red and orange. Before catching a midnight flight to another country in the region, I always went for a jog through the countryside to loosen up.

I ran through the outskirts of Shi'a villages. The animosity between Shi'a and Sunni had heated up and the Shi'a villages were restless. A group of Shi'a teenagers threw a few insults and stones at me. I growled and made as if to chase them, and they fled wildly. That wouldn't work too many more times, I thought. Still, even during troubled times, most of the region was safe—unlike, say, Baghdad.

I traveled to Muscat, Oman, the prettiest of the Gulf Arab countries. Muscat had roadside art and sculpture and its buildings were constructed with an attention to detail and craftsmanship. In other Gulf countries, buildings were often little more than functional, cinderblock affairs. In the rest of the Gulf, men wear a white thobe during summer and a gray or black one in winter. In Oman the men wear pale lavender thobes.

Not seeing many potential sources, I moved on to Syria, where I'd lived as a child. I'd been very young and of course my memories were faint, but I wanted to see the place again. I rented a car and drove around Damascus.

I remembered the name of the neighborhood in Damascus in which I'd lived more than twenty years prior, and drove to see it. It all came back to me. I turned a few corners and found myself gazing up at the apartment building in which I'd lived. Older buildings quickly became run-down and people in the region usually built new ones rather than bother with upkeep or renovation. Our old place was now used by immigrant laborers. There were extra doors on our landing, showing that the apartment had been divided up, and twenty pairs of shoes were lined up outside the doors. Cement blocks where my father had installed a swing set for the neighborhood were still there, the swing set itself taken down probably years ago.

Across the street was a cluster of "temporary" cinderblock buildings constructed for Palestinian refugees during the 1960s. I remembered walking to the bakery one day with a few coins in my pocket. A mob of Palestinian boys moved toward me, and I ran, but more boys came from the opposite direction. I took the coins with which I'd meant to buy bread and flung them in the air. The mob shifted direction like a school of fish and headed for the coins, giving me time to flee.

During the Six Day War in 1967, our Palestinian neighbors believed Arab radio reports that Arab armies were pushing the Israelis into the sea. They loaded up their cars and headed back home, only to be stopped far from the border with the news that things hadn't gone so well after all. But then, Palestinians have an uncanny ability to support the loser. In the first Gulf War, Palestinians in Kuwait had backed Iraq. The Kuwaitis returned to power and promptly ejected the Palestinians.

As a police state, Syria kept our people on edge. I wasn't able to develop operations at that time in Syria, though in later years I developed a couple of minor targets.

Moving on to Kuwait, not long after the Iraqi occupation, war damage was still visible in shoddy bunkers and burned-out buildings. The Agency's relationships in Kuwait seemed set up merely to communicate between the two governments, with few Agency operations independent of the Kuwaiti government. I didn't see much I could do there, so I moved on.

DUBAI WAS A THRIVING PORT CITY in the midst of a huge construction boom. The conventional wisdom was that it was taking the lead in the Gulf as an offshore banking center, and today it even competes with New York and London as a financial hub.

Dubai was also the region's trading center. Iran was under a variety of sanctions and its markets were dysfunctional, so Dubai had become the place to conduct Iranian business. When Iranians wanted to buy military hardware or weapons technology, they generally had it shipped to Dubai and then diverted to their own country.

When I first started traveling to Dubai, the Agency had a "stand-down" on operations against Iranians there. It lasted for several years. Its origins were murky, but it appeared that HQs was concerned that the Iranian government would retaliate dramatically against Agency interference. It wasn't clear what form that retaliation was meant to have taken—maybe terrorism, maybe aggressive surveillance of US diplomatic installations. In either case, our "stand-down" communicated to the Iranians that they'd cowed us without, as it were, firing a shot.

In conversation with HQs and the local turf managers, I implied that I'd been running into people during the course of my software solutions sales. It made my activities seem less risky. It looked to me like there would be serious operational potential in Dubai, so I made phone calls, knocked on doors, and set up appointments.

New CIA managers in the region agreed with me that we shouldn't cease Iranian-targeted operations just because there were hazards involved. Together we were able to chip away at the stand-down policy, until at last we were given approval to initiate activity.

I traveled to Dubai as often as once a week, staying at the airport Marriott and setting appointments with shady Iranians and possible terrorist bankers throughout the city. Some of the old city still existed but it was quickly being demolished to make way for the construction of new office and apartment towers. From its high-speed powerboat racing, golf courses, and Russian prostitutes, it was easy to see what element Dubai served.

I paid a visit to the offices of a trading company involved in shipping weapons components to Iran. "I'm Ishmael Jones," I said, "from Acme Software Solutions. We need shipping in the region for some of our products, and I wonder if I could get some quotes on pricing and delivery terms." I wasn't sure yet whether the office was an Iranian government entity or whether it actually did some legitimate business, but two Pakistani men responded to my questions and we exchanged business cards.

The Agency shied away from recruiting Gulf Arabs, for fear that if something went wrong, their governments would be offended. Pakistanis, however, were ideal; they were in the country solely to make money, most of which they sent home to their families. The Gulf Arabs considered them inferior. In my situation, I considered them a godsend.

I left the office and, several days later, called the more knowledgeable of the two men I'd met. "I am still evaluating different shippers," I said. "On a different topic—well, let me be blunt. Your English is strong. You obviously know your business. My company is getting a foothold in the region, and I wonder if you'd be interested in working for us. I'd like to speak to you further, in confidence, of course."

He agreed to meet, as I'd expected. Pakistanis had no job security and were eager to keep abreast of new opportunities. We met in a back room at my hotel. I explained that I needed someone like him to help my company in Dubai by keeping me informed of the flow of trade in the region. I handed him $500 to get him thinking about my offer. I ended the meeting abruptly, to encourage the impression that I was a very busy man, and we made an appointment to meet again the following day. I hadn't obtained permission from HQs to pay the man. There hadn't been time.

During our next encounter, I explained what I wanted from him: descriptions of the goods his company shipped, and where they were shipped to. He agreed to provide the information.

The case moved into the ordinary drudgery of espionage. We met in hotel rooms, where he fed me reams of material. I studied it carefully and turned the results into intel reports. I also studied books and periodicals to learn which of the materials were applicable to weapons manufacture, and my Pakistani friend helped by pointing out which of the shipments were mislabeled or contained items not on their manifests. Some weapons parts seemed commonplace or had other commercial uses. A small cooling mechanism, for example, turned out to be a missile guidance component, used to cool missile guidance systems in order to make them accurate. In the movies, the vapor seeping out of missile heads as they prepare to launch is caused by these coolers.

As the operation progressed, the Pakistani man became more concerned for his security, so we began to hold our meetings at Al Ain, an oasis on the border with Oman. (Al Ain means "the source" in Arabic.) The oasis was a good place to glimpse the old Emirates-style architecture, but it was hot as ever, shifting only from coastal humidity to dry heat inland. In Al Ain, we usually met in a hotel room, but occasionally we met out in the oasis. In the date grove it seemed almost dark, and the temperature dropped a good 30 degrees.

I made progress in Dubai, but apart from moments of calm at Al Ain, the afternoons were dull, still, blazing hot, and lonely—the times I missed my family the most.

I VISITED PAKISTAN to generate further operations. On my flight to Karachi, I looked over and saw the Godfather a few seats away. He recognized me and winked. He showed off his charisma by meeting and engaging everyone sitting nearby. The man lived on airplanes and in hotel rooms; he seemed to be everywhere at once.

Outside the airport in Karachi airport, the Godfather disappeared into a waiting limousine while I waded through a throng of competing taxi drivers. Karachi was like a post-apocalyptic British village, with British-style street and traffic layout. At the hotel, there were employees everywhere, milling about on every floor. The walls, lampshades, books, and so on looked like they'd been handled by thousands of hands.

After a few hours of sleep, I woke up eager to explore the city. Karachi buses were decorated colorfully, and there were lots of three-wheeled cabs. I rented a taxi for the day and my driver took me to the zoo, where we watched lions lolling behind alarmingly flimsy-looking fences. Then we headed for Muhammad Ali Jinnah's massive mausoleum. Jinnah was the founding father of Pakistan, having played an important role in the partition of India, in which hundreds of thousands were murdered and millions fled their homes. Today he is revered—in part, perhaps, because he died well before the effects of his policies took hold.

Always on the lookout for a new location in case my current assignment fell through, I evaluated every new country as to how easily I might move my family there if necessary. I evaluated the local housing and the schools. The Clifton Beach neighborhood was nice. Sometime ruler Benazir Bhutto, who was assassinated in December 2007, had a house in Clifton Beach with its own gun turret. On the banks of Karachi's river a massive outdoor laundry spread like a quilt, different colors for different tanks of dye.

At the end of my trip, I sent a long message to HQs listing the most boring details of the trip, to lull them into thinking that my visit posed no risk. But I wasn't able to generate operations in Pakistan. The Agency bureaucracy wouldn't respond. Rumors within the Agency suggested discord among our people there. Soon after, an officer received a one-way ticket home for mishandling firearms; another got the boot for his relations with a local girl, whose father complained.

I ROAMED THE GULF REGION attending events. I went to an oil conference in Bahrain where the region's distinctive garb was on full display. Omanis wore the lavender thobes with their distinctive wraparound cloth headdresses, without the agal, the black loops used by other Arabs to hold the headdress in place. Iranians wore dark suits and white shirts without ties. Saudis wore red and white checked headdresses held in place by the agal. Arabs from the Levant preferred black and white checked headdresses. Southern Gulf Arabs wore white headdresses with black tassels hanging from the agal.

The American ambassador held a cocktail party for conference guests. He was a real estate developer and had been appointed to his post by the President. Since I wasn't a member of the State Department, the ambassador didn't know about my relationship with the Agency and confided that he got his job by donating $200,000 to the President's campaign and another $100,000 about a year later. Despite this method of obtaining his appointment, he seemed just as competent as a career diplomat. At any rate, Arab countries tend to prefer an ambassador with a personal connection to the President.

I got myself appointed to a couple of company boards so that I could look busy in a legitimate way. I went to the king's majlis—a ceremony in which anyone may meet or petition him—and joined the long line to exchange Ramadan greetings with him.

The Moon Sighting Committee prepared to do its duty. Ramadan is a lunar month and in order for it to begin, the committee has to confirm the appearance of the new crescent moon. The holiday is marked by daytime fasting and evening feasting. Extra shipments of live sheep arrive from New Zealand and Australia, and the abattoirs run around the clock. Many people put on weight and sleep most of the day.

ON A TRIP THROUGH CYPRUS, I spotted Max at the Larnaca airport. We glanced at each other, realized that neither of us was engaged in an operation, and sat down at an outdoor café to catch up.

During our lengthy training course, Max had used his spare time wisely, creating a self-study course with an impressive reading list, and then visiting HQs during slow days in training to press experts for answers to his questions. He was putting this knowledge to good use in his overseas assignment. His operations had a violent bent. His focus was the elimination of terrorists—long before this became a matter of such urgent necessity—and his strategy was to identify them and then to pass their information to the country most likely to want them dead. At one point he'd found a way to tap an enemy communications cable, and the Agency had given the how-to to an allied secret service. Our ally did a good job of setting up the tap, but unfortunately they also booby-trapped it to prevent tampering. The local police and security services investigated, triggered the booby traps, and ruined the operation.

In an unrelated operation, Max had been assigned to handle an agent who was giving us good intelligence. Before taking over the case, Max read the agent's file at HQs and learned that the agent had been recruited in textbook fashion. A case officer serving as a State Department diplomat had bumped into the man at an embassy cocktail party. Realizing the man had access to intelligence, the case officer learned they shared a passion for golf. Three golf outings later, the man agreed to provide intelligence and became an agent for the CIA.

Something about the case bothered Max. It was just too perfect, too easy. Yet the agent's record since recruitment was excellent. His intelligence was frequently corroborated, and when he said something would happen, it did. The case officer who recruited the agent was praised and later assigned to a management positions at HQs.

Still, Max questioned the agent relentlessly, until one day the agent broke down and admitted he was a double agent. He worked for the same allied intelligence service responsible for booby-trapping the cable tap.

Our ally had set us up from the beginning. They knew our modus operandi. They had spotted our case officer attending diplomatic parties and learned he was an avid golfer. They confirmed that their man knew how to play golf and assigned him to meet our officer at the next party.

In a further twist, the intelligence supplied by the double agent was indeed accurate and valuable. The ally had created the operation because they thought the CIA would take the intelligence more seriously if it came from an agent than if it were delivered to the CIA by the ally. For example, if the Turkish government, an ally, delivered information to us on the nefarious deeds of the Greek government, we might not take it seriously because of the history of conflict between the two countries. Max's case entailed the same concept.

He and I continued to compare notes. Max had some intelligence leads located in areas in which I would have more hope of gaining HQs approval, and I had several leads for him, and we continued to exchange ideas until we left for our separate flights.

I MADE SEVERAL MORE TRIPS to Pakistan and after each one typed up an innocuous after-action report. I couldn't get any traction with our bureaucrats there. They continued to permit me to make an occasional visit, but wouldn't reply to the operational proposals I'd begun to send. I kept trying.

In January of 1993, an illegal immigrant from Pakistan named Mir Aymal Kasi fired on Agency employees in Mclean, Virginia who were sitting in traffic, waiting for a light to change so they could turn left into HQs. He murdered two Agency employees and wounded three others. He fled and made his way to Afghanistan.

The search for Kansi (Kasi's name was misspelled as 'Kansi' at the time, and it stuck) pushed other operational activities aside in Pakistan and derailed my hoped-for operations there. It then spread like a cancer to other operational areas in the region. Our people in Pakistan suddenly had no patience for my requests for approvals to do ordinary intelligence work on topics like nuclear weapons proliferation. Now, whenever I sent inquiries to our offices in Pakistan, replies came back stating they had no time for such things because they were "chasing Kansi."

A strange dynamic had overtaken the Agency's operations in the region. No one was truly chasing Kansi; Kansi was no closer to being caught than he'd been in January 1993. Rather, "chasing Kansi" had become a new excuse to avoid the meat and potatoes of intelligence work. Chasing Kansi gave bureaucrats the opportunity to spend money and devise grandiose plans without really doing anything.

Martin, my colleague from my first assignment, was involved in one of the Kansi boondoggles. He went to Afghanistan with several colleagues, all posing as businessmen and asking around for anyone who may have seen Kansi. Martin was unsettled by it all. "My Agency companions left me in a field in a rural area of Afghanistan and I didn't know where they'd gone or when they'd come back to pick me up. I walked to the outskirts of a village, waited and worried. Finally, after dark, they came back and picked me up. We didn't learn anything during the operation, but we all got medals for our good efforts."

The Kansi chasing slowed my operations for a year. Then a representative of the Inspector General's office, a retired case officer, came to the region on a routine visit. I picked him up in my car and we drove around the city, talking. He asked if I had anything I'd like to report.

"I think the 'chasing Kansi' thing is a scam," I said. "Our stations are using it as a reason to avoid intelligence work. 'We're very busy chasing Kansi and we don't have time to respond to your request' has become a boilerplate excuse."

"I agree," he said. "The IG staff has already come to the same conclusion. During this trip, I've seen a lot of what you're talking about. We mean to put an end to it."

Soon after his visit, the "chasing Kansi" work avoidance scam indeed came to an end. The IG instructed stations that it was a law enforcement matter for which the FBI was well equipped.

Kansi was eventually captured in June 1997 by the FBI when Pakistanis who knew Kansi volunteered to turn him over to the FBI in exchange for a large reward[18]. Kansi was executed in Virginia in November 2002.

I was never able to get any traction in operations in Pakistan. I asked the Godfather for advice on Pakistan. "Don't ask me, my friend. I haven't been able to get anything moving in Pakistan either."

HQS SUMMONED ME BACK from the Middle East to attend a seminar in Langley. My colleagues and I arrived at the conference center in the evening and were assigned rooms for the night. My Mormon roommates got ready for bed by stripping down to their distinctive underwear, a wife-beater tee shirt and boxer shorts combo. Being disinclined to roommates of any kind, I left the room and prowled the building until I found an empty room with a single bed in it. I wrote "Ishmael Jones, COM/SEC/RRF" on a card and stuck it to the door. The initials meant nothing, but they sounded official and kept everyone away.

The next day, I asked for news about Randy, the fourth member of my training class. Only four members of my training class had made it overseas.

"Yep, I remember Randy," an HQs officer said. "We sent a technician to meet him to discuss a surveillance operation. The technician arrived at Randy's apartment, but when the door opened the place was full of Chinese men. We don't know where Randy was. We don't know what happened and there was never any explanation." HQs sent Randy a one-way ticket home to a CIA station in Massachusetts, where he stayed for a few months before leaving the Agency. Now only Max, Jonah, and I remained from our class.

Jonah had made it overseas, but unfortunately not for long. He'd become suspicious that one of our colleagues was working for the KGB and that management was covering it up. I didn't believe a word of it and guessed that Jonah was beginning to lose it. Many people at HQs were unhappy with him. Jonah's wife was, too. She informed a HQs bureaucrat that she was leaving him, and the first Jonah heard about her intentions was when his local boss said, "I'm sorry to hear that you and your wife have split up." His paranoia and deteriorating personal life eventually earned Jonah a one-way ticket home.

I chatted with Charlton. He'd been involved in one of the more expensive "chasing Kansi" fiascos and HQs had praised his performance. He was in a good mood, never complaining, not even gossiping. He couldn't understand why anyone would complain, because the Agency paid so much money and asked for so little work.

James Woolsey, director of the CIA at the time, arrived in the afternoon with a group of congressmen and Agency mandarins. Several of my colleagues gave brief talks about the operations they were running. The trend at the time was to hire foreigners. Some of my colleagues spoke halting English; others told entertaining tales of high adventure and derring-do. The congressmen didn't seem to notice that most of the officers they met were stationed in the United States, that their hair-raising tales had all been set in the US. A colleague who was in an OJT training assignment in a US city told the assembled congressmen that he had cracked the Iraqi intelligence communications network.

Charlton told the congressmen that he'd interdicted the flow of significant terrorist funding. I had been working on the same project and knew that his story was nonsense. Charlton was looking good, smiling, utterly unflappable. Well, deceiving Congress was the Agency's specialty.

Another colleague told a tale about how he'd found evidence that the European company Airbus was bribing customers to buy Airbus airplanes. Following the collapse of the Soviet Union, the Agency searched for new missions, and one of the ideas was "economic intelligence." I suspected that Boeing could play the game just as well as Airbus. A friend at the airport in a Middle Eastern country told me he'd had to escort Gulf Arabs through customs when they came back from Seattle, to make sure their bags of cash weren't opened.

WHEN THE SCHOOL YEAR ENDED and the heat became unbearable, I took my family to the airport to send them away for the summer.

I stood on a bench so I could see them and wave goodbye as they walked through customs.

I continued my exercise jogs through the outskirts of Shi'a villages near my house. Troublesome teenage boys, formerly a mere nuisance, threw stones at me with increasing force and accuracy. My trick of turning at them and taking a few steps as if to give chase no longer worked. Instead of fleeing wildly, they just took a few steps back and threw more stones. I realized it was time to end my jogs through that part of the country.

About a week later, an annual charity marathon passed through my old route. Lying in wait, the boys attacked the runners with stones and clubs. The boys increased the intensity of attacks as the slower runners passed through. The injuries were superficial, but frightening.

My wife became involved with a large charitable organization. In preparation for its annual meetings, she visited the ballroom where it was to be held, met the hotel staff, and discussed the requirements, such as tables, chairs, and refreshments. She left. That afternoon, a terrorist's bomb ripped through the lobby, blowing out windows and slicing up bystanders with shards of glass.

Later, my wife surveyed the damage and decided to hold the meeting anyway. The province's interior minister telephoned her and thanked her for not allowing the terrorists to affect the organization's meeting plans.

I DROVE EACH NIGHT to meetings with agents and with Horace. Horace handed me sheaves of water-soluble paper with messages from HQs about "connectivity," "being transnational," and "reorienting." In late 1995 and early 1996, HQs bureaucrats had been spending a great deal of time at off-sites—excursions away from HQs, where they'd try to let their hair down and create new ideas, often with the help of motivational speakers. After each off-site they'd send a message to Agency offices worldwide retailing all the good things they learned about themselves. The messages referred to top level bureaucrats by their first names. Messages kept me updated on HQs's various awareness weeks, and the employee art displays in the HQs hallways.

Horace said he'd be traveling to an off-site meeting in Virginia next week. He asked whether there was anything he should pass on to our HQs managers.

I said, "Tell them they need to stop having off-sites, and pick up the phone once in a while to make appointments with intelligence targets."

I continued to make cold calls and set up appointments. Most organizations give people incentives to make cold calls, but in the Agency it was seen as nothing but a risk. Blaise Pascal wrote that, "All the unhappiness of man stems from one thing only: that he is incapable of staying quietly in his room." Surely he'd be surprised to learn that, in fact, millions of government employees are quite happy never to leave their rooms.

I HADN'T BEEN TO BOMBAY since I was a child, and all I remembered was a bad case of food poisoning. On my nonstop Air India flight, I noticed that the cabin interiors were poorly maintained, ripped, and dirty, and wondered whether the same standards applied to the mechanical parts, as well. I counted the seats to the exit, so I could make my way out in case the cabin filled with smoke. The noises coming from the engines didn't sound right. A friend of mine, a pilot with Gulf Air, liked to say, "Indian airlines fall out of the sky with alarming frequency."

A crowd of happy families awaited the arrivals at the Bombay airport. Shouldering my way past the pitchmen and the shills, I found a taxi. The taxis smelled like the drivers slept in them, because they usually did. Halfway to downtown Bombay, we crossed the bridge over Shit River, a vast open sewer that may once have been an actual river. Sleeping people lay on the sidewalks. We passed a business with the sign, *"Dead Bodies Shipped Here. Any How. Any Where. Any Time."* We turned toward the Taj Hotel. The taxi driver tried the standard tricks—"I've got no change" and "the fare is double at night"—but I didn't fall for them.

The next day I walked the streets of the city. Generally speaking, there were only two cars in India, both locally produced. The taxis were Padminis, based on a 1950s Fiat design and painted the usual black and yellow. An "executive" car called the Ambassador was based on a 1950s Morris Oxford, a car whose production had been discontinued in Britain decades ago. The Ambassadors were usually white. Any other type of automobile was rare.

After independence, India had switched to a strictly regulated socialist economy dubbed the License Raj, in contrast to the British Raj. The new economy required licenses to produce anything, and the kleptocrats and influential families who obtained those licenses were able to produce goods without competition. The results on the roads were a measly two models of pathetic automobile, produced inefficiently and expensively.

Wherever I went, I ate the local food. I loved Indian cuisine, particularly the vegetarian dishes.

The influence of the British Empire was everywhere in Bombay, especially in its architecture. The British built Bombay to inspire awe, and the city's magnificent buildings continue to do so today. Still, when the British left, they took with them their capacity for upkeep, so that now the vibrancy of the city commingles with a crumbling, post-apocalyptic feel.

One morning I walked to the arch at the Gateway to India and then turned back into the city. Beggars were out in strength, the most persistent ones small girls clutching half-dead babies. Dark alleys contained young men offering hashish and prostitutes. Victoria Terminal was astounding, massive, adorned with gargoyles watching a million people pass through each day to board trains.

Has any other nation been so desperately poor for so much of its history? What would it take to survive in such an environment? I hoped that I'd never have to find out.

I went to lunch with an old friend. He was a Catholic, and about to be married. He'd gone to pre-marriage counseling with his priest.

The priest had looked at him closely and held his hand. "Always consider your wife and children first of all, and then your parents," the priest said.

I wonder what he means, thought my friend.

"She will be your wife. She will be your family now. Orders from your parents will be overruled by your orders."

At last it dawned on my friend: The priest was counseling against the practice of bride-burning. The groom's parents, were they unhappy with the bride's dowry, would be the ones to order it.

THE INDIANS HAVE RENAMED almost everything in their country, but many continue to use the old names. In time the new names will probably catch on. I walked past Flora Fountain, which has a new name, then through Bombay University, whose bell tower once played "God Save the King" and "Auld Lang Syne." I visited the Afghan church, an old Anglican church with plaques commemorating British soldiers killed in the Afghan wars, long forgotten. I visited the Prince of Wales Museum, built in honor of the Prince to house artifacts of Indian history.

I found the book bazaar I had been looking for next to the university. While browsing for books a young man standing next to me struck up a conversation. He said his name was Thomas. He was a Christian, and had come from Goa to study veterinary medicine at the university. Goa had been a Portuguese colony until a couple of decades earlier.

We walked through to the end of the book stalls and continued to walk north. "I don't have any more classes today," he said. "I'm taking a break from study to go to a festival." He said that the festival welcomed people of all religions, and I decided to join him.

We walked west, passing the Alliance Française and Churchgate Train Station; there, we headed north in the direction of the tracks. Thomas pointed out a small church that Mother Teresa had visited once. I was unaccustomed to the climate and hadn't had anything to eat or drink during the day, so I felt a little dizzy.

We passed a Parsi temple and Thomas explained a bit about the Parsi religion. We peeked into the temple; only Parsis were allowed inside. "The Parsis were originally from Persia." he said. "They believe that during life one eats a lot of good food, and upon death it is time for one to give oneself back to the creatures of the earth." The Parsis carry this out at the Tower of Silence on Malabar Hill in Bombay. They lay out the dead bodies of Parsis on the tower, and vultures eat the bodies. (My friends in Bombay took pains to point out that the meat is all gone by the time the remains are washed into the sea. But I'd read otherwise in the newspaper. There had been more dead Parsis lately and the vultures were having a tough time eating them all, and were becoming lazy, only eating the best parts. Neighbors were complaining; the vultures would grab a hunk of Parsi, such as a leg or an arm, and then flap up to the balcony of a nearby apartment building to enjoy the meal in private.)

Our pace picked up and I started to sweat in the heat and humidity. We passed a row of religious markings on a wall—a Muslim crescent, a Christian cross, and a Hindu symbol. Thomas pointed to these as evidence of the festival's religious unity. He said that earlier that day a building had collapsed in Chinatown and over 100 people had been killed. He described the different burial practices of the different religions.

We walked by a stack of wood on the sidewalk. Thomas said it was used for cremations. A few yards later he announced that we'd reached the festival. We turned into an ancient passageway which led past more stacks of wood into an interior courtyard.

It gradually became clear that by "festival," Thomas meant

"funeral ceremony." We passed a Muslim graveyard as we first walked through the "festival." (The Muslims bury their dead without markings.) We turned into a small room with pictures on the wall of Hindu holy men. Thomas pointed to the pictures one by one, explaining the significance of each one. As my eyes became accustomed to the light, I saw that the room was filled with dead bodies. Some were rolled up in carpets, some were in winding-sheets bound with twine. A hand here and a foot there jutted out of the wrappings.

I began stammering.

"Don't be concerned," Thomas said. "We have permission to be here." (All very well and good, but did we *want* to be?)

A man approached who appeared to be in charge. He had hair protruding out from inside his ears like bushy whiskers, a good two inches on either side. He assured me that I was welcome, and ushered us into the next room.

It had an open roof. In it was a roaring fire in which a body lay sandwiched between two layers of burning wood. The wind and smoke blew in our direction and a light layer of ashes covered my shirt. A second pile burned another body. Thomas and the manager led me toward a crowd of relatives and friends of the deceased.

"I don't belong here," I said, but they would have none of it.

They pointed to a sign requesting donations for the poor to buy wood. *I can make a donation and then get the hell out of here*, I thought.

We passed the human fires and abruptly turned to a cemetery for babies. Hindus do not cremate children who die before their second birthday. The cemetery was disorganized, with holes dug at random and unmarked. My guides showed me the fresh graves of babies buried that morning, and small, empty holes waiting to be used. I felt light-headed.

My guides led me through the baby cemetery until we reached a gnarled tree at the far corner.

They explained that this tree had a mystical significance, like a wishing well. They didn't waste many words on this, however, because it was donation time. Several Indians appeared at once, men with large red dots on their foreheads like the Indian women wear. Behind them was a growing crowd of Indians of different ages. "You must make a donation to these men, they are too poor to bury their relatives," my guides said.

In a daze, I pulled out my wallet and gave the first man 500 rupees, about $12. I gave the same to the second man, but the manager and my guide said the second man was burying two people that day and needed 500 more. Then the manager wanted a donation. I gave him 500, too, but that wasn't good enough. Both he and Thomas said it was an insult for the second man to have been given 1,000 rupees and for the manager to get only 500.

By this time, sense was starting to leak into my dazed brain, and I realized that the whole thing was a setup. Although my back was to the far corner of the cemetery, and the crowd was in front of me, I realized that I could fight my way out fairly easily. But they didn't want me to fight my way out—they only wanted to fleece me fair and square. I began to move across the baby cemetery toward the exit. They pressed me plaintively for more money "for the babies," but I pushed past the cemetery, past the burning bodies, outside, and moved down the street.

My guide and friend Thomas was still with me. Thomas shook his head, disappointed. "How could you have given the manager less than the others?" he said. "Oh well. Would you like to see Chinatown now?"

I looked up and down the street and saw that we were alone. "Thomas, you did a fine job of fooling me, and I'll have to thank you for the lesson. It was well worth the price."

"Then give me money. You must give me money."

I ignored him and got in a taxi.

I was no match for a simple street scam. I'd just had a relatively inexpensive lesson: Never feel smug or superior, and always stay alert. I also appreciated that when the motivation is there—when facing the horrific poverty of the Bombay street—people come up with some pretty creative and resourceful ideas.

HQS SUMMONED ME for meetings. I found an assortment of officers in limbo, some after receiving one-way tickets home, others still struggling to get an overseas assignment. A man who'd done poorly in his interview with a station chief had just had his planned assignment cancelled. A female officer had been given her ticket home when the Agency found out she'd been having an affair with an agent. She thought they were going to marry, but the agent had no such plans. She planned to sue the Agency.

By this time, I'd become obsessed with avoiding the dreaded one-way ticket. The reasons for getting one *seemed* varied, but they had a common cause: The bureaucracy didn't want non-State Department officers overseas. In the Marine Corps, everything is about leadership. If each of the forty Marines in a platoon fails, the Corps will not assume that each one is truly a failure; it will recognize a leadership problem and replace the commander. In the Agency, the failure of large numbers of individuals was judged to represent just that. Managers were never held accountable.

At an HQs lunch meeting I sat at a table with a man wearing bright, colorful Wall Street power suspenders. He was trim, fit, and dynamic. He looked me in the eye as he discussed the operations he was managing at HQs. Suspenders was impressive.

I mentioned my meeting with Suspenders to a colleague. He was skeptical. "I worked in Suspenders's group for three years, and we didn't do much. But he was promoted twice during the three years I was there, so he must have been doing something right. I think he's a good briefer. He's good at standing up in front of a group of senior managers or congressmen and he looks and sounds so damn good that they can't help but promote him. But I've never seen him do an intel operation."

I wasn't able to get much information out of HQs during this visit. HQs was still in its "off-sites" phase, with senior managers holding meetings at resort hotels away from the Washington, D.C. area, still singing, holding hands, and celebrating diversity, so I caught the next flight back to the Middle East.

ABDUL QADIR KHAN, the assembler of Pakistan's atomic bomb, was coming to our Middle Eastern city. The Pakistani ex-pat community was excited. He was a national hero— a sort of Pakistani George Washington.

My wife and I attended a large reception in a hotel ballroom and listened to Khan give a speech. Everyone was friendly and polite, happy to be in the presence of this Great Man. I approached him after his speech, shook his hand, and exchanged a few pleasantries. He was mobbed by admirers, so I backed away and struck up a conversation with some of the young scientists in his entourage. I invited them to lunch the next day.

Following our lunch, I made arrangements to meet one of them separately. My first impression was that he would be the most likely to accept recruitment.

Our station in Islamabad would hear none of it. The Agency had no interest in contact with Khan or his subordinates. I'd written up some of his remarks; the station argued furiously, irrelevantly, against them. Khan had boasted of Pakistan's great scientific strides when in fact he'd merely stolen or bought most of the technology used to make their bomb—that was the station's big revelation.

"I didn't say I agreed with him," I wrote. "I was merely recording his remarks. Let's move on this. A. Q. Khan is one of our most important targets."

Our people in Pakistan flatly refused my plans for further contact with Khan's minions. They reminded me pointedly that they were busy "chasing Kansi." Later, the Agency learned that Khan was even more important than they'd known at the time. He'd been selling and exporting nuclear weapons technology to other rogue states, including Libya. The technology he developed and sold may one day be used in an attack on a US city. For that reason, my brush with Khan was immensely frustrating, and a good example of the Agency's refusal to pull the trigger when it counted most.

MY TRIPS TO INDIA CONTINUED. There were so many people on the streets in Indian cities that the Indian security service could form networks of virtually invisible static surveillants. A little man begging on a corner might be in the pay of the Indian service. And once a surveillance target moved out of *his* vision, he might be picked up by another man squatting on another corner.

In reality, surveillance was usually more obvious. An officer under surveillance would leave his home to find a man waiting to follow him. Luckily, the enemy was a bureaucracy, too, and could be as clumsy as we often were.

China presented problems similar to India's. My colleagues complained that it was impossible to spot surveillance in such densely-packed crowds.

I'd explored most of the region. Every city had its Agency gatekeepers, some more aggressive than others in their operations. Some areas refused to allow me in at all; some let me in but blocked the exchange of information. In Pakistan our gatekeepers did nothing; in Dubai they did more; and in India they were the best. After a few trips to India, I'd earned the confidence of the gatekeepers there.

Most gatekeepers preferred that the case officer beg and grovel for permission to recruit a human source. Not our people in India. They gave me the Glengarry leads, a list of a dozen entities of interest to the Agency—pre-approved and ready to go.

The instant I received the list, I headed straight for the first address. It was the office of a company that sold potential biological weapons components. (The components also had industrial uses.) I invented a reason to be there and exchanged my card with employees. I walked out loaded with cards. Later, I marked the cards of those who'd seemed the most eager to help.

In the office of a producer of a compound sought by chemical weapons programs, an employee accompanied me out of the office and down the stairs.

"I would like to give you my personal card," he said, "in case you are finding other opportunities for investment in India. I would like to be involved." He described the business activities of his friends and family and the good ideas that they could produce.

I called him back and invited him to lunch at the Taj Hotel. He hadn't spent much time in restaurants, it seemed, and the food was soon all over his face and staining the tablecloth in concentric rings around his plate. But he was eager to help me. I told him I needed to know everything about how his company's trade was conducted, and that this would help me determine the direction our business should go in.

During this and later trips to India, I worked those dozen targets and succeeded in producing intelligence from every one of them. We learned details of the buyers and sellers of components used to make chemical and biological weapons, pieces of puzzles that could be put together to identify weapons constructed by rogue states and the locations of those weapons. It was a productive time.

With so much travel to India, I came to recognize the same mutilated beggars at the same corners. The poverty seemed lessened somewhat. The brilliant and entrepreneurial Indian people needed only to be released from the prison of their command economy. India was no longer subject to a colonial power, and it wasn't a dictatorship, a monarchy, or a Communist state, just ruled by a bureaucracy that inhibited its people. In that regard, it was not unlike the Agency itself. As the years passed, India weakened the License Raj, and to each new gift of freedom, Indians responded with creativity and enthusiasm.

Our people controlling the India turf were the best, but they weren't perfect. There were nuclear targets I wanted to approach, but they refused, telling me in 1995 and 1996, "We have the nuclear target wired." We didn't. Later in the decade, on May 11, 1998, the Indians set off a series of nuclear bombs that came as a complete surprise to the Agency—all because we had no reliable human sources. Had we known in advance, the US government might have been able to stall the Indian government and prevent the South Asian arms race. In response to India's explosion, Pakistan set off a series of nuclear bombs on May 28, 1998. Pakistan's response was more or less expected, though we'd had no warning of that either. Decades of CIA bureaucratic risk aversion in Pakistan meant that we had no good human source in its nuclear program.

ONE EVENING, back home in the Middle East, my family and I felt a powerful pressure wave run through the house. It shuddered, and although the windows were shut, the curtains blew in as if a gust of wind had come in. It felt like it did when young Shi'a men blew up gas canisters nearby, but this time there was no sound. I went outside in the street and found my neighbors out in front of their houses as well, looking at each other, wondering what had happened.

The wave was an effect of the blast from the June 1996 bombing of the Khobar Towers building in Saudi Arabia. The building was full of American servicemen; the bomb killed seventeen Americans and one Saudi, and wounded 372 others of many nationalities. The terrorists were members of a Saudi branch of Hizb'allah. A federal court in the United States later found the attack was authorized by 'Ali Khamenei, then the ayatollah of Iran.

This came at a time when I'd already begun to feel that after five years, it was time for me to leave the region. Non-State Department officers' tours were loose back then, and I could have stayed as long as I wanted, but I was eager to move on. I haggled and negotiated with HQs and wound up with an assignment to Eastern Europe, working on Russians and former Soviets.

My assignments hadn't been stuck within a geographical

division, so I'd had more choices. The Agency was strictly divided, each sphere with its own HQs mandarins. An officer assigned to the Middle East division—where none of the assignments were cushy—might be in nasty assignments for his entire career, while an officer assigned to the European division—where all of the assignments were cushy—might have cushy assignments for life. Some of our people loved life in the Middle East, though, and I knew three of our case officers who had converted to Islam.

We'd done some good work preventing rogue state banks from laundering terrorist funds. We'd blocked some WMD production in India and in the Emirates. Yet I hadn't accomplished the things I *really* wanted to get done in the region. I hadn't recruited Indian or Pakistani nuclear sources, al Qaeda sources, or Iraqi sources. Neither had anyone else, and I knew that this was a very serious problem.

I'd appreciated the freedom to pursue different leads. In 1995, for example, the Aum Shinrikyo cult used sarin gas to kill twelve people on a Tokyo subway. The group had also experimented with botulinum toxin and anthrax.[19] I was interested in stopping the use of these horrifying weapons and began to look more closely at biochem targets. An advantage of receiving no direction from the Agency was that I could create my own initiatives.

By Agency standards, I'd had a long and successful tour in the Gulf. I was proud of my survivability. In percentage terms, of the non-State Department officers I'd known in the Middle East, about 15 percent had been successful. About 70 percent had failed quietly, usually leaving after a short time in the assignment. The remaining 15 percent had failed spectacularly, resulting in their beatings, arrests, kidnappings, being chased out of the country by the secret police, or having to be evacuated by a special forces team.

Driving by the hotel we'd stayed in on our first night in the country, I thought about the riot we'd seen. I could still make out the hole where a car had punched into the hedge.

★ 7 ★

Morning in Eastern Europe

> Freedom replaces the ancient hatreds
> among the nations with comity and
> peace. Freedom is the victor.
> *Ronald Reagan*

I met my new boss, Stefan, in a small, bare-walled, windowless conference room at HQs. "You'll report directly to our office at HQs," he said. "This will remove the local station where you'll be living and will make for a clearer chain of command."

I could see at once that he was a dynamic fast-tracker, dedicated and physically fit. He'd served in exciting and dangerous posts, and had a strong military record preceding his Agency work.

"You'll be fully supported by experts here at HQs," he said. "They'll select and analyze your targets. We won't be doing any trolling for leads. We know whom we want to target, and we'll go straight at them."

His deputy chief, Bettie, nodded her support. She was equally clear-eyed and energetic, full of ideas. I wanted to work the big targets, the truly destructive ones—nuclear, chemical, and biological weapons targets and their command structures. Working in the new unit with Stefan and Bettie was ideal. The fact that I'd report directly to them rather than to a local office, as in the Middle East, simplified things, and I knew this arrangement would dramatically improve efficiency.

I was eager to start working on new targets. During the transition to my Eastern European assignment, I'd met a Russian at a cocktail party. His background was intriguing, so I asked HQs to trace him. Sure enough, they identified him as an ex-KGB officer. KGB officers were of interest to us, naturally, and I was determined to find out whether *ex*-KGB officers were even better.

First to kick off the new program, Stefan and Bettie had organized a conference back at HQs.

At the conference, I took a seat next to Martin, my old friend from my domestic post. He couldn't stay awake for very long when seated in a warm room, and he started to nod off almost immediately. After a few introductory remarks by Stefan and Bettie, an HQs manager strode confidently into the conference room and stood facing us in a military posture. It was Suspenders.

"Your mission," he said, "will be to recruit our most important human targets in the former Soviet Union and Eastern Europe. The Agency has top-tier requirements in foreign leadership and command targets which must be met, and in nuclear, chemical, and biological weapons. We need human sources among top leaders and their cabinets and among top military commanders."

As he continued to describe our targets and the urgency of the mission, I thought: *This is exactly what I've been wanting.*

Toward the end of his speech he made what seemed like a serendipitous aside: "We want sources in the intelligence community as well. In fact, we're also interested in any ex-KGB officers you may run across. Although they may not have access to the most up-to-date information, their memories will contain an enormous amount of intel."

I jumped out of my seat, startling Martin awake. "I've got your man," I shouted. "I just met him last week!" Suspenders acknowledged me with a slight nod of his head and continued to talk. I sat back down, impatient for him to finish. When he finally did, I shouldered aside a couple of sycophants to get to him. (Suspenders had been promoted rapidly through the ranks and was well on his way to being an Agency mandarin.)

"I'm running late," he said. "I need to be off to my next appointment."

He left the conference room, so I followed, just barely squeezing into the elevator with him. When the elevator door opened downstairs he charged briskly through the lobby.

"What do you think of the ex-KGB officer I just met?" I asked. "He sounds like just the guy we're looking for."

Suspenders's strides lengthened until he broke step, shifting his pace from a brisk walk to a slow run. He kept up this gait until we reached his car. Keys in hand, he quickly opened the door and got inside. "We'll be in touch on this," he said through his car window. Then he sped away.

I walked slowly back through the parking lot and rode the elevator upstairs.

A wave of laughter greeted me in the conference room. My colleagues had been watching Suspenders trot through the parking lot. They couldn't tell what we were talking about, but whatever it was, they could see that it'd made him take off in a hurry.

After Suspenders's visit, the conference proceeded, with the usual parade of Agency personnel droning on without notes or lesson plans. We learned that many former Soviet weapons scientists were now unemployed and looking for ways to make ends meet. Fortunately, most of them had precious few years left, but others were selling their services to rogue states.

We'd had a few walk-ins at our embassies with information on chemical weapons. A speaker speculated that these volunteers were motivated by the sheer nastiness of biochem material; the mere thought of these WMDs could actually provoke pangs of conscience in a rogue state scientist. Except for these few, we'd had nothing but "dangles," agents pretending to be volunteers in an attempt to supply false information and waste our officers' time.

Our last speaker at the conference was a rising HQs manager in charge of running counter-proliferation programs. He didn't discuss counter-proliferation, but instead offered us advice on promotion. "As a young officer," he said, "promotion was important to me. I didn't just sit back and wait to get promoted. Even if you're a hotshot young case officer—and I was—you need to push your promotions forward. I studied the requirements. I found an office in HQs that handled promotions, and I went down there and said, 'Tell me what I need to do.' And they told me."

And *he* told us, in turn, at great length. I wanted to hear about counter-proliferation and what we could do to stop it—not about what a superstar this speaker was. But he had a certain charisma, and his visit was memorable. His words stuck with me and I thought about him from time to time as the years went by.

MY FAMILY AND I FLEW to Eastern Europe. We arrived in the afternoon and checked into a hotel near the city's central square, where we later relaxed at an outdoor café. The kids played in the pleasant late summer weather. Near a statue in the center of the square, the kids found some ancient coins wedged between cobblestones. I interpreted it as an omen of good fortune to come.

In the evening, I went jogging in the park across the river from the town square. A commanding statue of a Communist Party boss in the park had been taken down and replaced, temporarily, with a statue of Michael Jackson.

The next day, focusing on mundane but important tasks, we registered the kids in school. We were relieved to see the teachers place nametags on their desks and welcome them. With the uncertain nature of our overseas tours, and the issuance of so many one-way tickets, many of my colleagues' children had had a very tough time in school. They changed schools often, sometimes at mid-year. Having the kids set in school was the top priority for my wife and me. We felt good.

We bought a car with Agency money. As I'd done in the Middle

East, I picked a suitably modest one, so as not to draw the envy of other Agency employees.

Before we found a house, we spent a month in a hotel. As it had been designed as a retreat for Communist Party bosses, its rooms were enormous, garishly decorated, and filled with outsized and masculine furniture. It was on the outskirts of the city in a quiet neighborhood. Rumor had it that the hotel had secret underground passages and bomb shelters to protect the Communist bosses in the event of a nuclear attack.

The housing selection was poor throughout Eastern Europe, where the Communists had built concrete apartment blocks honey-combed with tiny apartments.

After a long search, though, my wife found a nice house. The owner had built it during the last decade of Communist rule. The Communists hadn't let people build their own houses, but they did allow the "proletariat" to build "socialist cooperative housing," so he'd signed up a group of relatives. His mother, brother, and cousins were suddenly a "socialist people's cooperative." He'd had to make the end result look like a collection of small apartments, so there were sinks, kitchens, and bathrooms scattered in unusual locations around the house. He'd had trouble finding building materials, and used whatever he could find, whenever he could find it. The house looked like the titular Cadillac of the Johnny Cash song about a factory worker who takes home a part every day, eventually assem-bling a '52, '53, '54, '55, '56, '57, '58, '59, '60, '61, '62 model.

It was difficult for our landlord to watch a renter move in. He left personal items in a small room downstairs and promised to move them out in a month or two. I knew he wanted to find out first whether we were decent people, and he was afraid to remove all traces of himself from the house. The laws of ownership weren't entirely clear in this post-Communist confusion. I guessed that he'd never have rented the house to another citizen of his country, wary of the cunning machinations of "squatter's rights."

There was plenty of weirdness in our new arrangement, but it was the best available, so we were happy with it. We'd looked at a beautiful house nearby—adjacent to a castle, in fact—but we'd had a bad feeling about it. Much later we learned that the landlord, who lived right next door, would enter the rental house in the middle of the night and roam around, frightening his tenants.

Saturday morning soccer started up for the kids in September and it was already getting cold. At the opposite end of the park, a long row of people trained their dogs to attack. Shouting *Hundekommandos*—that's "dog commands" in German—the owners ordered their dogs to *Komm*! (come), *Voraus*! (go), *Aus*! (let go). An instructor wore a shaggy, heavily padded protective suit. On his command, the owners ordered their dogs to attack, and the snarling dogs bit the man's padded arms and legs. I thought to myself that every country is a Petri dish and its policies the culture: Communism had produced fearful people who trained vicious dogs for protection.

For our part, we adopted a stray cat.

The switch to a new assignment was a critical period for an officer who did not belong to the State Department. This was the point at which most of my colleagues had run into trouble. There were always obstacles, different in each place and for each person. At each successive move, the law of averages caught up, so that while many officers eventually arrived at their first assignment, few made it to a second assignment, almost none made a third, and I'd never heard of anyone who had had a fourth successive consecutive assignment. Max and I were the only members of our original training class still overseas.

One obstacle that worried me was our house. My wife had begun to complain that it was dreary and menacing. I didn't really mind it that much; we had heat and a roof over our heads. The place was not far from a forest and we could take the kids down to play near a stream. But the important thing was that my family got settled—the assignment depended upon it.

One day, the phone rang. A man asked, "Are you the new tenants at 13 Dzerzhensky?"

"Yes, we are."

"I rented that house six months ago," he said. "It was awful. The landlord's a nightmare. He's unbalanced and dangerous. He turned off the electricity and the heat and forced my family out of there."

This didn't sound good.

"Has he kept the electricity bills in his name?"

I said that he had. The landlord had promised me it would be better that way.

"He'll be able to cut off your electricity at will. Did he keep some personal things in a room downstairs?" At this point I began to grow anxious. The man went on, "He'll use his access to that room to ensure that he can come and go in the house as he pleases.

"It wasn't just me who had problems with him. The same thing happened to three previous tenants: a Chinese diplomat, a German banker, the principal of the French international school. We've filed a lawsuit together, and you're welcome to read our affidavits."

The next day, we got copies of the affidavits, and spread them out on the floor for study. Each affidavit told the same story: The landlord's modus operandi was to become irrationally angry at the tenants, turn off their power, and send a gang of thugs to harass the tenants until they took off.

We were concerned, but we didn't have any better ideas—and I had operations to focus on.

I TRAVELED BACK to the HQs area periodically for meetings, and each time I spent my flight imagining the scenarios I might encounter upon arrival. The bureaucracy was always full of surprises. A polygraph operator might be waiting in the reception room, ready to hook me up to the Box; HQs might pull me into a conference room and inform me that the KGB had learned my identity.

I sat on the plane lost in my thoughts. An ex-Communist boss sitting next to me took off his shoes and the stink shocked me back to reality. I moved to another seat. Most of the other passengers were surly former party bosses in purple suits. Good manners had been a mark of the bourgeois and the bourgeois were the enemy of the proletariat, so the bosses had cultivated what they perceived to be the ways of the working man: unpleasant odors and poor manners.

When I arrived at my hotel room in Washington, D.C. my contact at HQs called me on the telephone. "There's a problem," he said. "The people from Due Diligence are on their way to you and they'll meet you in your hotel room in thirty minutes. It's not your fault. They've discovered some things of concern to HQs. Listen to what they have to say. No decision has been made yet."

I worked through various possibilities in my mind: Should I give a domestic assignment a shot, or just resign from the Agency straightaway?

Two big-bellied, middle-aged men arrived at my room and sat down on the edge of the bed. One of the men gave me a disapproving look and leaned over to turn on the television set. HQs people thought loud television sets masked conversations and were good tradecraft. "We're from Due Diligence," they said. "You're Bill Jones?"

I nodded. Close enough. One of the men went to the bathroom. The other man pulled out a notebook.

"You own two pieces of real estate," he said. "You rent an apartment. Your children go to St. Mark's Episcopal School. Your parents are divorced and your mother lives in Portland. Your father lives in Seattle. You enjoy reading books about the Civil War."

The man gave me a wry smile. I was speechless. His partner returned from the bathroom.

He said, "You play golf and have a low handicap. You studied history as an undergrad. You earned your undergraduate degree from Chico State in California and a graduate degree from George

Washington University. Your wife is from Maine. She is a graduate of Smith College, where she was a member of the Alpha Delta Pi sorority."

Finished reading their lists, they closed their notebooks.

"We've found this information using the Agency's new Due Diligence computer software. This information gives you an idea of how much can be learned about a person from publicly available databases. Hostile foreign intelligence services have access to the same databases. The characteristics we've found show that you're just an open book to the KGB. These characteristics don't jibe with the types of operational approaches you are doing. We think that if a sophisticated intelligence service—and the KGB is a sophisticated intelligence service—takes a close look at you, it'll be a simple matter to blow your cover. We think it may be dangerous for you to travel to Russia."

They paused for dramatic effect.

I was relieved that this was the only surprise I'd have to swat down.

"Bill Jones is an alias," I said, "and I hadn't even begun to construct the documents and cover legend for that one. I've never used it. It looks like you've gathered some random information on a person, or several people, named Bill Jones. I chose Bill Jones because it's such a common name. When you do a database search of the name, you'll come up with so much information that it could be anyone. As of today, though, all I've done is pick out the name. I haven't done anything with it yet. None of the information you've compiled is accurate, or even close."

Their expressions turned dull.

"I wear a light disguise with the Bill Jones alias," I said.

"Looks like a disguise to me," said one of the men, "but it might work on someone who doesn't have a trained eye."

I wasn't wearing the disguise.

I thanked the men and ended the meeting. I leapt for the phone and called my HQs contact. "Ishmael's blown to the KGB" could spread through the bureaucracy quickly and haunt me for years if I didn't squash it right away. I told my contact what had happened and asked him to alert Stefan and Bettie that the rumor should be stifled. It took them a couple of days, but they were able to do it.

It turned out that the Due Diligence was an early version of an Internet search engine. It could compile lots of information on a person, as it had about the phantom "Bill Jones." Imagine how many "hits" a Google search would have turned up.

The key to aliases in the modern day is to use common names. If a person's name is Bill Jones, it's tough to corroborate different search results. The Agency likes the "Xavier X. Xylophone" types of unusual names to ensure that two officers never used the same one, but it's an ordinary name that provides true anonymity.

Each time I visited HQs, I found that Stefan's personal appearance declined. He was putting on weight, getting a donuts-and-Coca-Cola-for-breakfast kind of fat, and he looked like he rarely slept. His head grew wider and heavier.

I spotted him and another man in a meeting room. "Hey Stefan!" I said, "You look like you were up all night! Those girlfriends of yours keeping you too busy?"

Stefan and the person he was talking to, an HQs mandarin, looked up and gave me dark glares. I realized they'd been deep in conversation. I regretted having made such a flat joke and I excused myself and left the room.

I wandered over to the area at HQs used as a holding tank for officers who were trapped in bureaucratic limbo. It was a windowless room with bare, scuffed walls, lit by fluorescent ceiling fixtures. The air was stale. Each morning these people arrived and took possession of small desks, spreading out their papers, pens, and other trinkets. Many of them were my friends. I talked to them to learn what had gone wrong, so that I could help them, or at least avoid making their mistakes myself.

I always opened with innocuous questions: "How about that game last night?" My colleagues seemed fragile and jittery. I displayed open body language. We're all aware of body language, but people in a strained psychological state are acutely aware—for instance, they might find arms crossed over the chest to be threatening. The bureaucracy had been burning these guys with cigarettes, figuratively speaking, and I wanted to be sure they didn't think I was one of the bad guys.

In one cubicle sat a pasty, out-of-shape creature.

I realized in horror that it was a colleague I'd worked out with during that conference several years back, an accomplished athlete.

"My marriage broke up," he said. "It was nasty. I'd been seeing other women. Then HQs ordered me to end my assignment and come back here. I'm trying to figure out what to do next. I've been under a lot of stress for a long time. I haven't felt healthy and I guess I've let myself get a bit out of shape."

I wandered a few cubicles away and saw Martin. "Watch out for that guy," he said. "He's told his girlfriends he works for the CIA. HQs thinks he's also told them the identities of some of our other colleagues. The girlfriends aren't US citizens. Looks like anyone who's served with him is going to get his one-way ticket. This guy is causing a lot of trouble to a lot of people."

Martin had recently recovered from a broken collarbone and a concussion. "I was injured while bungee jumping from a bridge," he said. "I hit hard and hurt my wrist. I couldn't figure out what went wrong because I always use the exact same length of cord from the exact point on the same bridge.

"I went bungee jumping a month later from the same bridge, and this time I hit *really* hard. That's when I got my injuries It took me a while to figure it out: I'd put on fifty pounds, so I dropped faster and harder than the cord could handle."

Unable to type, he'd had to dictate his operations reports to his wife. "My chief was furious when he found out my wife was typing my reports. My wife didn't have any security clearance. He accused me of exposing my wife to secret information.

"But HQs came to the rescue and told my boss that the situation was different for non-State Department officers. HQs told him that our spouses were authorized greater access depending on the situation. Since no one else from the Agency was around, it was okay for her to type my reports."

He was correct on that point. I discussed operations with my wife whenever I needed a second opinion.

Martin's station didn't sound like much fun. His manager had made him send in an hour-by-hour activity report each day.

"My manager backed off on the issue of my wife typing reports, but there must have been residual anger, because he also told me I couldn't write well and had to take a remedial course back here at HQs."

That's what Martin was doing there that day, hacking away at the kinds of typing exercises that new trainees are often assigned. It seemed to have little other purpose than humiliating him. He'd done well during our domestic assignment, but somehow the persona our US managers had found witty and creative had struck his overseas managers as bizarre and abrasive.

Martin's prediction came true—several officers known to our colleague were withdrawn from their field assignments and brought back to HQs. A few weeks later, Martin's manager used the news of our colleague's indiscretions to decide that Martin had been blown as well, and Martin received his one-way ticket home. It sounded like there was a lot of animosity in that station, not just involving Martin. A couple of months later the boss received his one-way ticket home as well. A rumor circulated that our colleague had been a convicted felon before being hired by the Agency, that the Agency had known about it but had decided to hire him anyway.

I thought carefully about the obstacles other officers had faced, and thought about ways to avoid or overcome them should they ever land in *my* path.

BACK IN EASTERN EUROPE, my landlord problem simmered. Housing was scarce and we didn't think we could find a better situation. We re-read the affidavits that the past four tenants had produced. In each case, the tenant had asked the landlord to fix something, and he had refused, thus prompting the tenant to threaten to withhold rent.

My wife and I prepared a plan: Be kind to the landlord. Don't ask him to fix anything. Never, under any circumstances, threaten to withhold rent. I didn't mind doing my own repairs. The only stumbling block to pleasant relations was that I couldn't have him living in the house with us. We decided to ask him to remove his belongings from the downstairs room. If he agreed, we'd stay; if he didn't, we'd leave.

Instead of renting an office, I rented a small apartment that could double as one. That way, in a "landlord" emergency, I could move in my family temporarily.

The weather turned cold, and neighbors lit coal fires in the basements of their homes. Eastern Europeans were still using coal for heat, and the coal available in the area was especially dirty. It fluffed heavily out of chimneys and poisoned the air. Household heating sources were rapidly being converted to natural gas, but it took just one old-fashioned coal-burner to turn a neighborhood's air into an ashtray.

In other ways, things improved rapidly. "We rarely had oranges, and almost never in the winter," a friend said. "Once, a truck full of oranges arrived at the local store during the darkest part of the season. We children received two each. I'll never forget that sweetness, what a treat it was."

I continued traveling to the Middle East and India and so had kept up my operational activity. It was lonely work, lots of long plane flights and nights alone in dreary hotel rooms. Colleagues in my unit weren't so lucky, however. They didn't have ongoing operations and could only sit and wait.

I hadn't received HQs responses to my operational proposals on Eastern European and former Soviet Union targets. I'd expected fast, aggressive targeting from Stefan's unit at HQs, but so far it was just another black hole.

I MET STEFAN AT HQS. He looked like a different person; his physical deterioration was striking. He'd gained forty pounds and looked exhausted, with pronounced bags under his eyes. His speech was vacant and disorganized. He counseled me to be patient; the operational approvals would come.

When I'd lived in the Middle East, I'd only visited HQs a handful of times. I'd been more or less ignorant of what was going on in the organization. Now that I was making more frequent HQs trips, I learned that the early and mid 1990s represented a period of intense budget and personnel cuts throughout the Agency.

Money had continued to flow into the non-State Department areas, though. Since I'd joined the Agency, there had been genuine momentum to get more of these officers assigned overseas. The training classes of the mid and late 1980s had been eviscerated, but the numbers of new hires continued to rise, and by the mid 1990s the number of officers had once again reached the level of the late 1980s.

There was an ongoing debate within the organization about whether the cost of fielding an officer outside the State Department was too high. Conventional wisdom said that it was much more expensive. I believed that it was dramatically cheaper. Basic expenses were the same: salary, rent, schools, a car. I rented an office, while they had a free office in an embassy or other State Department building, so this expense may have been greater for me.

But the major cost, the one that was already stratospheric and would continue to grow exponentially during my time in the Agency, was security. Billions of dollars were spent on our fortress embassies to make them more secure from terrorist attack. No money was spent on my security.

Even in these years before 9/11, the cost of protecting embassies from electronic eavesdropping was enormous. The embassy in Moscow was the most expensive structure, for its size, on earth.[20] It all depended on how you fiddled with the numbers. HQs argued that they needed vast numbers of managers and administrative personnel to support officers like me in the field. I didn't think any of those people were necessary. They were just layers of bureaucrats and I couldn't identify their tasks. There was the woman who was supposed to send me my salary, which usually arrived a year late. I didn't think it was fair to burden us with the cost of maintaining all these HQs people.

A case officer in an embassy had an array of support people that I didn't have and didn't want: the man who arranges to rent an apartment for you, the people running the PX. Each of these people cost hundreds of thousands of dollars a year.

The embassy ran a child care center for its officers. The American taxpayer didn't have to run a child care center for my children.

My secretary cost $1,000 each month. My counterpart in an embassy would have a secretary with an overseas pay and benefits package running into the hundreds of thousands of dollars a year.

It was fairly safe to say that the embassy workers were doing a better job of, if nothing else, draining the Agency's coffers.

IN LATE 1996 and early 1997, blowback from the Ames and Nicholson arrests spread through the case officer corps. In February 1994, FBI agents pulled the CIA mole Aldrich Ames out of his Jaguar[21] and arrested him. In the backseat of the FBI car, Ames repeated to himself, "Think, think, think."[22]

Although the Agency later said Ames had been tracked down

by a group of clever spy catchers within HQs, Ames was actually revealed as a traitor through information provided by a Russian source.[23] Much has been written elsewhere about Ames and his nine years of unrestrained spying on behalf of the KGB. When a rash of the Agency's Soviet sources were arrested and executed by the Soviets in 1985, the Agency's mandarins took no effective action.

The KGB's ability to expose Agency spies in Russia made it appear omnipotent. Unaware that the KGB was able to uncover Agency operations using sources within the Agency and FBI, some Agency officers came to believe that the KGB had developed an advanced form of surveillance; they called it "ultra-discreet surveillance."[24] This explained the training exercises in which instructors informed us we'd been under surveillance when in fact we were not, designed to put us in awe of the power of surveillance.

In November 1996, Harold J. Nicholson, another mole, was arrested. Both Ames and Nicholson were case officers who had sold secrets to the KGB. Over the course of their careers, Ames and Nicholson had had access to the real names of many covert Agency officers, as well as access to some officers' personnel files during the course of promotion panels. Some of my colleagues had worked with them on specific operations; others had met them at HQs or during training courses.

The Agency sought to keep the identities of its officers secret, but with the extraordinary number of layers of HQs bureaucrats, it was a difficult thing to do. If an employee had access to an officer's identity, then so would his many managers. One reason it had been hard to pinpoint Ames as the mole within the Agency's Soviet programs was the existence of such a large number of bureaucrats at HQs who had access to *all* of the information available on Soviet agents.[25]

Ames had been privileged with near-perfect access, and in 1985 he "betrayed every active espionage and counterintelligence operation that the United States was running against the Soviet Union at the time."[26]

At least since 1985, the Soviets had been aware of the identities of CIA sources in the Soviet bloc. After the fall of Communism in Eastern Europe, we learned that the East Germans had known the identities of all of our agents in their territory. (Much of the intelligence supplied by these agents was disinformation.) It's possible, in fact, that the Soviets had a lock on most of our sources throughout most of the Agency's history. Beginning in 1961 and continuing until the mid 1970s,[27] Soviet agents vanished in droves.

"Ames looked like any other guy at HQs," Jonah said. His knowledge of HQs was better than mine and he thought Ames would have been just another gray man at HQs if not for the organization's culture. Every organization has its bottom 10 percent. The Marine Corps can take its bottom 10 percent and turn them into heroes. The Agency seemed to push *its* bottom 10 percent off a cliff. Perversely, the opportunity to be a traitor had given Ames something he could be *good* at. The KGB rewarded him and gave him the positive feedback that he didn't get at the Agency. I don't intend these as excuses for Ames—I think he should have been executed. But had he been properly led and motivated, he might not have turned on his country.

Nicholson's work for the KGB wasn't as damaging as Ames's because Nicholson's access wasn't as total. Agency bureaucrats spread the story that Nicholson had been, like Ames, a loser with a career going nowhere. Jonah disagreed: "Nicholson had a good reputation, was promoted on time, and was politically well-connected within the Agency." The Nicholson case was in a way more frightening within the Agency than the Ames case because Nicholson had had a reputation as a good case officer.

Ames and Nicholson had passed all of their polygraphs. Later, supporters of the test within the Agency argued in vain that a more careful look at Ames's charts indicated that he hadn't actually passed.

Prior to one of his polygraphs, Ames had been nervous and had asked his KGB handler for a foolproof way to pass the polygraph. The man told him to relax and establish a good rapport with the Box operator. Ames was disappointed. The KGB was the most sophisticated intelligence service in the world, and this was the best they could do?

Then he cooled down and realized that the KGB really *was* the best intel service in the world—if they told him to do something, he'd do it. That was all it took for him to pass.

HQS INFORMED ALL OFFICERS potentially compromised by Ames or Nicholson that they could no longer serve overseas. They were welcome to find other jobs within the Agency at HQs.

Returning to Langley for another round of HQs meetings, I found the cubicles filled with officers who'd been purged. I joined a group of four sitting around a table.

"Have you been purged, Ishmael?" an older man asked.

"I don't think I'm going to be. At least, I haven't heard anything. I'm back here for operational meetings."

"I think you're back here to watch everyone being purged, Ishmael. You like this, don't you? It just means headroom to you, doesn't it?"

The other men laughed. The Agency had limited numbers of senior pay grades available, so opening up "headroom" by eliminating officers senior to me would mean I would be promoted faster.

"That's not true, you guys. I didn't join the Agency for promotion. I'm only here to work," I said.

"Bullshit, Ishmael, you love all the new headroom."

"Headroom, headroom for Ishmael!" the three other men chanted, laughing.

HQs handled the purge efficiently, meeting each purged officer with a special team: a couple of managers, a finance officer, a personnel officer, and a psychologist. The team headed off resistance by firmly informing the officers that the decision was irrevocable. There was some rancor, and one of the purged officers picked up a chair during this meeting and threw it at the wall. But few purged officers left the Agency. They accepted their one-way tickets home to jobs at HQs.

"I knew I'd be purged, and I didn't have a problem with it," said the older man. "I'd been in a hotel room in a dangerous country, getting ready for a meeting with an important agent.

"My meeting wasn't scheduled to take place for an hour, so I turned on the television to watch the news. Nicholson's ugly mug flashed up on the screen, and I knew I was done for. I knew him well, and had worked with him on a bunch of operations. He'd have identified me to the KGB for sure. The local police had close ties to the KGB.

"I scrambled to the airport and got out of there. I didn't want to go to the fingernail factory."

A pretty blonde woman named Valerie came into the office and sat down at our table. She said she had received a message to return to HQs and wondered what it was about. Moments later, a group of managers beckoned her to join them in the conference room. "She's about to be purged," said the older man. Twenty minutes later, the woman returned, weeping softly.

A THEORY DURING THIS TIME held that the purge had nothing to do with security in the aftermath of Ames and Nicholson—that it was strictly budget-driven. The non-State Department program had overspent and in an era of big budget cuts something had to give. Pulling officers out of the field and moving them back to HQs collapsed expenses. I discounted this theory at first because it sounded too conspiratorial—surely none of our managers could be so devious. But as time went on, two top HQs manda-rins, both division chiefs, confirmed this theory to me in separate, private conversations, and today I am convinced the purge was the result of bureaucratic agendas. The Godfather, after all, had not been purged, and his identity was known to multiple hostile intelligence services. (The sheer volume of the Godfather's intelligence operations and his recruitments of such a large number of foreign spies had left foreign governments with no choice but to acknowledge that the Godfather was probably a CIA officer.) The purge, in the end, cut half of our non-State Department officers overseas.

OUR LANDLORD CONTINUED to slip into the house and lounge around in his little room downstairs. We crossed our fingers that he would move out permanently.

Each time I saw him, I gave him a cheerful hello. We gave him bottles of wine; he gave us some smoked salmon and a picture book. We listened to and pretended to agree with his political conspiracy theories. I wrote him "happy letters," just like I'd once sent to my old chief, Horace, notes full of happy news that required him to do nothing. He'd associate my name with fine feelings. I continued to pay the rent in advance and made sure never to ask him to fix anything.

Finally, he surrendered the little room and moved his stuff out. We were happy. So far, I'd read him correctly. He just wanted his rent money and he didn't want any hassles. We'd convinced him that we weren't evil, and so had solved the landlord problem. Day-to-day obstacles like this one had ended many officers' overseas tours.

DEEP INTO THE EASTERN EUROPEAN WINTER, I scheduled a meeting in Dresden, in eastern Germany, with an agent who would be traveling in from the Middle East. I took my family along. We drove through Slovakia, into the Czech Republic, and then north through the crumbling villages of the former Sudetenland. Beginning about twenty miles from the German border, prostitutes appeared along the road, some in raingear with umbrellas, some behind windows with few clothes on.

"Why are those ladies dressed in short sleeves and shorts in this cold weather?" my young daughter asked.

The kids were hungry. "Why don't we stop and get some lunch?" I said. We looked for a restaurant.

We stopped at the "Paradise Rest Stop" and the "Miami Beach Restaurant," but they turned out to be whorehouses so we got back in the car and kept going.

After crossing into Germany, we finally found a real restaurant. Dresden was a beautiful city and much of the war damage had been repaired. I left my family at a hotel while I conducted my agent meeting, and then I picked them up and we drove home.

We traveled back by the same route. About a third of the population of Czechoslovakia prior to World War II had been ethnically German, and the presence of this large German population served as the excuse for Hitler's invasion in 1939. During World War II, Czech cities were not bombed and Czech men were not conscripted. The memoirs of German soldiers describe traveling through the country without difficulty.

Just as the populations of many other parts of Eastern Europe had done, the Czechs helped the Germans identify and round up Jews. Czechs served as guards in the holding camps used to imprison Jews and Gypsies before they were moved to the extermination camps in Poland.

Concentration camps for Gypsies were conceived, constructed, and manned entirely by Czechs and one of the camps, Lety, was conceived by the Czech government even before the Nazis had invaded Czechoslovakia. Lety sent 500 Gypsies to Auschwitz; another camp for Gypsies, Hodonin, sent 863.

The existence of the camps was not officially disclosed until the early 1990s. Except for a few reprimands, none of the people who operated the camps were punished. (In 1994, a beauty contestant gained world attention by stating that she planned to go to law school so she could become a prosecutor and clean up the "Gypsy problem." Eastern European audiences welcomed her comments, finding her to be a breath of fresh air.)

Resistance to the Nazi occupation was light, and Reinhard Heydrich, the Nazi governor of Bohemia and Moravia, often drove alone in an open-topped car. He was one of the chief architects of the Holocaust. In 1942, he was assassinated by two Czech men trained in Britain. In retaliation, the Nazis obliterated the town of Lidice, near Prague, and murdered its 340 inhabitants. After this, there was virtually no resistance in Czechoslovakia until the end of the war.

While crimes against the Czechs were relatively light, the German occupation did humiliate them. They brooded darkly throughout the war. In May 1945, after the German army was defeated, the Czechs attacked and tortured, killed, or expelled its ethnic German population. About three million Germans, a third of the prewar population, were gone by the end of the year. Their property was confiscated. Most of the Germans moved to Bavaria, where they have complained about their 1945 treatment ever since. A few German politicians with large numbers of Sudeten German constituents have paid lip service, but no one else in the world cares.

Estimates of the numbers of German civilians killed by the Czechs vary wildly, from 10,000 to 100,000. The killing was up close and personal, with guns, axes, and knives. It was not state-sponsored, but a sum of individual acts of violence.

WE RETURNED TO OUR CITY of assignment. That night, we went to dinner with an American friend. His grandparents were natives of the country and when he visited during the 1980s he looked up some distant cousins. "I found their address, and I knocked on the door. They wouldn't invite me in and they asked that I leave immediately. They were terrified.

"Just last week, I went to visit them again. This time they were gracious. They remembered who I was, invited me in, and apologized for not having invited me in when I'd visited before.

"They explained that the secret police had visited them the day after my visit, taken each family member into a separate room, and questioned them. I guess the secret police were satisfied, because that was the last of it."

A friend who had fled his village as a child in 1956 said, "I go back to my village to see my friends and they look twenty years older than me. Some are dead; most of the rest are drunk; most of them are unemployable; most are toothless. They look like hell, and they're depressing to be around."

People respond to the sets of rules to which they're subjected. The people of India under the License Raj and the people of Eastern Europe under Communism reminded me of my colleagues in the CIA. Subject to a maze of restrictive bureaucratic rules and procedures, human creativity and productivity are blocked.

The younger generations of Eastern Europe, freed from the restraints of Communism, were growing up indistinguishable from young people in Western Europe. The economy was growing rapidly and life was improving dramatically.

I CONTINUED TO RUN operations in the Middle East and South Asia, but so far none of my operational proposals for Eastern Europe and Russia were getting any traction at HQs. Those replies I did get from HQs were evasive. I cursed and paced the floor. Our intelligence gaps were huge—so much work needed to be done.

A colleague arrived in my city of assignment. He picked up surveillance almost immediately. Rather than go about his life in the most mundane fashion in order to bore the surveillants into thinking he was an ordinary businessman, he rounded up some of his friends and confronted the surveillance team.

"What the hell do you guys want? Why are you following me," he said, exactly as we'd been taught not to. He told HQs what he'd done, and HQs rewarded him with a one-way ticket to the Oak-wood. There seemed to be an overwhelming human need, rooted firmly in pride, to inform surveillants that you knew they were there. It was hard to maintain the self-discipline necessary to bore a surveillance team.

I DECIDED TO TRAVEL to HQs again to see what I could do to push operations forward. My wife gave me a ride to the airport. When I opened my car door to get out, the edge of my door hit the side of a taxi. I apologized to the driver, but he got out and started shouting. I lost my temper, cursed him, and pushed him out of my way. Other taxi drivers began to mill around, and one of them stood in front of my wife's car, making as if to prevent her from driving away. She was a graduate of the Agency's hostile driving course, and she drove right at him, making him jump aside. I pushed the loudest driver out of my path and got into the safety of the airport terminal before the little mob could advance any further.

Once I arrived at HQs, I headed to an appointment with Stefan. I waited for an hour and he didn't show up. A thin, gray man arrived in his stead.

"Stefan's gone," he said.

"Well?"

"Can't talk about it. That's all I can say. He's gone."

I badgered managers at HQs to find out what had happened. The official line, that he was gone and that no one should ask questions, satisfied most of my colleagues. They were afraid of retaliation from mandarins. If CIA management felt that Stefan should disappear, that was fine by them.

I finally found a manager willing to talk. He explained that Stefan had failed his Box exam shortly after I had joined the new unit. It took the Agency a long time to come to a decision about what to do with him. During the many months that the Agency took to ponder his fate, Stefan had been worried and stressed out, and he had overworked himself in the mistaken belief that displays of spirit and dedication would save him from the failed Box.

When the Agency finally fired him, men from the security department arrived to escort him out of the building. Later I heard rumors about why he'd been fired, the most likely of which was that he'd had an unauthorized Russian girlfriend. We were supposed to report our girlfriends to HQs, especially if they happened to be Russian. I remembered the unfunny crack I'd made about girlfriends to Stefan while he was speaking to a HQs mandarin. No wonder it had fallen so flat.

All information about Stefan's departure was innuendo. Bettie couldn't tell us anything, and no rumors were ever confirmed. His personal appearance had been the "lab rat" look a person gets when they lose control over their lives. They eat an atrocious diet, sleep poorly, and worry constantly.

I found a friend of Stefan's. "I went to his house to see him last week," he said. "HQs ordered me not to visit, but I explained that it was a good idea to keep an eye on our colleagues who had been fired. Otherwise they could go off the deep end like Edward Lee Howard. Stefan would never do that, of course, but my explanation worked, and HQs said it was okay for me to make the visit.

"Stefan told me he'd been under continuous surveillance by FBI teams. He went jogging and ran like hell so the surveillance teams would have a hard time keeping up.

"Doing a turn while driving, he noticed a helicopter banking overhead. Now he thinks he had helicopter surveillance."

★ 8 ★

Physicists Who Knew Sin

> In some sort of crude sense which no vulgarity, no humor, no over-statement can quite extinguish, the physicists have known sin; and this is a knowledge which they cannot lose.
> *J. Robert Oppenheimer*

Bettie was now in charge of our unit, and HQs was ready to approve my operational travel to the former Soviet Union. I started with a trip to Belarus. First I needed a visa, so using an alias and a mailing address and phone number supplied by HQs, I went to the Belarus embassy in Washington to get one. The embassy put the visa into my alias passport and mailed it back to the address HQs had provided. But the address bounced it back to the embassy marked "return to sender."

The Belarus embassy telephoned the phone number I'd given, and the Agency man who answered acknowledged it was the correct number but would not give them the address. The embassy tried the phone number again the next day, and this time another guy answered the phone and gave them a new mailing address. This address bounced the passport back to the embassy, too. I called the embassy and told them to hold on to the passport, and then I went there to pick it up in person. This wasn't, needless to say, a good way to start alias spy trips to Belarus.

I had some alias business cards printed and acquired a driver's license. The man who operated the license machine showed me a collection of celebrity license photos that he'd pinned to the wall next to his machine.

I tested the alias credit cards to make sure they worked. There was a fundamental flaw in the credit cards that made them look unusual. They were real cards, and they worked fine, but there was an obvious flaw. If I were hauled in for interrogation in Belarus, the interrogators would notice the flaw. But I didn't want to sit around whining that the credit cards weren't in order.

Just as they'd promised to do when I'd joined the unit, Bettie and her people identified an important military officer with access to former Soviet nuclear stockpiles. I called the target on the telephone, gave him my cover story, and set an appointment for a meeting in Minsk.

WITH MY "BILL JONES" ALIAS and disguise, I traveled to Minsk via London. My family had traveled to London to meet me. There was a risk involved in tangling my real and alias personas, but I was prepared to take it; I hadn't seen my family in a long time. I missed meeting them at the airport and searched for them at the hotel, but the hotel had been overbooked and they'd been placed somewhere else. I finally found them and was overjoyed. That night we went to dinner at a scraggly pizza place in Piccadilly Circus, and then we went to see the show *Oliver*, which the kids enjoyed immensely.

My family left London the next day and went back to Eastern Europe. I spent the night alone in the room. I went for a walk past Harrods, to Leicester Square, and took the Tube back to the hotel, wandering around until my plane was ready to leave.

MINSK, LIKE MANY FORMER SOVIET CITIES, was rebuilt after the war in drab, utilitarian blocks. There weren't any hotel rooms available, so I rented a short-term apartment accessible through a long, dark passageway. I dined at a new McDonald's nearby, the only source of convenient food within a few blocks. I figured I could work off the burgers later.

My target didn't show up for the meeting. I telephoned him; he hemmed and hawed and said he'd be late, giving all the usual signs of reluctance and anxiety. I'd seen the signs before. I had done this sort of thing enough to develop a sense. I scanned the hotel lobby several times, in case he had misunderstood our meeting location. I hoped to see a man wearing the large, distinctive hat of the Soviet military officer, but I knew before looking that I wouldn't find him there.

I didn't want to return to HQs empty-handed, so I went out into the city to troll for other intelligence targets. I made my way around Minsk on the city's impressive subway system. Its stations had been constructed deep underground, to double as shelters from American nuclear attack.

I located government buildings, and tried to enter the Ministry of Foreign Affairs to see who I might meet, but the security out front was too strong. Winging it, I said, "I'd like to speak to someone from your Middle Eastern department. I'm here to gather information on the feasibility of establishing a trading company in Minsk on behalf of Gulf investors."

The guard was unmoved. In typical Soviet style, he said, "Give me a written list of questions first, and I will submit them through proper channels."

It wasn't worth the trouble, so I moved on.

I decided to avoid other traditional government leadership targets. Belarus was no threat to the United States. Individuals involved in weapons proliferation were far more interesting to me.

I visited a few banks. I'd done a great deal of bank work and thought I might find a good target: a bank with shady Middle Eastern ties, or bankers involved in terrorist or rogue state money flows. Visiting the first bank on my list, I approached employees and asked vague questions about foreign investment. Most of them stared at me, uncomprehending, but one had a suggestion. "I know the Agricultural Institute develops new agricultural products, and they're looking for investors. I have a friend there. Here is his card."

I had to show identification in order to leave the bank. This was a peculiarity of closed countries, the requirement to pass security both entering *and* exiting a building. I went back to my apartment to think about what to do next. I decided to give the agricultural scientist a call and we set a meeting for the following morning.

I put on a Wall Street suit and went to the agricultural institute, an impressive building constructed in the late 1800s. Now rundown and filthy, it reminded me of the buildings the British had built in Bombay. Other structures nearby, newer but even more dilapidated, had been built by German POWs in the 1950s. (The Soviets held German soldiers well into that decade.) The Soviet Union had had some of the world's most advanced scientific institutes, which had since decayed from lack of funding. The scientists were still there, but they weren't doing much. As I walked up the main stairwell, a rat ran for hiding in a pile of trash.

I introduced myself to the scientist as an investor interested in agricultural projects. He gave me a tour of the institute and led me into a large room where a group of about fifteen scientists conferred at the far end of the room.

They turned, looked at me, and without a word began walking across the room in my direction. They were older, gray-skinned men, and their slow but inexorable movements reminded me of zombies in a B-movie chanting "brains...brains."

They crowded around me, explaining their pet projects. Some had papers or bits of agricultural implements grasped in their hands, which they showed me as visual aids. If only these men had been good human sources—it would have been all too easy to recruit them. Unfortunately, Soviet agricultural information was of no value to the defense of the United States.

Of course, other institutes might contain similarly eager scientists—ones who worked on weapons instead of agriculture.

I collected the zombies' cards and asked about other Soviet institutes, most of which had been devoted to weapons development at one time or another.

Another scientific institute was across the street and I walked over and wandered around inside. Things were different now—had I strolled in during Soviet days, I'd have been arrested immediately and subjected to days of bright-light interrogation.

Just as at the agricultural institute, these scientists were eager to talk about their plans and ideas. They worked on small, innocent-sounding components. By themselves, the little gadgets were clever solutions to mechanical problems, and they often had commercial applications. But combined in just the right way with other innocent-sounding components, they had the power to reduce human beings to blood and dust.

I built a matrix of contacts with these people, using them to provide bona fides for me to meet progressively more significant weapons scientists. I filled my schedule with lunch and dinner meetings with scientists. We met at fashionable new restaurants in the city. The scientists were old-school Soviets, unfamiliar with table manners. They leered at the waitresses and seemed unsure of how to behave in a trendy, Western European-style restaurant. But embarrassment was a small price to pay for information.

SATISFIED THAT I'D ACCOMPLISHED enough for one trip, I headed for the airport.

A newspaper I found on the plane had an article in it about Stefan. The article didn't mention him by name, but I was sure he was the subject. It said he was suing the Agency. The story in the article sounded close to the rumor I'd heard. He'd been engaged in some unauthorized activity with his Russian teacher and hadn't told anyone until he was on the Box. I was disappointed that Stefan of

all people had let the Box break him down. I've never had an unauthorized Russian girlfriend, but had I, I'd have known better than to
admit it to the Box.

Having a Russian girlfriend was strictly against the rules. The
Russians and the Soviets before them had utilized women as "honey
traps" to recruit Americans. Marine Sergeant Clayton Lonetree, a
guard at the US embassy in Moscow during the early 1980s, was
convicted of espionage. He'd been recruited by the KGB through an
affair with a Soviet translator within the embassy.[28]

My trip had gone well, and I returned with extensive contacts. I
downplayed the manner in which I'd met them—HQs would have
been uncomfortable had they known I was knocking on doors like
a vacuum cleaner salesman. I implied that I'd run into the scientists
during the day-to-day operations of my software solutions business.
HQs didn't understand the software business, and no one seemed to
wonder how a business solutions salesman could run into weapons
scientists while going about his ordinary business. Maybe there was
some element of "don't ask, don't tell": We don't care how you do it
so long as you don't get into trouble.

I traced the new contacts, and some of them looked like they
had good access. I met a plethora of HQs managers to discuss my
Belarus trip. Mostly they were decent men interested in getting the
mission accomplished, though one of my new targets was suspected
of proliferating chemical weapons. An HQs man murmured, "No
interest in chemical weapons."

I ignored him, but he said again, "HQs isn't interested in chemical weapons."

I turned to him and said, "HQs *is* interested in chemical weapons."

He didn't reply.

Operations moved forward after the Belarus trips. There was the
usual drudgery of intel operations—the basic blocking and tackling,
meeting men with bad breath in hotel rooms.

I RETURNED HOME. The taxi from the airport dropped me off at my house. I set my suitcase down to open the gate to our yard. When I stooped to get the suitcase, a vicious dog slipped past me and bounded into our yard. It caught our cat in its jaws, shook it violently, and killed it instantly. I cursed the dog's owner, and chased the dog out with a stick. The owner shrugged helplessly. My wife and kids were heartbroken.

After just a short visit, it was time to begin trips to Russia. This would be in "true name," so I would be able to dispense with the hassle of going back to HQs to make alias arrangements.

The Agency had been tricked and one-upped by the Russians on many occasions, so internal Agency obstacles to Russian operations were fierce. Espionage was one of the few areas of human achievement in which the Soviet Union had outperformed the United States. Only bad had come of the Agency's Russian operations, and it seemed reluctant to keep trying. HQs seemed to think that all Russian diplomats and businessmen were KGB officers. When I ran across an unemployed weapons scientist, HQs would suspect him of being a KGB officer. It was possible, but it seemed unlikely that a foreign intelligence service would deploy its spies under cover as desperately unemployed.

HQs sent me to a series of briefings to prepare for travel. Russia was going through a rough period and, like a nation slowly committing suicide, it was suffering from a population decline unheard of in modern countries. Life expectancy for men had dropped from 64 to 56 years old, about where it was 100 years ago. This, combined with a low birth rate, meant that there were 700,000 fewer Russians every year. The fall of Communism showed how poorly the socialist system motivated people. You can beat people into making steel, but you can't beat them into writing good software.

HQs briefers told cautionary tales of failure in Russia. It was easy, they said, for foreign intelligence services to mislead or waste the time of our State Department officers. One of our officers went to a store to buy a bottle of wine. While he was speaking to a sales clerk, a Russian man sidled up to him and said he'd like to practice his English. The officer and the man had only spoken for a few minutes when the man mentioned casually that he was a nuclear scientist.

About a week later, the same officer met a foreign service national (an employee of the US embassy who was a native of the country) for lunch. Another Russian man walked by their table and the foreign service national introduced the man. The man joined them for lunch. After a few moments, he told the officer he was a nuclear scientist.

The next day, the officer went to the airport to fly to Washington, D.C. The Russian man sitting next to him on the airplane struck up a conversation, and mentioned that he was in what was beginning to sound like a very popular line of work.

A case officer in Africa was developing a Russian. They'd been meeting socially, playing tennis and having lunch and dinner together. Our case officer decided that the time had come to recruit the Russian. In the assessment message he sent to HQs, he jauntily described the great relationship he had with the Russian, and said that the Russian was already recruited "in principle."

During the next meeting, the Russian unexpectedly brought along one of his associates, who bluntly asked our case officer to work for the KGB.

An HQs briefer told me that we'd assigned an FBI agent to Moscow who had transferred from the FBI office in New York. While in New York, the agent had arrested a KGB officer. The Russians had been upset with the arrest and they hadn't forgotten the FBI agent's role in it, so when he arrived in Moscow they harassed him until he left one month later.

A pervasive HQs excuse for avoiding operations in Russia was the belief that the Russian government would like to catch a non-State

Department case officer like me in order to exchange him for Aldrich Ames. Since Ames would probably live for several more decades, use of the excuse would likely persist for many years to come.

A briefer discussed overhead imagery from satellites and examples of denial and deception. People on the ground know that they are being watched by satellites, so they take measures to disguise their behavior. The briefer showed a picture of Russian submarines, in port during the early 1970s. One day, following a storm, the satellite showed that one of the subs had broken loose and bent in half. It had bent in half because it was a rubber submarine; the real one must have been out to sea.[29]

Although we'd had few human sources, CIA analysts had done well with other sources of information, such as imagery and signals intelligence. Analysts had accurately estimated Soviet missile capabilities and deployments.[30]

A paper written by a college professor of ethnic studies described the many different ethnic groups in the Soviet Union. Although there were about 400, there were only three large ones: Muslims, Russians, and Eastern European Slavs. An obscure group located near the Volga had practiced cannibalism well into the modern age. The professor had been chided by the Soviet press for reporting this, and the Soviet press stated emphatically that the ethnic group did not eat people at present.

AS ALWAYS, I had to reassure the bureaucracy that my visits to Russia were taken in the course of my software solutions business. As long as I made it clear that nothing would happen, that no intelligence activity of any kind would take place, they'd be happy. In briefings to Congress, they'd be able to say, "We have another man traveling to Moscow," while not having to worry that anything would go wrong. HQs provided no operational ideas or leads. As was so often the case, it was up to me to find my own.

I wanted to keep a low profile during my first trips to Russia, to lull the bureaucracy into a sense of security. I'd turn up the heat very gradually until I was engaged in more productive operations.

In preparation for my first visit, I met with a Polish friend who had operated a company in Moscow. He'd had his business taken away by a gun-toting former partner and was bitter and angry. "Don't go there," he warned. "The new Russians are nothing but white Nigerians. Power and guns rule—no laws."

THE LONG LINES at the Moscow airport didn't bother me; I was happy to be in Russia at last. Although the Cold War was over, Russia remained the only country with a weapons arsenal capable of destroying the United States, and it was an excellent destination for espionage travel. I stayed at the Metropol Hotel, near Red Square, built at about the same time as the Taj Hotel in Bombay and with the grandeur of pre-Communist Europe.

In order to learn my way around the city, I called an old friend who lived there and met him at his apartment, a grand place in the French style of the 1890s. Moscow was the Wild West, and my friend wasn't happy. He was tired and angry and just wanted to go home to his native Austria. We sat talking for hours, until the sun went down. When I remarked about a commotion in the street below, my friend said, "That's the open air prostitution market." We went to the window and he pointed to a line of women. Prospective customers drove by; some got out of the cars to inspect the women, crudely grabbing their breasts and lifting their dresses.

Later, we walked past the line of women on our way to a Scandinavian restaurant. The guards at the restaurant's entrance carried pellet- and tear gas-pistols.

The next day I bought a book and map and played tourist. I'd seen many of the sights when I visited Moscow as a child, and it was strange to revisit them in my current circumstances. The downtown was undergoing a cleanup in preparation for the city's 850th anniversary celebration. The weather was warm, so I bought a suspicious-looking bottle of water from a street vendor. It was probably tap water in a used bottle. They never missed a chance to short-change.

I made a brief visit to another friend who lived up Tverskaya Street, an American who was growing wealthy from his chain of restaurants.

I walked past a comatose drunk, followed by several unsteady but still upright ones. A man walked by with his shirt off, displaying the large tattoo of Lenin on his chest. He approached an outdoor bar to get a drink. The security guard gave him an exasperated look one might give a child, one that asked, "What am I supposed to do with you?"

I left the city having conducted no espionage activities, and sent a windy message to demonstrate just how uneventful the trip had been. HQs continued to approve my trips to Moscow, just as I'd expected them to do.

THE AGENCY had reasons to avoid risk, and reasons for me to worry, as well.

Hugh Francis Redmond, a highly decorated World War II combat veteran, joined the CIA in the postwar years. He was assigned to Shanghai, China, as a case officer under cover as a salesman for a food import and export company. In 1951, he was arrested by the Chinese government on suspicion of being an American spy.

Redmond's mother knew that he was a CIA officer. The Agency did not notify her of her son's arrest, however; she learned of it six months later in a newspaper.

Redmond had been in China for four years by the time he was arrested, and it appears that during that time the Agency had somehow forgotten about him. He had become a "vague memory, a series of dusty file jackets in the bowels of a confused bureaucracy."[31] While in China, Redmond had married a Russian woman.

He must have understood that marrying a Russian woman could end his assignment, so, like the Godfather, he decided not to tell anyone. After his arrest, his wife made her way out of China and wound up in Milwaukee. At some point in the 1950s, the Agency caught wind of a woman claiming that her husband, a CIA officer, was imprisoned in China.

Other westerners who were taken prisoner by the Chinese and subsequently released reported that Redmond had been interrogated and tortured for years. He was ill with beriberi and near-constant diarrhea. He lost all of his teeth. Redmond's captors executed two Chinese men in front of him, men who'd been accused of working with him. Redmond remained defiant throughout his interrogations, consistently denying that he was a spy.

It's possible that the Chinese government would have released Redmond had the US government admitted that he was a spy. In any case, Redmond was left to rot until he died nineteen years later. The circumstances of his death were unclear. His wife had long since divorced him; after years of courageously holding out, his life had simply drained away from him. The Chinese said he'd killed himself by opening his veins and bleeding to death. They delivered an urn of ashes to Redmond's family. Whether the ashes were Redmond's is anybody's guess.

Redmond had gone straight to Shanghai after being hired by the Agency. He had never spent any time at HQs, had never networked with Agency colleagues, and had few connections or contacts in the Agency. His fate was probably sealed when his case went static. When his 1951 arrest and imprisonment didn't get the Agency's attention, time passed, and the managers on duty at the time of his arrest moved on to other assignments. Inertia prevented subsequent managers from doing anything. What difference would it make if Redmond were in prison tomorrow or the next day, they'd wonder, as the clock struck five o'clock and it was time to go home.

The Redmond debacle occurred decades before I joined the

Agency, but I could see it playing out today. The Agency made one attempt to get him released, a scheme involving a ransom payment. In order to hide the source of the funds, the Agency recruited American celebrities as fronts. The plan failed.

In 1952, two other case officers, John Downey and Richard Fecteau, were arrested and imprisoned in China after their airplane was shot down. In 1953, an Agency panel concluded that they'd died when their airplane crashed. Even if they hadn't died in the crash, the panel decided, the men would have been eaten by wolves. (Apparently, there were wolves in the area, though the supposition retains a certain fairytale quality.)

Fortunately, Downey and Fecteau *had* survived. They were held in a Chinese prison until their release nineteen years later.

I never expected the Agency to come to my aid in the event of emergency. Kind-hearted individuals within the bureaucracy might try to help, but I knew the bureaucracy too well to believe it capable of decisive action. If I were arrested, I could only hope that my wife would not also be, because my only escape plan was to rely on her. She'd know better than to believe that I'd been eaten by wolves.

AFTER LOTS OF UNEVENTFUL TRIPS to Russia, I figured I could start turning up the heat. I adopted the same routine I'd used in the Middle East and Eastern Europe, in which I'd purposely sought out and met with potential human sources by knocking on their doors or telephoning them to set meetings. I agonized over the tone of my HQs after-action reports, softening the appearance of the contacts by implying that the meetings had come about as the result of routine business.

I visited laboratories, offices, and government facilities that would have been closed tightly during the Cold War. I found people willing to talk, people who would have been terrified to speak to me during the Cold War. Russia wasn't adequately paying the salaries of weapons personnel, and they were looking for new opportunities. Its weapons scientists and former intelligence officers had been given special treatment under Communism, treatment they no longer received.

Rogue state intelligence services and weapons proliferators could meet these former Soviet weapons experts as easily as I had.

Russian diplomats were available for meetings as well. I met them in front of the huge Stalinist Ministry of Foreign Affairs building, and had drinks with them at John Bull's pub nearby.

During one of my trips to Moscow, an American businessman was arrested on suspicion of espionage. He wasn't a spy and had no connection to the Agency, and he was released a few days later. My HQs contacts learned of the arrest and were in a frenzy until they were able to confirm that the arrested businessman was not—me.

BACK IN EASTERN EUROPE for about one week, I went for a nice run through the forests on the outskirts of the city. A vicious German Shepherd bit me and I shouted curses at its owner, who stood motionless and silent, watching me.

When I got home, I looked around for an antiseptic and couldn't find anything, so I splashed vodka on the wound instead. I looked out the window and pondered whether I ought to have a doctor take a look at the bite.

I MADE A ROUTINE TRIP to the Middle East, and, on the way back, HQs ordered me to Amsterdam to meet a colleague who was having trouble adjusting to his overseas assignment. I had a good reputation at HQs for overseas survivability, so they occasionally asked me to speak to other officers to see if I could help them.

I walked up and down the canal paths in Amsterdam waiting for my meeting. Immigrant men on street corners muttered, "Hey, cocaine. Hey, cocaine."

I recognized my colleague. We sat on a park bench.

"The first thing," I said, "is to get your kids set up in school."

"I can't do that until I get my residence permit."

"I didn't have a residence permit until I'd been overseas for a couple of years," I said. "Go ahead and get your kids set in school."

"I need the permit. Can't do it until I get the permit."

I sighed. "All right, then. What about your housing. Have you rented a place yet?"

He had. I knew the address, too. He'd rented a place near the coastline, where sewage was discharged into the sea and the air stunk all the time, especially at night.

"Your wife will go nuts," I said. "Move to another house."

"I've already signed the lease."

"Break the lease. The Agency will pay the cost."

"Can't break a lease."

I did my best to help him out, to break down his "can't do" attitude. He seemed to pay attention. Our meeting drew to an end. I asked him if he had any questions.

"I'm a firearms collector," he said. "Can I bring some of my collection with me?"

He was a true firearms aficionado, the kind of collector who buys obscure rifles for which ammunition is no longer produced, then fabricates the ammunition himself in his garage. Unfortunately, gun control laws are draconian in most countries.

"No, definitely not," I said. "They'll clap you in irons if you arrive with *any* firearms."

"I just thought I'd ask."

"I mean it. It will end your assignment. Really. Don't bring any firearms."

"Point taken!"

I also advised him to inspect his household goods before shipment. While moving furniture prior to my first assignment, I noticed an odd metal edge sticking out from a small bookcase our elderly landlady had given us when we'd rented her house in Virginia.

I jiggled the metal edge and a secret compartment popped open. Inside were CIA personnel records and files belonging to her husband, a man who had died a decade ago. He had been with the Agency in the 1950s.

As we parted, he walked across a foot bridge over a canal. When he was about a block away, I turned and shouted a final reminder: "No guns!"

His supervisor in his country of assignment had been booted out of another country by *its* American ambassador for having a sexual relationship with an underage girl. Even before *that*, the supervisor had been booted out of still another country, a European one— and also by order of the American ambassador—for having sex with an underage girl. An advantage of putting CIA officers in the State Department's embassies was that the system tolerated people with self-discipline problems. If that statutory rapist had been working in a non-State Department assignment, he'd have earned his one-way ticket home and would never have seen the outside of HQs again.

The situation didn't look good for the man I'd just interviewed, but his perseverance and thick hide kept him overseas for several years before events beyond his control led to his one-way ticket home.

I continued on from Amsterdam to another HQs seminar in the Washington, D.C. area. On the plane, halfway across the Atlantic, a woman on board had a baby, and the pilot decided to return to Shannon airport. I would be late for the conference and I hated to be late. I was angry, but the other passengers seemed to think it was cute. "Maybe we'll be on TV," one of them said.

BETTIE WELCOMED US to the seminar and introduced our first speaker, the ubiquitous HQs manager Suspenders. As always, he appeared fit and commanding, and he certainly dressed well.

Suspenders's dynamism and charisma had continued to blossom. After a brief speech, he lined up all of the case officers present. He walked down the line like a commander of paratroopers, inspiring his men before the big battle.

"HQs will determine individual strategic targets. You'll each be given specific individuals and you will contact them using the tradecraft and recruitment skills you have been taught." He paced back and forth, looking each one of us in the eye.

"You will be given close support by HQs and by our stations overseas. I will ensure that each of you is given a personal contact within HQs who will assist you in processing your operational approvals.

"You will recruit your strategic targets. We will make every effort to assist you. These targets are of the utmost importance to our nation. You cannot fail. You will not fail."

Suspenders shook hands with everyone and left the room. My colleagues were impressed. My colleague Loman had been assigned to our unit, though he was currently in a domestic post. Loman had once been in the Navy and he loved what he heard from Suspenders, who sounded like successful commanders he'd known.

"I want to believe him, myself, but I've seen him before," I said. "You'll never hear about his action plan again. I'm sorry, my friend, don't be angry with me—I'm only the messenger."

A speaker arrived to discuss restrictions on operations in France. Our focus was the former Soviet Union, and none of us planned to do anything in France. A worldwide cable had advised us not to because that summer, the summer of 1998, the World Cup would be going on. The cable said there would be lots of tourists and it would be difficult to get a hotel booking.

"You're kidding," I said. "We're afraid to do any operations in France because of a soccer game?"

"Well, that's what it says," the speaker said. "Hey, HQs told me to come over here and talk about the stand-down in France. I'm just trying to be helpful."

He continued talking. I was bored and jet-lagged, and my thoughts drifted to my wife and children. I smiled. The speaker smiled back at me, thinking I was enjoying his lecture. My relaxation increased and I drifted off to another part of the globe. The speaker on French non-operations disappeared and another took his place.

At one point, I heard, "We're looking for some good Greek targets to recruit."

Greeks? This woke me up.

I asked, "Did you just say we should find Greeks to recruit? There's no intelligence value in Greeks. No threat to America. Last thing in the world we need is Greeks."

"The station in Greece," he said, "wants to recruit some Greeks."

Stations could be myopic when it came to their own turf. A station in Timbuktu would want to recruit people from Timbuktu, even if they had no value whatsoever to our worldwide missions.

Maybe this Greek thing had come from an HQs mandarin seeking to please George Tenet, the director of the CIA. Tenet was of Greek heritage and the press had written a lot about his being the child of immigrants. He surely had no interest in recruiting Greeks, but maybe a mandarin believed that he did.

Tenet had replaced John Deutch as DCI. All the DCIs I'd known were nice guys—friendly, albeit mediocre men who had spent decades in the corridors of Washington, D.C. buildings. They'd been members of various staffs, had sat through endless meetings. But Deutch, DCI from May 1995 to December 1996, had been a little bit different. He'd recognized that the US military's culture was more effective than the Agency's, and he'd had some ideas for change at the Agency. Deutch noted that Agency employees seemed beset by personal problems.

The Agency's bureaucrats hated Deutch; they chewed him up and spit him out. When he left after his brief tenure as director, Agency security officers searched his personal computer and found 17,000 classified documents on it.[32] Deutch had used his personal computer to connect to the Internet, so a hacker could have gained access to those documents. This computer may also have been used to access pornographic websites.[33] The Agency canceled Deutch's security clearances. Today, he isn't allowed to get anywhere near US government secrets. Some mandarins spread rumors that the Agency had bungled the investigation and that Deutch's security violations were actually even *more* serious.

I VISITED A HOLDING TANK at HQs for officers who had returned from overseas.

Moe, the office manager, was seated at the reception desk. I liked him, and we struck up a conversation.

"Have you ever thought about becoming a case officer?" I asked. He seemed like a solid guy, with common sense and good academic credentials.

"Actually, I have. I even filled out an application. But I don't have much hope.

"I checked on the status of my application a few months ago. The place was a real mess. There were stacks of applications and résumés spread out all over the room. Piles were everywhere, and I could see papers that had slid behind the desk onto the floor. No one could give me an update on my application."

The holding tank was quieter than it had been during the Ames and Nicholson purges, but there were still a few of my colleagues hanging around. One lurking around the cubicles said he'd come home recently to find his spy gear opened and displayed on the floor of his living room. Nothing had been stolen or broken. It was a message from the local security service.

Another, a State Department officer, had mistakenly left a bag of money and secret papers in a restaurant.

Several colleagues with sick spouses or children who couldn't go overseas moped around. The Agency does a good job of mede-vacing sick family members, but when a family member gets so ill that they need to return to the US, the officer's tour is usually cancelled.

BACK IN EASTERN EUROPE in the winter, Loman came through the city and gave me a call. We went out for a drive in the Eastern European countryside and stopped at an ancient inn for goulash and half-liters of excellent beer for the equivalent of about 35 cents a glass. We discussed our desire to recruit higher-priority human sources.

Loman had just terminated an agent who'd worked for us for nearly thirty years. The agent lost his access to secrets when he'd retired from his government job. Over the course of his career, we'd paid him some money and promised to put additional money in a bank account. The account existed in ledger form at HQs, not in a bank. When it was time to end our relationship with the agent, the amount of money owed the agent had become very large. HQs summoned Loman for a meeting, and told him to probe the agent's memory to see if the agent remembered how much money he was owed. If the agent didn't remember, Loman was to give the agent a much smaller sum.

Loman refused and paid the agent the amount he was owed.

★ 9 ★

Always Be Closing

A-B-C. A–Always, B–Be, C–Closing.
Always be closing, always be closing.
Glengarry Glen Ross

Easter of 1999 came, marking the beginning of spring. On Easter Monday, in a local tradition, the men fashion whips with which to beat women. Traditional men fashion their whips by braiding willow or birch strands. It's a festive occasion, involving a good deal of drinking, and the men roam the streets and houses with their whips. Many women approve of this tradition, which has its roots in an ancient fertility rite, and the women are expected to reward the men with an Easter egg or a ribbon. Proud men display their whips, decorated with the many ribbons received from the women encountered that day.

I received an unexpected influx of cash from the Agency. It was a pleasant surprise.

The garbage men came by our house each week, but would take only a limited amount of trash. When our cans filled up with too much, I'd take the excess bags and dump them in someone else's Dumpster. I pulled my car up near a Dumpster that sat behind one of the big Communist apartment buildings.. After making the drop, I got back in my car and, fumbling for the keys, sensed movement out of the corner of my eye. A wizened old man had appeared out of nowhere and stood in front of my car, blocking my exit. Snarling with rage, he gave me the most hateful glare I'd ever seen.

I gave him a quizzical smile—*who, me?*

"You bastard," he said.

I pressed the car's accelerator to make the car surge forward. The man spryly jumped out of the road. Looking in the rearview mirror as I drove away, I saw that he was still cursing, twisted up in rage. I stopped visiting these Dumpsters.

In the spring the Eastern European forests exploded in beauty and I enjoyed long jogs down wooded paths. All of Eastern Europe was blooming with prosperity as well. The signs were everywhere: new roads being constructed, nice new houses—instead of small, drab apartments owned by the state—built and owned by families, new cars on the roads, new restaurants and bars, new stores filled with fresh fruits and vegetables. Every month the air seemed to get cleaner and the people happier and more prosperous.

I USUALLY WENT all the way back to the US to pick up my alias documents. It was easier to do the long-haul flights than to go through the complex arrangements of meeting a State Department officer from a field station to pass me the papers.

Preparing for another trip to Kiev, I traveled first to HQs. When I arrived at HQs, a man was waiting for me in the reception room.

He asked, "What kind of car did you buy for your assignment to Eastern Europe?"

I described the modest, unattractive car I'd purchased with the funds earmarked by the Agency for that purpose. It was a model not sold in the US, so I compared it to similar American budget models. "It doesn't have air conditioning," I said, "but then it doesn't get hot there very often."

"Thanks," he said. "I've been sent over by the division chief. He wanted to know what kinds of cars you guys were buying. Seems one of you fellows bought a big black Mercedes convertible, and the chief wanted to find out who it is."

I scrambled to acquire my alias papers and disguise, and I left my true name materials in an office in Washington, D.C. The disguise materials were high quality: a hairpiece, glasses, and makeup, which in combination altered my appearance a great deal. Were I captured and interrogated the separate pieces probably wouldn't look like parts of a disguise. The hairpiece felt itchy and ugly. It took a while to get used to, but after a while I was satisfied that it looked right and that nobody was staring at me.

HQs had assigned me a new home address for my alias. The address was in a city not far from Washington, D.C., so during the weekend before my trip I got in my rental car and took a drive to look at the place. It was a dump in a virtually abandoned neighborhood full of prostitutes and drug addicts.

I put on the hairpiece and headed to the airport for my flight to Kiev via London. On the airplane from London to Kiev, I sat in the midst of a bunch of pirates. They were actors, going to the Crimea to film a "Horatio Hornblower" series for BBC television, and they were getting into character. The actor sitting next to me had been cast as a sailor, and was in a scene in which he had to fight rats with his teeth for the entertainment of his fellow sailors. He said the Crimea was rough duty for an actor; the facilities were poor and the natives were depressing. The Crimeans called the British actors "smiling monkeys."

I arrived in Kiev and went to my hotel, a Communist-built monstrosity with lots of adequate but Spartan rooms. I had a strong case of jetlag and I might have been a little sick as well. When I woke up, I couldn't guess what time it was. Unfortunately, it was only midnight, so I had many hours of darkness before the day began.

I ordered room service from the limited menu—chicken Kiev, of course, was the only thing I can remember—served by a man with a mouthful of shiny Communist dental care. He demanded cash on the spot for the dinner.

I went to some of the appointments I'd made, and walked in to offices cold in order to set up other meetings. At some government offices, I entered and stood in the middle of the office area, without a script, using method acting. I thought: *How can I make money here?*

Between appointments, I walked around town. A Ukrainian friend was worried about crime, and he thought my walks were foolish, that I was red meat in a tank of sharks. Crime was up from its zero level during Communism, so to Ukrainians the country seemed lawless, but Washington, D.C. was still far more dangerous than Kiev.

The people were friendly and I was lucky to be there during fine weather. I walked across a footbridge over a highway. It was rickety and missing planks. Pedestrians could see traffic speeding by below through these gaps, but no one seemed to mind. I bought some bread and a caviar-like substance, sat in the park, and enjoyed life. No one hassled me during these strolls. I visited the few historical and tourist attractions not blitzed during the war. I took a longer walk to Babi Yar, a ravine where, during World War II, the Nazis had murdered more than 100,000 people, most of them Jews.

Having squeezed all that I could out of my trip, I departed Kiev by way of London, then returned to the US, back to my city of assignment. Before I'd left, I'd had to leave my wedding ring at HQs with my true name documents because it was inscribed with my true name initials and the date of my wedding. Somehow, during the exchange of alias documents, my wedding ring was lost.

AFTER PASSING AN AIDS TEST, as required for Russian visas, I flew to Moscow for a routine visit to laboratories and government facilities. In between meetings, I walked through Red Square and stood in line to see Lenin's preserved corpse, stuffed and yellowing, on display in a darkened mausoleum. A young woman walked past; I thought that she'd looked at me.

Leaving the mausoleum and Red Square, I walked inside a museum, an ancient boyar's house which had belonged to a family of middling nobility. It had been built hundreds of years ago and was located across from a huge Communist-era hotel block. I bought a ticket to enter. As I stepped away from the ticket window, I realized the seller had short-changed me. When I turned around, I saw the young woman from Lenin's tomb. She approached the window and bought a ticket. (Had I been on an intelligence operation, I wouldn't have turned back toward the ticket seller—doubling back on surveillance is a suspicious move.) As I wandered through the rooms of the house, I was in view of the young woman the entire time. We were the only people in the house.

Leaving the boyar's house, I walked toward the river, looking for an old section of the city wall I had read about in my guide book. Because I was searching for the wall, I doubled back again, and as I did a young man behind me did a slight double-take. It was subtle, but he seemed startled when I rounded the corner and walked at him.

These incidents were the closest thing to surveillance that I'd ever encountered. It wasn't unusual for a person to go to Lenin's tomb and the historic boyar's house; that was a typical tourist route. The young man I saw near the old city wall could have been anyone. Even if this had been surveillance, it might have been the routine surveillance to which the Russians subject all visitors. I was sight-seeing, not performing a surveillance detection route. I wouldn't have done a detection route in a tourist area, anyway.

So nothing was sure, except for one thing: If I had reported these two incidents in my after-action report, it would have made me look confused, amateurish. It would have ended my trips to Moscow.

The weather had turned cold and the Russians wore their characteristic fur hats. I walked back to the hotel from an appointment, a walk of about forty minutes. There were thousands of silver dollar-sized frozen spit circles on the ground. Heavily dressed, thickly padded prostitutes trudged about, taking periodic breaks to warm up by sitting, tightly packed, in dilapidated Soviet cars. The windows steamed up while madams negotiated with customers in the street.

From my perspective, the trips were going well. A troubling aspect, however, was that I wasn't getting any traction at HQs on Russian biological weapons programs. The Soviets had been well advanced in biological weapons, and, as with nuclear weapons, the Russians possessed an arsenal capable of great damage to Americans. The arsenal and its secrets could also attract rogue states interested in building comparable programs.

THE CONTACTS I'd made in Russia and Eastern Europe were now ready to become recruits. My plans for advancing the cases sounded risky to HQs managers, and I endured a few days of managers' lectures on tradecraft. None had ever recruited anyone, and few had ever had an overseas assignment, but all had a lot to say. The four days of these meetings were brutal, but I reminded myself that I rarely had to live the HQs experience, while most Agency employees underwent these endless meetings every day of their working lives.

While at HQs, I spoke to a colleague who had just returned from a foreign assignment. His wife was pregnant and HQs had given him his one-way ticket home because they'd decided his wife would receive better medical care in the US. My colleague disagreed, arguing that hospitals were fine in his country of assignment. HQs was firm. He eventually got another overseas assignment, but only after five years of domestic drudgery.

Another officer at HQs had had a sick child in urgent need of medical attention. The care in his overseas city of assignment was poor. Instead of getting his child to competent doctors and hospitals in another country, he contacted HQs and asked for advice about his child's health problem. People at HQs rushed about trying to find information. One of the managers at HQs had a daughter who was a physician, and she provided some helpful information. Finally HQs realized that it didn't have much medical knowledge and told the officer to send his child to a decent hospital. But the officer had no cash available, and the stress led to his requesting a one-way ticket home.

The Agency is not a hospital, I thought. *Got to take care of your own problems.*

My wife and I discussed my job with the Agency endlessly, trying to figure out where my career was heading, what we should do. The main advantage was that, whenever I was able to cut through the bureaucracy, I could make progress for the good of our country. On a basic level, the job allowed me to control my time, and paid for most household expenses, even if the money did come in a year or two late. We lived in interesting places, which we enjoyed immensely. The disadvantage was the power of the bureaucracy and the difficulty of pushing through intelligence operations that achieved anything of value.

I HAD AN OPERATION in St. Petersburg, formerly Leningrad. I also attended a telecom conference and a few scientific conferences, and set meetings with individual targets as well. I stayed at the Grand Europe Hotel, a beautiful pre-Communist-era hotel with massive rooms. I didn't explore the city at first, because it was spit-freezing cold.

The conferences went well, and I met several possible sources. Old Soviet political bosses at the conferences grumbled whenever they heard anything with which they disagreed. A European Union representative discussed the lack of competition in the growing Russian markets, and an old Communist boss turned off the EU representative's microphone and said, "No one has time to listen to you pontificate. You must stop your speaking. You are criticizing the government."

The EU representative sheepishly sat down.

Eventually I bundled up and walked around St. Petersburg. The fresh snow made the city beautiful, especially as it contrasted with the golden domes of the palaces. The Neva was frozen except where sewage flowed into it. I watched a man kindle a fire under his car in order to get it started, just like the Germans had done to get their tanks moving during the Russian winters of World War II.

Returning to the conference, I saw that the Twins had arrived. I'd seen them at other conferences and knew that they were scientists who worked for us as access agents. The Twins approached a circle of Russians, introduced themselves, and exchanged business cards. The conversation between the Twins and the Russians seemed friendly and animated, but after the Twins walked away, the Russians held the Twins' business cards out so that their comrades could see, and tore them into small pieces, dropping the pieces on the floor. The Agency sent the Twins to too many conferences; perhaps they were getting too widely known as CIA personnel.

In addition to the Twins, I spotted another odd individual at the conference, a man I'd never met before. His reasons for being there weren't clear. He latched onto me for about fifteen minutes and had a creepy, cloying personality. Later, I checked with HQs to see if the man was connected with the Agency, and was advised that he was connected. I was careful not to mention that I'd thought the man unusual: I was just curious. At least he was trying, and I didn't want to torpedo his career.

I collected all the business cards I needed and left the city the following day.

MY WIFE AND I were expecting a baby. I hadn't mentioned the pregnancy to HQs.

Naturally I wanted to be at the hospital when my child was born, and I wanted to be available to help my wife for at least two weeks after the birth. Since the birth date can never be determined precisely, I figured I'd need a travel-free window of about a month. To inform HQs not only that my wife was about to have a baby but also that I didn't want to travel for a month would have set me up as a target.

I fashioned three sensible but risky operational proposals, scheduled them for my wife's due date, and asked for HQs approval. I'll go to Russia and walk into Missile Command Headquarters looking for leads, I proposed. I'll go to Athens and try to meet the Iranian intelligence service representative there. I'll go to Damascus and meet the North Korean ambassador. They were good proposals, and as the years passed I wound up pursuing all three. Had HQs approved the operations then, I would have been delighted, even to the point that I would have accepted the risk of leaving my wife alone during childbirth.

I knew HQs wouldn't approve the proposals, though. It takes a lot of hard work to come up with creative reasons why an operation can't be undertaken. Each proposal demands a written response.

The proposals were so strong that they froze up the system. HQs went silent. No one wanted to talk to me, and no one spoke to me or sent me any messages during the window of time that I wanted.

The due date approached, and my wife felt signs that the baby was about to arrive. Our doctor had a fine reputation, but he telephoned and said, "My car is broken down and I'll need you to give me a ride to the hospital when the baby's birth is near." He gave me directions so that I could pick him up when the time came. I worried that if the baby came in the evening, he might be drunk.

My anxiety proved to be unwarranted. The hospital was in a beautiful old 1890s building near the river. Under Communism it had been reserved for the bosses, and we had a huge private room with a balcony and a view of the river. I called it the Communist Boss Special. The doctor was excellent; the hospital staff did a terrific job. My wife spent a leisurely five days in her suite and said that the birth had been a more pleasant experience than in the US—surprising, as she'd been unable to obtain pain medication. The anesthesiologist only came to work on Tuesdays and Thursdays, and the baby was born on a Sunday.

The next day I walked the grounds of the hospital carrying the new baby. The hospital was attached to the wall of an ancient fortress city. I walked to a beautiful, albeit garbage-strewn, cupola, which looked down upon the hospital and the river. The stimulation of new sounds and smells put the baby to sleep immediately.

I OFTEN ENJOYED LONG WALKS throughout the city where buildings built centuries before Communism were an architecture student's dream. The Natural History Museum was located in the city center. During an uprising in the country, Soviet tanks sent to quell the rebellion sprayed bullets at the museum, apparently mistaking it for a government building. Discolored patches still mark the spots where the bullets hit. In 1945, mobs tortured and killed German civilians in front of this building. Ghosts haunted the city.

As I was walking past the museum, a familiar figure approached. "Ishmael!" he said. It was Vinnie, a man I'd met in college.

"The last time I saw you," I said, "you were in the middle of a freeway scalping tickets!" He'd been an entrepreneur during high school, walking between lanes of traffic by the football stadium, hawking tickets to a college game.

"I've been in Eastern Europe for a month, Ishmael. I love it here. I'm working in investment banking." He hesitated. "Well—actually, I'm working in a chop shop."

We stopped at an outdoor café and ordered some liters of beer for 35 cents each. Vinnie explained that the chop shop was a boiler-room operation, full of thick-skinned men who spent twelve hours a day on the phone, selling worthless securities to gullible buyers. They'd chosen Eastern Europe because the region had not yet developed a law enforcement system sophisticated enough to sniff out such a set-up. Vinnie and his gang were selling the bogus securities to people located in foreign countries, so they weren't cheating any locals, and this seemed to give them additional legal protection.

"I like this job. Each day I get to wake up and talk to people all over the world. I might talk to a Saudi, then a Greek, then a German. It could be snowing here and I'm talking to a man in Australia where it's blazing hot.

"We get in at 7:30 in the morning. The doors are locked at 7:45, so anyone who comes in after that is locked out and won't make any money that day. There aren't any chairs—everyone stands up. The company supplies us with lists of leads they've purchased for a few cents a lead.

"We learn a few details about the security we're selling that day and then we start calling. We've got phones with long cords so we can pace back and forth."

The bogus securities were for shares in companies with descriptions designed to make them sound interesting: water purification companies, vitamins and nutritional supplement suppliers, cures for common ailments, gold, diamond, and uranium mines.

I wanted to learn what motivated this bunch of entrepreneurial scammers.

"When the money comes in from a sale I've made, the floor managers stop all activity in the office, and everyone watches while he hands me my commission. Everyone claps and shouts, and then we get back to making calls. Every few hours we have a pep rally where the top sellers are praised.

"Every few days, during a pep rally, a guy who isn't making sales is called up in front of everyone and fired. So we've got carrots and sticks. It breeds competition and makes for a pretty wild working environment.

"The company's owners come from Salt Lake City. Salt Lake is a chop-shop center, probably dating from the uranium mine scams of the 1940s."

Later that week, Vinnie introduced me to some of his "colleagues." We met at a topless bar. The dancers swung about on their poles for a while and then picked one of Vinnie's friends out of the audience, brought him to the stage, and made him dance with them. He was a clumsy dancer but a good sport. The strippers insisted he disrobe; they pulled off his trousers, exposing a singularly unpleasant male form.

"Okay, okay, let's go!" I said. I'd had enough of that for one night. Vinnie and I left the topless bar and wandered over to the town square. When we entered the square, out of the corner of my eye I saw a couple of Gypsy girls approaching. One of them grabbed Vinnie's hand and the other grabbed his crotch. We shooed them away, recognizing it as a blatant pickpocket attempt. There was something childlike in the Gypsies' criminality. We had drinks in several outdoor cafes and then called it a night.

Vinnie's chop shop fascinated me. These men weren't afraid to make the call, and they had skills the Agency generally lacked. The Godfather had those abilities, but he was an exception. Most Agency people were afraid of the humiliation and rejection that were an inescapable part of the sales process.

In the Agency, this fear of humiliation manifested itself in the creation of layers of managers and in a pathological disdain for human contact. Agency people would huff, "We shouldn't make cold calls," but making cold calls was the best way of making contact with people we'd never met but urgently needed to meet.

Vinnie and his gang were criminals, but where foreign laws were concerned, so was I.

Eventually, his fellow scammers left the city in the dead of night. They weren't fleeing the people they'd bilked. They weren't fleeing local securities laws. The real reason was more mundane: They'd racked up massive bills with the local telephone company and didn't want to pay up. They set up shop the next day in Prague.

MAX DROPPED BY for a visit. We met for a lunch of pork sausages and beer in a smoky inn on the Danube. A month prior, he'd met his chief in a hotel room:

"I think the local security service has placed you under surveillance," the chief told him.

"No way. I've been doing good surveillance detection routes and I haven't seen a thing. What makes you so sure?"

An agent had told the chief that the local security service was following an American. The agent didn't know the identity of the American, but the chief had a "gut feeling" that it was Max.

Max left that meeting thinking: I don't believe I'm under surveillance, but if my chief feels so strongly about it, perhaps I should take it seriously.

He decided to hire a gang of local thugs.

"Listen," he told them. "I'm worried that I'm being followed by someone who plans to kidnap me. I want you to follow me and see if you can spot anyone."

The thugs followed Max at a discreet distance. Max was living in a Third World country in which kidnappings were all too common, so the gang of thugs didn't find his instructions unusual.

Meanwhile, Max's chief had left the meeting thinking: Max is under surveillance and won't admit it. I'm going to follow him; I'll detect the surveillance myself.

The gang of thugs spotted Max's chief. They grabbed him, threw him to the ground, smacked his head into the sidewalk, circled him, and kicked him until they were exhausted and Max's chief was severely injured. The thugs never saw anyone else following Max.

The chief never mentioned it again.

MY RUSSIAN AND EASTERN EUROPEAN cases moved along and I began holding meetings in safe countries, places where hostile security services, such as the KGB, had less control. I didn't have to worry as much about surveillance and bugged hotel rooms in these countries as I would have in Russia or Belarus. I traveled a great deal to meet potential human sources, and I slogged through technical topics with the targets and wrote up long reports. It was boring, and offered little potential for promotion, but it was the fundamental task for which the Agency had been created. I enjoyed learning from the sources, who recommended books for me to read. I tore through many texts about missile guidance and nuclear and biological weapons science.

For meetings with agents in safe countries, I'd often try to combine the meetings with visits to some other kind of venue that might have potential human sources, such as scientific conferences. This way I could kill two birds with one stone.

My style for scientific conferences was to walk in, find a list of attendees, pick out the ones who looked promising, and seek them out. If I couldn't find them, I put a message on the bulletin board telling them that I wanted to meet. I approached each target in a commercially direct manner, saying that I had a problem in their field that I needed to solve. It didn't produce secrets at first, but eventually it did.

PASSING THROUGH HQS back in Langley, I learned the latest Agency news. A man named Douglas Groat had been arrested by the FBI for threatening to reveal secrets to foreign governments. Groat had done some breaking and entering of foreign facilities on behalf of the Agency, and he wanted $500,000 from the Agency in exchange for silence. This amounted to blackmail, so the Agency called the FBI to haul Groat away.

An officer named Dave was responding infrequently to HQs communications, and when he did respond, he did so with listless, whining, contradictory messages about having too little work or work that was too hard. Dave seemed to have gone into a depression. He'd just returned from a conference where he'd been sent to meet an important Russian target. In an after-action memo, Dave wrote that he *had* approached the target, but that upon seeing Dave the target had "turned ashen-faced and moved away." HQs wanted a more detailed explanation, but that was all that Dave had written.

Dave had somehow become known as a CIA officer. HQs sent him his one-way ticket to a station in California.

Like most organizations, the CIA had its own stationery. Its official envelopes had "Central Intelligence Agency" written on the return address. The Agency mistakenly used this stationery for a mailing on its new diversity policy—a mailing sent to officers, including Dave, who were working under deep cover in foreign countries. We hoped that no one had seen the return address on the envelopes. In any event, according to a friend at HQs, this incident led the Agency to destroy its entire stock of stationery.

My old friend Martin had handed in some spy gear to an OFTPOT (the husband half) who worked at his local embassy. A year later, the Agency asked him where the gear was. The OFTPOT denied that Martin had given it to him. The Agency started the paperwork to fire Martin.

Martin insisted he had turned in the gear, and so the Agency decided to put Martin and the OFTPOT on the Box to see what would shake loose. On the Box, the OFTPOT admitted that Martin had given him the gear and that he'd then lost it. He'd been afraid to report the loss.

Martin's name had been cleared, but his managers didn't like him, so they assigned him to a remedial course in surveillance detection. Then he was given a "disgruntlement" Box, designed to determine whether his degree of "disgruntlement" posed a security threat to the Agency.

I met a HQs manager for lunch in the Agency's cafeteria. He'd just completed an operation involving the Godfather. "Dozens of managers at HQs spent a year planning and coordinating every detail of the operation," he said, "and then Godfather ignored the whole plan and just did what he wanted to. That's the trouble with Godfather: You assign him a mission and he'll look at it and then follow his nose."

Godfather's productivity was legendary, though. The Agency

considered a case officer successful if he recruited a new agent every year or two. The Godfather recruited dozens of new agents in a year. His recruitments weren't always perfect, as some agents would agree to work for the Godfather but then refuse to work for anyone else. All the same, the Godfather was worth 100 case officers.

HQS TOLD ME to hand over one of the sources I'd developed to a new case officer based in the US. The source had the ability to travel to western countries and could do the meetings in the west. The turnover was a good idea because it would free me up to find new sources.

Although my relationship with the source had advanced to the point where I was meeting him clandestinely and he was providing secrets in exchange for money, HQs didn't consider him formally recruited. He hadn't gone through the paperwork. I knew what HQs was up to: They'd take this guy, call him a mere "lead," and then, a month or two later, they'd declare him to be a new recruitment and shower themselves with kudos. But I didn't mind this trick because it would motivate the officer taking the case to do a good job.

I planned to meet Mabel, the new case officer, in the lobby of a hotel in Philadelphia. She sent me an elaborate description of her height, weight, eyes, hair, and clothing. She would carry a magazine folded under her left arm. I was to ask, "Can you tell me the way to the parking lot?" and she was to reply, "Are you looking for the hourly parking?"

Since the meeting was in the benign city of Philadelphia, I wrote, "I'll be the man in the lobby who comes up to you and says, 'Hi, Mabel.' We have each other's telephone numbers, and can call if one of us has difficulty making it on time to the hotel lobby."

I met Mabel in the hotel lobby as planned and we went to my hotel room to discuss our plans for the turnover.

"I have a boyfriend," she said.

She must have been nervous about meeting a man alone in a hotel room. Maybe she'd had some bad experiences.

"I'm glad you said something," I joked. "I was about to start taking my clothes off."

We discussed the turnover and agreed on a plan. She went to her hotel room and I went to the airport to greet the arriving agent.

Mabel and I each had many layers of managers above us, and because we were doing the turnover in the US, our managers weren't far away. They called us frequently and sent lots of emails to a throwaway Yahoo address I'd created.

"What's your assessment of the agent's mood?" they asked.

"He seems to be fine. I picked him up at the airport and took him to his hotel. We had a friendly conversation on the way to the hotel. He's in a good mood."

"HQs needs more. What did he say? Is he worried about being in the US? Has he been having any trouble back home? What does he think about meeting a new case officer? Where's your assessment?"

"Don't worry, it's a simple operation. The agent doesn't have a choice about whether he wants a new case officer or not. I'm going to introduce the agent to Mabel and it will go fine. She's competent. She has a good understanding of the operation."

I realized that a dozen managers were sitting in an office at HQs eager to direct the turnover. The phone kept ringing with managers requesting updates.

I stopped answering my telephone. I met the agent for dinner and introduced him to Mabel. Everything went well. I knew Mabel would do a fine job.

My telephone started ringing again the next morning. I decided to pick it up.

"My God, Ishmael, we stayed in the office until 7 PM last night, waiting for more assessment!" said HQs. "Why haven't you responded to our emails?" I checked the Yahoo address. Sure enough, it was full of frantic message from HQs.

HQs was in a panic. I said, "Look, the turnover went fine and Mabel knows what she's doing. The agent seemed happy to meet her. I said goodbye to the agent and when I walked away the two of them were talking and getting along fine."

"You weren't supposed to do anything until you gave us the assessment."

"Am I going to have to come back there and kick somebody in the ass?"

I said it with a smile, but truth is often spoken in jest and my meaning was clear. HQs stopped calling me and turned their attention to Mabel, who was relatively new to the Agency and easier to harass. Mabel and I met later to review the turnover. Everything had gone well. "HQs has been going ape, though," she said. "I hope I'm not in any trouble."

"You did great, and the operation went well. I think there were just a lot of managers hanging around HQs with nothing to do."

When I returned to HQs, a manager handed me a cable containing plans for the turnover. The cable had been written just after both Mabel and I had gone to Philadelphia, so we hadn't had a chance to read it. It called for me to meet the agent, assess his mood, and then go to the Agency office nearby in Trenton, New Jersey to type a cable describing the situation. Based on that information, HQs would then decide if the agent's mood was conducive to making a turnover to a new case officer. If yes, I was to meet him and sound him out on a turnover to a new case officer. I was then to return to the Agency office in Trenton and write another cable about the agent's willingness, in principle, to accept a new case officer. HQs would then decide whether the turnover meeting should occur.

In other words, Mabel and I had carried out the turnover without approval. Everything had gone well; everyone was happy.

But I realized that the point of HQs's behavior had been to pin
responsibility on us in case anything went awry. Where there's a
will to avoid responsibility, there's always a way.

AGENCY EMPLOYEES RECEIVE written annual evaluations, like
report cards. The evaluations are important documents used to
decide promotions and assignments. The writer of the evaluation is the boss—he or she can advance or destroy an employee's
career. The origin of the system of annual evaluations was the
military's fitness report system, in which a soldier is evaluated by
his commanding officer.

My annual evaluations had many writers. When I executed
operations on someone else's bureaucratic turf, they'd often add
comments to my evaluation. These were generally favorable, and I
appreciated them.

Unfortunately, however, numerous HQs people were also able to
write my annual evaluation, which started to look like a blog, with
every fool inserting his opinion regardless of its merit. The different
administrative staffs, such as the accounting people, each controlled
a section. If they didn't like the way I filled out my accountings,
they could write nasty comments. Some of these people I'd never
met; all of them were junior to me in grade. Some had been hired
recently out of high school or college.

When I returned from the turnover meeting in Philadelphia,
the woman in charge of handling my accountings, Flora, summoned me to a meeting in a conference room at HQs. I sat down
in the empty room. A few minutes later, I heard the whirring
of an electrical motor as she rounded the corner on a motor-
ized chair. Flora was a huge, red-faced, friendly woman. "Your
accountings look good," she said. "You have a good reputation
here at HQs." I knew that already: I'd gone to great lengths to
keep these people happy.

"HQs is having a display of collections," she said. "I collect

Cabbage Patch dolls. It's an obsession. On weekends I go to doll shows and look for garage sales."

She confided that her collection was a drain on her finances. There were some nice pieces, a certain pink dress and accessories for the dolls, that she'd like to buy but she couldn't afford to right now. Her kids had bad teeth—weak teeth were hereditary in her family— and dental care cost more than the Agency could provide.

Our meeting ended and she repeated that I was her favorite case officer because I had no personal problems or complaints. As usual, my pay was about a year in arrears, and I'd just finished shuffling around some investments in order to fill up my checking account. My ability to go indefinitely without being paid was one of my most important tools for longevity overseas.

Just a few sharp words to the Cabbage Patch fancier and I'd be paid. But, given that she was one of many writers of my annual evaluation, she was, in effect, my boss. By not raising hell, I was better able to stay overseas to do my duty to my country.

I STOPPED BY the "holding tank" at HQs to see if any friends were in town.

A female officer was in limbo for a sexual relationship with an access agent.

An officer had given a large amount of money to an agent to buy some real estate for an operation; the agent had disappeared with the money.

Another man told his girlfriend that he was a spy, and then told HQs what he'd done.

Another told an old college friend that he was a spy, and then informed HQs.

Loman was in Washington for a routine visit and he'd rented a Mercedes at the airport. An HQs mandarin had spotted him swanning about in the car and had called Loman in for a browbeating.

A group of officers had returned from trying to put a bug in a target's office. Everything had gone wrong. The radios didn't work, so the guys who were standing watch outside the building couldn't warn that someone was coming; the man who was supposed to delay anyone who might show up panicked and fled; the team fled in the wrong direction; when the police arrived, the team said they were from Australia, even though they had only US passports. It had been like Keystone Cops meets Watergate.

WITH Y2K APPROACHING, the Agency spun up to prepare for the anticipated problems. It was a non-issue that provided plenty of opportunities to spend money and appear busy. As the years go by, it's easy to forget the Y2K scare: On the first day of the year 2000, the whole world was supposed to shut down. Computers had been programmed to represent the year with only two digits, and thus could only understand dates through 1999. Airplanes would drop out of the skies; power plants would explode; nuclear-tipped ballistic missiles would launch. The Agency devoted enormous resources to preparing for this.

Charlton was deeply involved in the Y2K issue. HQs sent deep piles of money to him to pay for broad, expensive Y2K projects for which he was not required to provide receipts. Charlton took Y2K a step further, and convinced the Agency that we needed to watch out for 9 September 1999 as well, because 9/9/99 might also make computers malfunction.

RETURNING TO EASTERN EUROPE after a long time away, I was glad to be home. The evening before my arrival, my wife had heard a noise outside. She'd peered out a window, only to realize that she was looking straight at the face of a burglar. She yelled at the intruder and called the police. The police arrived half an hour later and told her that intruders had tried to break into three houses in the neighborhood that night. An alarm frightened the burglars at the first house, and a resident had scared them way from the next.

They managed to break into one house, but the resident ran them out of that one, too.

The day I landed, my secretary called to say that our downtown office and apartment had been robbed. I ran down to the apartment and found everything in order. The other apartments and offices in the building had been ransacked and there were crowbar marks on our door, but the thieves must have run off before they could break in. Crime had increased in Eastern Europe following the end of Communism, as the various countries adjusted to new governments. Gypsies took the blame for the increase in crime, but the burglars arrested never seemed to be Gypsies. The burglar my wife had seen wasn't a Gypsy.

The Agency loves the idea of "trolling" for intel leads by attending social functions. I thought we knew most of our targets already and just needed to start calling them, but I still did some trolling myself now and then. I thought it would be a good idea to go to the Indian dances, an event sponsored by the Indian Embassy, so the children could have an outing and I could meet some new possibilities. The performers danced listlessly. Indians, normally so warm and friendly, seemed standoffish and unhappy. After conversing with an Indian diplomat for a while, I learned why.

"The Eastern Europeans think we are Gypsies," he said. "They treat us like dirt."

★ 10 ★

Restless

Restlessness is discontent—and discontent is the first necessity of progress. Show me a thoroughly satisfied man—and I will show you a failure.

Thomas Edison

One dark, cold afternoon in Eastern Europe in late 1999, HQs sent me an order: Move to an assignment in Western Europe. My wife spoke German and Italian and had lived in Germany, Switzerland, and Italy, so she was excited. She already pictured herself walking down a street in Vienna or Amsterdam.

I'd never thought of Western Europe as a possibility for an assignment. I thought we were afraid to engage in operations there after the Paris Flap.

In 1995, the French government, possibly for its own internal political purposes during an election season, closely surveilled our station in Paris. The French gathered detailed information on our station's activities, including the identities of case officers and agents. Our tradecraft was poor and our people hadn't realized they were under surveillance. The former CIA inspector general Frederick Hitz also describes "a female American spy who was operating in Paris under private business cover. Reportedly, she involved her Swiss-Brazilian lover in efforts to cultivate well-placed French officials, but all the time, he was reporting her contacts to French intelligence." [34]

The French government divulged some of its findings in the

French media, which wrote articles about the station and US espionage activities in France. The French government also approached the American ambassador, Clinton appointee Pamela Harriman, and asked her to send several case officers home, including the chief of station, Dick Holm, which she did. (The ambassador's other major achievement in Paris was to end embassy sponsorship of the local Boy Scouts troop and forbid its use of embassy facilities.)

I was accustomed to watching the overseas tours and careers of my colleagues fizzle, so having a few officers in Paris given their one-way tickets home didn't seem out of the ordinary. But the bureaucracy treated the Paris Flap as a catastrophe, and it has affected American intelligence operations ever since. Information about the Flap is available in many open sources, but the most revealing is a book called *The American Agent—My Life in the CIA*[35] by former station chief Richard Holm. When Holm returned to HQs after leaving Paris, no job or position awaited him, and he felt like a pariah. He'd been in the organization for more than 30 years and thought his treatment following the Flap was unjustified.

HQs conducted a formal investigation of the events leading up to the Flap and concluded that station officers had used poor tradecraft, and that station management had been incompetent. The human sources the station had been pursuing were not valuable and had provided information that was available through open sources. HQs wrote up the results of its investigation in a 360-page document. In the little windowless office to which he'd been assigned at HQs, Holm and one or two other former Paris station case officers went to work rebutting the HQs's document line by line, eventually producing a document of similar length.

"Have you read both of the documents?" I asked several HQs people who had briefed me on the Paris Flap.

"Of course we've read them," they said.

Squinting like Lee Van Cleef, I asked again, "Every page?"

"Well, uh, no, not *every page* exactly. But a lot of them. Parts of them, anyway."

Holm was a brave man who had operated in several combat zones. During the Simba rebellion in the Congo in the mid 1960s, he'd had a lot of close calls. During a reconnaissance flight in which Holm sat in the back seat of the airplane, his pilot got lost, ran out of fuel, and crash-landed. Holm's plane had been accompanied by another plane, which also crash-landed. The pilot of the other plane was captured by a Simba patrol and was killed and eaten.

During the crash-landing, Holm was badly burned and blinded. He and his pilot found a friendly village where a witch doctor saved his life with a traditional burn salve. Holm spent about a week in the open jungle being eaten alive by bugs before help came. The first doctor who examined him thought it unlikely that Holm would survive. When he got back to the US, doctors removed one of his eyes, and it was many months before an operation was able to restore vision in the remaining one. Holm subsequently underwent more than thirty operations, including painful hand operations and skin grafts, and it took him two years to recover. The Agency did everything it could for him, ensuring the best transportation and medical care. Holm had frequent Agency visitors during his hospital stay, including visits by all of the top bureaucrats.

But being given his one-way ticket home from Paris and being treated as a pariah upon his return were harder for this brave man to endure than any physical pain.

Years later, while discussing Holm's book, a colleague told me, "Well, don't feel too sorry for old Dick. When the Paris Flap broke out, he tried to solve it by pinning the blame on a subordinate. The subordinate was a friend of mine. Dick hounded the guy so badly that he was forced out of the Agency." Everyone has his side of the story, I suppose.

The Paris Flap had immense repercussions not only for operations in France but also for the Agency as a whole. It was a seminal event in risk aversion. Its effect was heightened by its occurring during the same period in which the Agency was accused of having recruited criminals as human sources in Central America. (In response to the Central American flap, Congress imposed restrictions on recruiting unsavory people as human sources, restrictions that lasted until 9/11.) The Paris Flap taught Agency managers that a complaint from a foreign government to an American ambassador about the espionage activities of the station could result in closure of *all* intelligence operations in that country and could end the careers of *all* case officers involved.

The French now wouldn't even need to make a complaint to the American ambassador. If the French merely surveilled a few of our people, and made certain that our people *knew* they were under surveillance, all American intelligence operations would shut down. The implications of the Paris Flap affected other Agency offices worldwide, especially in other Western European capitals—and in my new city of assignment.

The bureaucrats' turf extended up into the heavens. A case officer planned to sit next to a potential human source on an airplane, engage him in conversation, and then pitch him to work for the CIA. The CIA station in Germany cabled frantically: Be sure not to pitch him while you're in German airspace.

The flight didn't begin or end in Germany, but flew over Germany for about thirty minutes. "Before the flight, I estimated by flight time when we would be over Germany," the case officer said. "During that period, I opened a magazine and didn't speak to the target." ·

Operations in Western Europe weren't aggressive even prior to the Paris Flap, because Western European stations were used as pre-retirement posts for Agency mandarins. After careers spent mostly at HQs, they sought painless assignments in beautiful cities. After three hassle-free years, they could retire at a higher pension, because retirement pay was based on the employee's highest three years' pay, and we paid our people between 10 and 30 percent more for overseas work.

"I was assigned to Western Europe when there were seven former division chiefs doing their pre-retirement tours as chiefs of stations," a colleague said. "There wasn't an American intelligence operation going on in the whole western half of the continent."

Flaps threatened the size of the mandarins' pensions and were a threat to their rest and relaxation plans. HQs couldn't put these top bureaucrats under any pressure to produce. After all, these were their former bosses and mentors, and, in due time, HQs managers would get their own cushy pre-retirement posts.

Sloppy as they may have been, Holm and his co-workers had at least been trying to do intelligence operations. After the Paris Flap, the message from HQs couldn't have been clearer: Don't try to do any intel work. It only leads to trouble.

So, since 1995, we hadn't done much in Western Europe, but time had gone by, and now we were considering "staffing up" again.

NOW, IN 1999, as I'd done in past assignments, I focused first and foremost on making a successful move. The American schools were full. American diplomats' children were automatically accepted, but mine weren't. We called on a kind-hearted relative to help us out, and secured places for the children in school. Later we heard that our kids had taken the recently-vacated spots of a famous actor's children, and that they'd edged out the children of the incoming Irish ambassador. Getting our children placed in school may sound straightforward, but lesser obstacles had sunk many of my colleagues' assignments.

HQs was behind in paying me and I was about $100,000 in the hole. I'd need to have plenty of cash available, so I gathered $150,000 in my checking account. The schools could cost $50,000, and a year's rent put down as a deposit on an apartment could be another $50,000. Showing up cold meant we'd have to put down a large deposit on the apartment. European landlords need large deposits because it's tough for them to remove a non-paying tenant; a non-paying tenant cannot be removed in the winter, for example. Had I waited until HQs got around to sending the money, I may have lost the assignment. A committee at HQs could have re-evaluated the assignment and decided it didn't need an officer in cushy Western Europe after all. My wife would've killed me.

The concept of a cover identity provided, as it were, bureaucratic cover for the management bloat at the Agency. That is, the US Department of State gave diplomats places to live and desks to sit at each day, people to help them deal with medical problems, and people who issued their airline tickets and paid their salary. The Agency figured that if an officer didn't have the State Department, he'd need another organization to take care of him. The truth was that I took care of all these things myself.

Cover was helpful, of course, in providing better access to intelligence targets. If the worldwide poultry industry were planning to attack the United States, for example, it would be great to have cover as a vice president at Kentucky Fried Chicken and Colonel Sanders' personal representative. This would give excellent access to intelligence on the plans and intentions of the poultry industry. But in reality, specific covers tended to be restricted to narrow targets and not very much worth the trouble. The Godfather never used much more than a smile and handshake. He'd print up some business cards, go to Beirut, and start making telephone calls. The skill in finding new human sources wasn't the development of complex cover, it was the ability to make that call.

Developing elaborate covers provided excuses *not* to make the call—the covers never seemed to be just right. Setting up covers had become a big business within the Agency. That's what Charlton did.

Back at HQs, a manager said, "This will be a great assignment.

You'll be able to run a top-flight company in industrial chemicals that will put you in touch with some of our most important targets. Your colleague Charlton helped us set up a relationship with this company. You'll be replacing a man, a new officer, who had some troubles getting established. We know you won't have any trouble getting set up."

It seemed my clean administrative record was the reason I'd been given the assignment.

Flora, the Cabbage Patch lady who handled my accountings, met me and we drove around in her van. "Well, there's more to it," she said. "The officer you'll be replacing—Jerry—had a lot of problems. I think he was about to have a nervous breakdown. The Agency spent a lot of money setting him up, and we didn't want the effort to be wasted. You never have admin problems, so you'll be able to step into his place and make the assignment work."

It had been poor Jerry's first assignment. It had been a very bad idea from the beginning—a fellow should go to a rougher place, a less pleasant country, first, so that his life goes uphill. Jerry had a sought-after assignment, but he wasn't able to appreciate it. During the course of his abortive tour, he offended everyone at HQs. He whined about every little problem. He asked for guidance in the simplest matters. He bought things, like a hairdryer and a sewing machine, which had no place in his authorized budget. Everyone at HQs who knew him disliked him. He didn't realize that all these support people were his bosses; they each wrote a section of his annual evaluation.

I went to meet the man myself.

"I recommend you buy a scooter," he said. "Traffic can be pretty bad, and with a scooter you'll be able to get around a lot faster." His hands shook and his eyes darted. He wanted to salvage some self-respect. He gave me lots of advice and recommendations based on his experience. I listened politely.

The chemicals company had complained about Jerry, too, and they wanted a new guy. Traditionally, when a non-State Department officer failed in a foreign assignment, we ended our relationship with his cover company. We weren't always sure what torpedoed the assignment, and may not have known exactly why it fell apart, but for safety's sake it was best to start over from the beginning.

I didn't want the chemicals company, but HQs was adamant that I take it over.

I learned why HQs was so eager to work with this company. "They threatened to sue us," Flora said. "They said their business would be harmed if they had to close their European office abruptly. The deal is that you get a cushy assignment, but you have to deal with this company in order to keep it."

I traveled to meet the managers of the cover company in a US city.

They were dressed in expensive suits and adorned with trinkets: pocket squares, rings on their fingers, expensive watches, glasses, and gold pens. They had expensive haircuts, the smooth skin of facials, even manicured fingernails. Evidently HQs was impressed by these displays.

The initial meeting was set up as a job interview. The chemicals company managers set the meeting in an expensive hotel room which they'd billed to the Agency. I knocked at the door.

"Open," they said. "Sit."

"That Jerry did us wrong," snarled one of the managers in lieu of a polite introduction. The interview was in the "stress" format, designed to fire tough questions to evaluate the applicant's ability to think on his feet while being thrown off his balance. "We want to see if you've got what it takes to make things right again, if you've got what it takes to be a chemicals man. Because if you don't, we'll shut this thing down."

I swallowed my pride, sat on the edge of my chair, and gave enthusiastic answers to their questions. I passed the interview.

After the interview, I asked an HQs manager, "Can we dump these guys? We don't need them for anything."

"No, you're going to have to use this company. Don't ask that question again."

HQs made it abundantly clear: I was to deal with this cover company or I could forget my assignment. I was stuck. I needed a way around the problem.

IN MY SIDELINE WORK in the software solutions industry, my spy skills often came in handy. I came across a company called ACLN, located in Antwerp, which bought used cars in Europe and shipped them to Africa. The principle behind the company was that used cars have little value to Europeans but great value in poor countries. The idea made sense, and the company's stock grew until it was worth hundreds of millions of dollars. The company listed its shares on the New York Stock Exchange (its symbol was ASW, earning it the vulgar moniker "asswipe") and the company's managers flew to New York to ring the closing bell at the Exchange.

ACLN shipped cars from Antwerp to Tripoli and Lagos, and I knew these ports well. Obtaining accurate information about ACLN's claims of shipping cars through these ports would be difficult for the (mostly American) investors who'd purchased ACLN stock.

I called the ACLN office in Antwerp and asked if I could drop by for a visit. They said no, so I visited them anyway. It reminded me of one of Charlton's Potemkin offices; there wasn't much activity to speak of. A few employees hung around listlessly. (The Yahoo message boards were full of wildly enthusiastic promoters of ACLN stock, another bad sign.) Checking with a contact in Tripoli and another in Lagos, I learned that ACLN wasn't really shipping any cars through those ports. ACLN was a big stinker and I sold their shares short.

Eventually ACLN was shut down by the Securities and Exchange

Commission. It had had few if any real business activities. Its founders were revealed to have personal histories of involvement in financial scams. The value of ACLN stock dropped to zero. The story was a black eye for the NYSE, the Securities and Exchange Commission, and ACLN's prestigious audit firm, BDO Seidman.

MY FAMILY AND I traveled to the US to take the medical exams required for the switch to a new assignment. During the blood test, the needle came out of my arm and sprayed blood around the room and on the nurse's uniform. The nurse was furious. When it came time to pay, I watched the doctor whispering to the secretary who was preparing the bill and I knew what he was up to. The doctor ripped off the US government to the tune of $5,000 for our physicals. Other peoples' money.

A routine Box exam followed. During the pre-exam interview, the operator asked, "Have you engaged in any criminal activity, or broken any laws, since your last polygraph exam?"

"Yes. I've engaged in a great deal of criminal activity. I've broken lots of laws."

"Excuse me. I meant American laws. Have you broken any American laws?"

"Oh, no, none of those."

After passing the medicals and the Box, we moved to Western Europe. As usual, everyone was a real trooper. The children got off to a great start in school. We saw our daughters walk by in a line of little girls at the school, talking to new friends and looking completely at home. I bet my sons they would make at least one new friend, and by the end of the day they each had several. So far, so good.

We had moved so quickly that I hadn't had a chance to shut things down in Eastern Europe. I returned to pack up our belongings and to close down the house and office. We'd had a woman house-sit while we were away. She'd heard some potential burglars lurking in the yard and had set off the alarm to scare them away.

According to the affidavits from former tenants, the landlord had hired security thugs to give them a rough time when they were moving out of the house, giving them dirty looks and muttering threats. I decided to get our things first, and to inform the landlord afterward.

The moving men arrived and worked hard. I went to buy them a bag of sodas and sandwiches. The checkout woman at the grocery store was in a bad mood, and took each soda can and threw it high in the air, each one landing hard at the far end of the check stand. I urged the workers to work hard and fast. I walked around handing out cash. They liked the spirit of competition, the sodas that exploded when opened, and the lunatic handing out tips, and turned it into a game, yelling and having a good time, seeing who could work the fastest. Every few hours, my phone rang with a call from my new company. "Where the hell are you? *Budapest*? Get your ass back here."

Most cover companies are full of patriotic individuals who want to help out with the national mission. But there are always bad apples. Sometimes companies expect to get a lot of money plus a slave.

"You need to get out and sell chemicals," the boss repeated during his daily phone calls.

"How about if you guys send me some money?"

The Agency had sent them half a million dollars; they were supposed to pass it on to me for operational funding, agent payments, personal funds, salary, rent, school costs, and so on. The idea was that sending the money through the company was more discreet than sending it to me directly.

"*That's* not going to happen," they said.

"Maybe we should set up the bank account so I can write checks for more than a few hundred dollars at a time," I said.

"*That's* not going to happen."

With everything moved out of the house, the landlord learned we were gone, and sent me a few threatening letters and phone calls. He wasn't angry about money, since I'd left him with much more than required by the lease. He was angry that I'd moved without his permission or knowledge. Sadly, his feelings were hurt, too; he didn't realize that I'd been kind to him only because of his ability to make life difficult for me. The humble Ishmael was now the Ishmael who would hurt him if he caused any further trouble. He didn't.

Eastern Europe's surliest cab driver drove me to the airport. The weather was overcast, smoggy. I was happy and eager to go west.

In Western Europe, I went to meet the company secretary. Although she didn't know it, she'd been hired by the company with Agency money in order to provide me with administrative support during my assignment. Ostensibly I was the new manager of the office, and I introduced myself as such.

A few hours later, I got a call from the cover company.

"What did you do?" the boss shrieked. "What did you tell her? You're not her boss. *That's* not going to happen. What were you thinking? Do not let that happen again."

The secretary put large potted plants on top of my desk whenever I went away. She disconnected the telephone and internet from my desk, and told me I couldn't sit at any other desks—she'd designated them for use by the company bosses when they were in town.

She locked all the cabinets in the office and hid the keys. She changed the door code and neglected to tell me the new one. Each time I saw her, she sent an email to the cover company documenting the encounter, and never in a complimentary way. She was a minor inconvenience, though, and didn't affect my operations in any way, so I didn't try to make her mend her ways. Luckily, her behavior improved as time went on.

AN ADVANTAGE OF being in a non-State Department position was
that I could still work on operations in Eastern Europe. If I were a
State Department officer, turf barriers would be strict, and I'd have
had to shut down my old operations. It would be unthinkable for a
State Department diplomat transferred from Budapest to Madrid to
continue to visit Budapest and do operations there.

I still ran my Eastern European and Russian operations, just
as I'd continued to run my operations in the Middle East while
in Eastern Europe. I knew that it could take a while before folks
in the European division were comfortable with my doing operations there. Our people in Western Europe seemed pleased with
my Eastern European and Russian operations. It meant I was busy
and posed no risk to them. I was about to make some decent new
recruitments, and I worked hard to create a good impression.

I flew to Washington, D.C. to prepare for my recruitments. The
chemicals company had also summoned me for a visit, so I stopped
over at their office in Houston on the way to HQs. The company
showed me a marketing plan they'd developed that would cost
about $100,000. *Go ahead and waste your money*, I thought.

When I got to HQs, Flora said, "Your chemicals company just
called. Did you approve and authorize them to spend $100,000 on
a marketing plan? They say you did."

"No way," I said. "They're lying. I didn't approve them to spend a
cent. Don't even think about giving those guys money for that plan."

I picked up my alias disguise and documents from a man I called
the Kid because, though he was in his thirties, he looked about
twelve years old. I traveled to a western city where I'd planned to
carry out a recruitment.

I met the target in my hotel room. It was a straightforward
commercial recruitment meeting where I provided a list of what I
wanted to know about certain weapons designs and the amount of

money that he'd receive to provide that information. We spent a lot of time covering the details of the designs. I liked diving into technical areas I didn't understand; I could learn from the agent. While he was teaching me, he'd also provide the intel we needed, and I'd be able to write it so that the layman could understand. I met him in three sessions each day of about two hours each, after which I would type up the intel reports and prepare additional questions for the next meeting session.

I was alert to any changes of behavior from one meeting to the next. The breaks between meetings gave him a chance to think, and he might wonder, "Hey, this guy's pushing me too hard; he wants too much too fast." If he felt as if he was being worked too hard or too recklessly, he might clam up at the next meeting. He seemed fine, though, and each meeting picked up exactly where the previous one had left off.

Since it was a commercial recruitment, I didn't tell him that it had anything to do with the Agency or with the US government. Nevertheless, I emphasized how important it was to keep things confidential, and instructed him not to be careless of his personal security.

These meetings went well, and I returned to HQs in a good mood and exchanged disguise and documents again with the Kid. It had been a decent, albeit not especially exciting, recruitment. With the fall of Communism, the counterintelligence threat was greatly reduced, and it was easier to recruit these ex-Soviets. Everyone at HQs was satisfied. I'd had to spend about $25,000 on the operation when authorized to spend only $10,000, but no one seemed to mind.

The Kid did a fine job of supplying my disguises and documents. But when I read through some documents at HQs, I came across a record he'd written of our meetings. He wanted to be a case officer some day, so he'd made a practice of documenting our meetings in detail. "Ishmael seemed pleased that I'd brought the correct documents and disguises," he wrote. "Ishmael frowned and seemed unhappy. Perhaps he was worried about his upcoming meeting." Another: "Ishmael seemed tired and cranky after his long flight."

"Hey, Kid," I said, "Don't document me. Just bring me the stuff I need. Don't write about my feelings."

I worked on the paperwork and the intel reports from my meetings with the agent. I visited Bettie at her office and she complimented the case. She'd put on a lot of weight and dark bags had begun to appear under her eyes.

"Bettie's been working like crazy," the Kid said. "She's in the office when I arrive in the morning, and she's still there when I leave at night."

I SPENT MANY sleepless nights trying to figure out what to do about the chemicals company. Every new assignment seemed to present a unique administrative problem. In the Middle East, it had been getting registered and obtaining residence papers; in Eastern Europe, the landlord; now, in Western Europe, it was strictly chemicals. I kept pen and paper next to my bed, ready to scrawl out ideas in the dark. In the morning the paper was always full of scribbles, some of them illegible.

The chemicals company was distracting me from my mission. The company hadn't sent me any of the Agency money earmarked for my operations. The company continued to take and spend the money as it pleased.

"Hey," I asked, "how about releasing that money to me?"

I tried to be as friendly as I could be.

"We're not gonna run this out of your wallet," came the reply. The problem was getting serious. I sent a message to HQs: Please stop sending these men money. HQs said that it was too late; they'd already sent the company all the year's money.

It occurred to me that my predecessor, Jerry, probably had possessed the talent to be a successful officer. He was intelligent, and had not only university degrees, but also solid business experience to his credit. But the chemicals company experience had turned him into a jellyfish. Now he'd never be of any use in achieving our missions. The company had treated him cruelly, drilling it into him that he was a failure. The company had caused him to be removed from his assignment.

The biggest factor in all this was that Jerry didn't have the money to pay his bills in Europe. Since he didn't have any money, he'd had to beg and whine to the cover company and to people like Flora at HQs. This led to the perception at HQs that he was a walking headache. The money was there, but it was in the hands of the chemicals company, and, as has been the case since time immemorial, they wanted to keep it.

I was able to finance my own operations, so I'd outlast the company. These peculiar internal obstacles seemed to be what caused most of our officers' careers and assignments to fail. It was rarely anything that we'd been trained to defend against, such as surveillance or counterintelligence.

Except for the chemicals company, the assignment continued to proceed successfully. The local Agency people were a fine bunch. My family was happy in the new assignment. My wife's foreign languages for that location were great and mine were adequate and steadily improving. We took long walks to explore the city and we found its people friendly and welcoming.

The phone rang from the company. "We want you back here for a meeting," they said. "Get on the next plane."

"Can do," I said. There didn't seem to be a purpose for the meeting. They just liked to show who was boss, that they could summon a case officer from a foreign country at will. I played along, but thought it was high time I set some limits.

I FLEW TO THE US and met some HQs managers. "We can do one of two things," I said. "We can put the brakes on this company, or we can cancel the assignment. Our goal is to do intelligence operations. Those guys are getting to be a serious obstacle."

I knew that my assignment was running so strongly that no one would want to shut it down, but I was ready for the consequences if they called my bluff.

I set up a meeting with the chemicals company managers. We met in their conference room. They started off with their usual snarling: "What do you want? You're wasting our time."

"No more insults from you people," I said. The room got quiet. "You haven't handled US government funds properly. You owe me roughly $280,000 in back pay and operational expenses. I want the money now. If you have a problem with that, I'll turn this situation over to the FBI." My tone was harsh, my body language confrontational.

They were taken aback. This was not the Ishmael to whom they'd grown accustomed. "Let's all cool down and take a break," they said. When we returned they said they'd initiated a wire of $50,000. I didn't push for more because I knew they didn't have it handy.

And that was it, the end of the problem. Their shift in attitude was immediate and total. They'd just been looking for a sense of boundaries in this unusual relationship. They never insulted me or behaved poorly again.

THE CASE INVOLVING THE AGENT I'd turned over to Mabel in Philadelphia had gone bad. Mabel had managed it for a while, but she'd decided to leave the Agency and had turned the case over to another officer.

This new officer subjected the agent to a test. The Agency had suffered from enormous numbers of bad agents, such as Cuban, East German, and Soviet doubles who fed us disinformation and wasted our time. Many double agents were hard to uncover because they fed us some valuable information to dispel potential concerns about their loyalty. The high quality of feed material created an uncomfortable dilemma. We couldn't tell if an agent was legitimate based solely on his intelligence production.

HQs had created a system designed to prevent this from ever happening again. Unfortunately, the new testing system proved to be an enormous pile of rear-end covering extra paperwork. As part of the system, case officers had to test their agents and then report the results. Lots of the tests were silly or inconclusive.

As with all paperwork exercises, this one included pointless changes in terminology. Agents were to be called "assets." Recruitments were to be called "acquisitions." Sycophants started using the new terms immediately. As the years passed, "assets" came into common use, while "acquisitions" largely went out of favor.

The new officer in charge of the Philadelphia case convinced another one of our officers to pose as a member of Italian intelligence and ask the agent if he'd provide secrets to the Italian government. By refusing this "false flag" approach, he passed the double agent screening test, but the experience bothered him so much that he didn't want to work for us. "Now I have the Italian people talking to me, asking me to spy for them," he said. "This is too much. This is too risky. I have to stop before it's too late."

I had to visit him, spend time with him, and calm him down before he'd agree to stay on at the Agency.

BACK IN EUROPE, our cushy lifestyle continued. My wife and I went to a small town to the north of our city to look for good sites for clandestine meetings. I located one and noted the ways I or the embassy person could enter and exit. I found another near the heights of our city. We sipped tea at a picturesque café. We'd never use the sites, though. In a real emergency, I'd just fly to the HQs area and communicate from there.

Another of my cases was heating up and getting ready for recruitment. I traveled to the US, met the Kid, and exchanged alias documents. Then I took a plane to Eastern Europe. When I finally arrived at the hotel, I slept for an entire day. No need to rush back into the first meeting after so many long hauls.

When I woke up, I called the target and set our meetings. I met him twice a day, each meeting advancing farther than the one before it. I accomplished my goals for the trip, paid the target, and everything went according to plan. The first night, the target and I went to dinner at a game restaurant, featuring venison and wild pigs. As men from the former Communist countries were wont to do, he leered at the waitress, showing gold dental work.

The meeting sessions were dry and straightforward: Here are the questions we need answers to, and here is how much we will pay you to provide those answers. The questions were scientific, so I'd had to do a lot of homework beforehand. But the agent was also helping me learn as we went along. As he taught me more, I could ask better questions. At the end of our meetings, he was providing the information I wanted, in exchange for a salary, so I decided to call it a recruitment. He was not a very high level individual, but his production was fine, and HQs was happy.

Loneliness had a way of hitting me on these trips, which were long and tedious, but it at least felt good to accomplish something.

I traveled back to the US and met the Kid at the airport. "Prepare to head out tomorrow morning to a meeting in Istanbul," he said. "We expect some big targets to attend a summit meeting there."

Excited, I went to my hotel and got on the Internet to make my travel reservations. Oddly, I couldn't find anything about the meeting.

The Kid returned later that evening. "Your trip is off," he said. "It turns out that the summit meeting took place a year ago. We just got a memo on it, and we didn't notice that it was a year old."

BACK IN WESTERN EUROPE, I had a visit from a chemicals company boss. The problems had been smoothed over, but I still had to interact with my employers occasionally. My wife and I went to dinner with one of the bosses at a restaurant near the parliament.

The boss was tired and emotional, and very rude to the waiters. He demanded an English menu. When the English menu arrived, he ignored it and grunted, "Just give me the special." There wasn't a special, so he grudgingly selected something from the menu. He was actually on relatively good behavior, probably because my wife was present.

"I want the special sauce," he said. "You know, the one with the asparagus in it." The waiters didn't understand which sauce he intended, but whipped up something that seemed to satisfy him.

The topic of sushi came up, eliciting his firm belief that it was cooked.

"Come on," I said, "everyone knows sushi's raw."

"It's cooked. The process cooks it. Sushi is cooked."

He responded to my wife's chirpy attempts at pleasant conversation with grunts of disagreement.

Seeking to make idle conversation, I mentioned a recent vacation we'd been on to Paris, and our visit to the military museum and Napoleon's tomb at Invalides.

"Napoleon's not there," the boss said. "He's buried on Elba."

We said goodbye outside the restaurant and my wife and I walked home. "That was the most difficult working dinner I've ever been on," she told me.

GODFATHER AND I MET in Tunis while planning an operation. I asked, "I've been meaning to ask you this for a long time. How do you handle administrative problems? I go an awfully long time without getting paid, for example. How do you deal with it?"

"Ishmael, I'm always hearing about how our colleagues have admin problems, and I don't understand why. I never have admin problems. I just don't have them."

He paused for a moment, and thought.

"Of course, there was the time I didn't get paid for eleven months.

"To solve this problem, I bought a copy of the local newspaper. Inside I turned to the classified ads. A company needed a man to drive a van, to make deliveries. I went to work for this company, driving the van.

"I told HQs, 'I'm working for this company, driving a van. When you send me my paycheck, I'll come back to work for you.' HQs sent me my paycheck pretty quick."

THE Y2K "BUG" was coming soon, and the will to squander money grew stronger. HQs sent employees a message: Advise HQs of the funds you need to prepare for Y2K.

Like most officers, I didn't reply to the HQs message. I couldn't figure out what I could possibly need the money for. But HQs was so desperate to spend money that a top manager sent us a personal note: *There's something you need to learn about working for the government. When they ask you if you'd like some funding, you say yes.*

The message was so insistent that I felt I had to obey. I sent a reply requesting Y2K funds, I received the money in short order. I bought camping gear, tents, sleeping bags, enough emergency food to last for a year, spare car parts, warm clothes—including new coats for everyone in the family—and plenty of miscellaneous goods.

Loman told HQs that his house was on the flight path of a nearby airport. When Y2K came and airplanes fell out of the sky, his house might be hit, so he requested that HQs send him and his family on vacation. This story earned him a one month paid vacation back home in the US.

On New Year's Eve, my wife and I flew to Paris with an important potential human source and his wife. (Our plane did not, as you may have guessed, fall out of the sky.) We had planned to go for a boat ride on the Seine, but a storm had raised the water level too high for the boats to pass beneath bridges. We went to a hotel party instead. The source's wife complained that we were right there in Paris but were the only people in the world not to see the Eiffel Tower light up on New Year's Eve. I'd neglected to call a limousine far enough in advance, so when the dinner and dancing were over, we had to walk to the Metro instead. It was closed. We walked back to our hotel, our wives moaning in their painful high-heeled shoes.

The Y2K scare turned out to be utter nonsense. The Agency had squandered more money and effort on Y2K than it had on the two issues that really mattered: Al Qaeda and Saddam Hussein's weapons of mass destruction.

I WANTED TO WORK biological weapons targets because of their potential for apocalyptic destruction. Little vials of biological toxins were theoretically capable of killing millions of Americans.

HQs never told me to do anything about these weapons. The Agency's mission statements, assembled by committee, ran to many pages, full of looping and turgid sentences. There was nothing of John F. Kennedy's lapidary "Put a man on the moon" or the Marine Corps's, "Locate, close with, and destroy the enemy."

I'd have to invent my own missions.

According to former Soviet biological weapons scientist Ken Alibek, in his book *Biohazard*, historical examples of the use of biological weapons include the poisoning of wells with dead animals, catapulting the bodies of plague victims over the walls of besieged towns, and giving blankets smeared with smallpox to the Indians. Modern examples include the Japanese bombing of Manchuria with bombs containing plague fleas. The World War II Japanese military facility, Water Purification Unit 371, experimented on prisoners of war with anthrax, dysentery, cholera, and plague.

According to Alibek, the Soviets may have used tularemia against

German soldiers just prior to the battle of Stalingrad in 1942 and possibly Q fever against German soldiers who were on leave in the Crimea in 1943. (Tularemia is an enemy of gardeners in Martha's Vineyard; it's the only place where cases of pneumonic tularemia have appeared in the US. One theory suggests that when, for instance, a lawnmower hits the body of a dead rabbit containing tularemia, it creates an aerosol spray of the toxin.)

In 1979, a worker at the Soviet biological weapons facility in Sverdlovsk removed a filter which was designed to prevent anthrax spores escaping from the facility. The worker went home for the day and the next work shift arrived at the facility, unaware that the filter was missing. Without it, anthrax escaped from the laboratory into the air outside. An unknown number of people living in the neighborhood, probably about 100, were killed by the spores.

Alibek suggests the Soviets may have used biological weapons in Afghanistan in 1982 and 1984.

I'd always wanted to make progress with biological weapons targets but had had little traction so far. I pushed Bettie, the Kid, and my other contacts at HQs to see if they could connect me with someone who understood the target. The Kid set a meeting for me with a scientist who worked as a biological weapons analyst at HQs and the scientist created a course of instruction for me. I read a stack of books he recommended and we discussed each one. After the course, I had a good understanding of the weapons and the threat they posed, but I wasn't any closer to finding human sources. The scientist knew his topic well, but he was an analyst, without any ability to help me locate anyone.

I knew Bettie could do something. She tracked down the man at HQs in charge of Soviet biological weapons targets. I recognized him; he was someone I'd met once in a meeting to discuss chemical weapons. He'd muttered that we weren't interested in chemical weapons targets. I'd contradicted him sharply. He was a retired army officer who'd been in charge of a chemical decontamination station.

I remembered these stations from training in the Marine Corps. Soldiers contaminated by chemical or biological weapons were to enter at one end of the station, disrobe, shower, get new clothes, and exit at the other end.

"I hear you've been looking for me," he said. I'm the Russian BW program."

You're *it*? *You're* in charge of targeting Russian biological weapons? Russia was the only country able to develop frighteningly effective bioweapons at facilities that today were guarded loosely at best.

No one else even worked with him. He was the CIA's entire effort aimed at the former Soviet Union's biological weapons capability, a program which even today has the ability to wipe out millions of Americans. I talked to him for half an hour, trying to wheedle and cajole information out of him. He was a nice person, but he had little knowledge and frequently veered off topic, talking about sports or the weather. I tried to steer him back to BW, but it was a waste of time. I turned to some reporting I needed to finish up from my last agent meetings. He talked about nothing for another 45 minutes. I ignored him. Finally, he got up and walked out.

I knew that HQs must have lists of BW targets. We knew the laboratories where these people worked; we knew the names of principal players; we knew their email addresses and telephone numbers. Many of the scientists and laboratories were looking for work now that Soviet military spending had been cut back. Some of these men even had personal websites.

My HQs contacts suggested that I do a newspaper ad campaign to seek BW targets. The Agency loved newspaper ads. You could spend months getting the wording just right and arranging the procedure for placing the ad itself, finding someone with the right credit card and backstopped alias who would contact the newspaper and place the ad. Then you could sit back and answer any responses that came in and set up interviews. It was easy activity, devoid of risk, and it could go on forever.

AT A CONFERENCE I'd attended years earlier, a man lectured on the proliferation of weapons of mass destruction. He'd had a certain charisma and I'd remembered his speech, because he hadn't actually spoken on weapons, but rather on his career, what a hotshot he'd been as a young case officer, how hard he'd worked to be promoted within the Agency.

In 1999, this hotshot was appointed to a high position in the CIA's clandestine service. Except for a couple of brief assignments in the early 1970s, he'd spent his entire career within the HQs facility. He hadn't been outside the building in over two decades.

WITH MY NEW RECRUITMENTS and several older ones, I fell into a routine of meeting agents, gathering and processing the intelligence that they produced, meeting new targets, and moving their cases forward. My annual evaluations were good. I was getting promoted. The managers I dealt with were all good people.

Sometimes I could schedule agent meetings in the US, which meant more travel, but fewer counterintelligence worries. It's tougher, naturally, for spy services to conduct operations in foreign countries. But in their own countries, they're at their best. Luxembourg's spy service may be insignificant on the world stage, for example, but they're the top spy service in Luxembourg.

My operational routine meant a lot of time away from home and a lot of time in hotel rooms meeting agents. The Kid was a tremendous help in meeting people all over the world, because he could use a diplomatic passport. He wouldn't be searched, so he could transport my alias documents and disguises.

One night in Bangkok, I met the Kid and, having some time to kill before our flights, we jumped on the backs of a couple of motorcycle taxis and headed for one of the red light districts. The one we chose had been a stand-in for Saigon in the film *The Deer Hunter*. We sat at a couple of stools on the balcony of a bar looking down at the parade of humanity walking by.

Something seemed familiar about a man walking below. As he got closer, I realized it was, surprise, surprise, the Godfather. He was accompanied by a Slavic-looking man and a couple of bar hostesses. I watched him, but never saw his eyes turn in my direction. Talking gregariously with the Slavic man, he suddenly paused, and then turned and looked directly up at me. He winked and continued down the street. Incredible.

The Kid and I made a game of trying to pick which of the bar hostesses walking by were actually ladyboys. The ladyboys were hard for me to spot, but the Kid was pretty good at it. He thought he could tell by their hands, but for me it was more of an instinct. They tended to be taller and thinner than real women, and they had sharper faces, thinner hips, and wore more make-up. They walked as if they were on a catwalk, while real Thai women just trudged by. The Kid and I had a great time, drank lots of beer, and ate the fried insects offered at a stand nearby.

THE NEXT TIME I saw the Kid was in Oslo.

"Bettie's gone," he said. "She was at her desk in the morning when I left to pick up some plane tickets. When I returned just half an hour later, she was gone. The pictures of her kids were gone and her desk was swept clean, as if no one had ever been there. Later that afternoon, security men came by and asked me some questions."

Bettie's disappearance shouldn't have come as a surprise. I'd noticed her physical deterioration, and had wondered whether the same factors that had caused Stefan to fall apart had been grinding down Bettie, too.

"I don't know why she'd be disappeared," the Kid said. "Her boss told me to keep it quiet in case she gets cleared and comes back."

The Kid and I agreed that her chances of returning were slim.

Bettie's boss told the Kid that Bettie's absence was not counter-intelligence related. Rumors at HQs suggested there was yet another mole who hadn't yet been discovered, but it wasn't her. HQs didn't suspect her of having worked for the KGB, so our operations were still considered sound. Rumors circulated that money had gone missing, that she'd had an unauthorized Russian boyfriend, even that she'd had an unauthorized Russian girlfriend. None of these hypotheses had a ring of truth about them.

I was disappointed in the news because Bettie had been a dedicated worker. As had been the case with Stefan, the investigation into her perceived wrongdoing had dragged on for a long time, which was why she'd doubled her efforts and let herself fall apart.

It sounded to me as though both of their firings were due to personal indiscretions, though I'm sure that whatever these indiscretions were, they didn't compare to Agency management's post-9/11 shenanigans.

When I got back to HQs from Oslo, I went around demanding an explanation for Bettie's disappearance, just as I'd done in Stefan's case. Managers tried to mollify me by insinuating that it might work out better for Bettie if I kept quiet. In hindsight, that was just a trick; Bettie never had a chance of coming back, and it might have helped her had I been more aggressive with the bureaucrats.

Later, the Kid told me that he'd bumped into her at a shopping mall and that she'd seemed fine. He said she sent me her regards.

IT WAS TIME for another seminar at HQs. We assembled in a large conference room and HQs mandarins began to drone. Across the room, I spotted an old friend sitting next to his wife.

Through sign language, I asked, "What's she doing here?" He gave me a broad smile. Later, during a break, he came over to see me.

"I got her a job with the Agency," he said. "It's great. Our household salary doubled. She can still spend a lot of time at home, and I can handle enough of her work so that she looks busy. The only downside is that now you're going to call me an OFTPOT."

I laughed and said, "Yeah, you're an OFTPOT now, all right."

I was happy for him, though. He was a competent officer, so I figured that if anyone was going to game the system, it might as well be him. His wife didn't speak English very well, and her native language was an exotic one spoken by only a few people in the Agency. HQs would be happy even if she just sat still and did nothing all day, because it would be able to claim another language specialist.

"The process was easy," he said, "because it's easy to get spouses through the Box. I told my wife to relax. You know—be one with the Box. You must *be* the Box."

My fellow seminar attendees included the usual array of colleagues whose careers were unraveling. A couple of colleagues were actually processing to leave the Agency and probably shouldn't have been invited to the seminar.

Another officer had recently taken over the handling of an agent. The agent didn't like him and complained about him to HQs, which removed the officer from the case. "Whenever there's a dispute between one of our officers and an outsider, HQs always believes the outsider," Jonah had once remarked.

A Mormon colleague had gotten in trouble for trying to proselytize; while attempting to convert some sinners, he'd come to the attention of the local security service, which had been monitoring the sinners as closely as he had.

Another man, who had just returned on a one-way ticket home from Africa, had been drunk in a bar. "I'm not just some little guy," he'd slurred to another patron. "I'm not a nobody. I'm a secret CIA spy." The other drunk turned out to be Loman, who dutifully recorded the incident in a memo for HQs.

"Does your wife think you're more important at work than you really are?" bellowed the voice of a latecomer to the seminar. It was Max. Everyone laughed.

Spotting me, Max yelled, "I killed some more terrorists!"

He'd continued to find information that could pinpoint the locations of terrorists. The Agency was more squeamish about dealing with terrorists in those days, but continued to pass the intel on to liaison contacts from countries interested in finding those terrorists. Generally speaking, they manifested that interest by sending military personnel to destroy the guilty parties.

It was always nice to see Max. Most of our original training class had left the Agency within the first few years, but Max, Jonah, and I were still there, twelve years on.

A case officer we hadn't met before sidled up to Max and me. He seemed like a nice guy, but he had double-pierced ears, which made Max uncomfortable. The man with the earrings confided that he also had a nose ring that he removed whenever he came to HQs. He showed us the little hole in his nose. He wore a foppish style of boots that the Sun King might have worn at Versailles, and his shirt was puffy and feminine. Max scowled. I reminded him that we weren't in the military, that it was the man's choice to be creative.

During breaks in the conference and at lunch, the man told tales about his vast personal wealth and influence. He said he'd known Fergie and Princess Diana, and had predicted Diana's death. He wore a huge watch with a compass that he advised was for use during his hobby, flying helicopters.

Each morning of the seminar while colleagues gorged themselves on donuts and coffee, the man described his sexual encounters with the Swedish gymnasts he'd met the night before. On the last day of the seminar, an HQs mandarin came to speak to us. The man put on a suit and took out his earrings for the occasion.

"Hey," I said, "I admired you for being your own man and wearing those earrings, and now I see that you're afraid of HQs bureaucrats."

"I have a bellybutton ring too," he said, and unbuttoning his shirt to show us. "I'll show it to the bureaucrats, if you insist."

"No, no!" I waved my hands to stop him. "Not necessary, my friend."

HQS ASKED ME to mentor some newly trained officers. These pro-tégés had been forced to spend many stupefying hours listening to the advice of older employees and were clearly concerned that I was just another blowhard who'd lecture them mercilessly. They didn't have any respect for me merely because I'd been around for a long time, and to say that I was experienced meant I was just another long-term government slug. I organized my thoughts and sent them advice in writing so that they could walk away from it if they wanted to. If they thought I had anything of value, I was ready to meet them and answer questions any time.

I wrote: "America needs you, but the bureaucracy hates you. Your service benefits your country but does not serve the bureau-cracy. The sooner you understand this, the sooner you will be able to protect yourself.

"Keep your marriage in order. Keep your finances in order. Ensure that you obey regulations on the use of government money and property. Make sure every dollar you have been given by the government is carefully documented. Never buy a fancy car or any personal item that will attract the envy of your colleagues. Make it a priority to set your children up in school so that they have access to good educations and are happy."

I backed up these exhortations with examples of colleagues whose careers had failed because they hadn't adhered to these rules. I'd compiled a lot of institutional knowledge and could give them numbers: Five colleagues had hit this obstacle; four colleagues had hit that obstacle, and so on.

"Wake up each morning and go through a mental checklist: Is your marriage in good order? Are your family members happy and in good health? Are your personal finances in order? Do you have your debt contained and is every dollar of your personal savings being invested wisely? Are your Agency accountings in order?

"Solve any problems in these areas first. Do not turn to intelligence operations until all aspects of your personal life are in order. Eventually, each morning's mental checklist will take just a few moments.

"If your personal life is not in order, you will be vulnerable."

I asked them to think obsessively about the mundane acts of making life overseas successful. The officers who don't obsess about these little things tend to receive one-way tickets home.

A couple of my protégés were still assigned to stations in the US and were worried that these assignments would go on forever. I gave them the same advice the Godfather had given me: Take any assignment. Do whatever you have to do to get overseas.

"Always be strong in your dealings with HQs. When you go through times of vulnerability or weakness, keep that hidden from HQs." Everyone loved hearing about how I'd frozen up the system with operational proposals so I'd have time to be at home when my wife had our baby.

As their trust in me grew, I gave them my darker secrets of operational success: chiefly, to obey the spirit of the law, not the letter. All of my successful ops had involved tricking the bureaucracy. I'd led the bureaucracy to think that operations were much less dangerous than they really were. I'd contacted targets without permission. I'd paid targets before obtaining permission; I avoided the dreaded layers of managers whenever possible. Had I followed the rulebook to a T, I don't think I'd have had a single successful operation.

All of the officers on the listening end of my advice did well and had successful overseas assignments. Maybe my advice was helpful. Maybe these officers had been squared away from the start. HQs had assigned several people to Charlton, however, and all of his protégés ended up receiving one-way tickets home. Maybe Charlton didn't care to part with his tricks of the trade. Maybe he didn't have any.

In later years, I asked these protégés to look closely at their motivations and desires in order to determine what they wanted out of a career in the Agency. If you want to run the organization, go to HQs and never leave; if your goal is to lead a quiet life, get involved in an expensive boondoggle. If you want to get things done—go out there and get things done.

MY CASES CONTINUED to move forward, and when I had one that looked easy, HQs often pressured me to hand it over to one of their less experienced case officers. I liked turning over the cases because it freed me up to locate and process new human sources. Handling an agent's administrative paperwork and intel production was hard work. It was more interesting, not to mention important, to find new agents.

Many of my colleagues thought recruiting human sources was crucial to promotion, but I disagreed. None of the mandarins had ever made any important recruitments, and many of them had never made a recruitment at all. This was a peculiarity of the CIA. In most organizations, the top people have had a record of important work. Among the top FBI managers, you'll find men who have caught criminals. Louis Freeh, then-director of the FBI, had put plenty of wicked men in prison. Most top Marine Corps officers have seen combat. This doesn't apply by a long shot to the Agency.

I spent a week in an American city conducting a turnover of an agent to another case officer, while at the same time meeting another agent. I'd picked a city in which neither of the agents had any friends or family, so that I wouldn't have to compete for attention.

I planned to meet the case officer who'd take over my agent in a hotel lobby. I'd never met him, but had heard of him, and he had a good reputation. Usually, before a meeting in a hotel lobby, officers sent me elaborate descriptions of themselves or complex meeting signals.

This man wrote, "You'll be able to spot me because I'll be naked, with a newspaper in my left hand. Don't forget that: a newspaper in my left hand."

We met in the hotel lobby, where, sure enough, he had a news-paper in his left hand. We adjourned to my hotel room. The day before, another American had been arrested in Russia on suspicion of espionage. The American had no connection to the Agency and was released. The Twins were still running around at conferences, and I wondered whether the businessman had spent much time talking to the Twins, which may have drawn KGB attention. The case officer and I were worried that the arrest might spook the agent we were going to meet. Fortunately, the agent never mentioned it.

I had to change my alias packages between each meeting and to perform surveillance detection runs to make sure no one could connect the two aliases. The Kid stayed in a hotel nearby for the entire week, just to help out. The turnover went smoothly, and the meetings with the other agent produced intelligence of fair quality.

I helped the agents with their cash management because they were building up decent savings accounts. I drove around with them, seeking the specific gifts and medicines that friends back home had asked them to buy. They appreciated it and gave me big gold-toothed smiles. I thought I saw more gold than I'd seen at our last meetings, and maybe their Agency salaries were responsible for that.

I LIKED TO TAKE long walks through cities to see the sights. Some cities had no convenient places for jogging, so for exercise I substi-tuted a one- or two-hour walk. About half an hour into a walk in a Western European city, I looked up and saw the red star of the Viet-namese embassy. Vietnam was beginning to warm to free markets. I quickly concocted a cover story.

The sidewalk in front of the embassy hadn't been swept, and the front door of the embassy needed paint. I knocked on the door and a short while later a man cracked it open. "My name is Ishmael Jones," I said. "I'm the manager of a software solutions company. I've heard about the rapid economic growth in Vietnam and I'd like to ask your commercial officer's opinion on market opportunities."

"No English."

"German?"

He shut the door and I waited. I was about to leave when the door opened again and he signaled me to enter. He led me through several darkened chambers, each containing an icon-like portrait of Ho Chi Minh. We passed by the embassy's backyard, which was scattered with trash. The ambassador's deputy spoke German.

I described my interest in business in Vietnam. He said that he was from Saigon; I was intrigued that he didn't call it Ho Chi Minh City. We had a pleasant conversation and exchanged cards. I set more meetings with this fellow in the future, and he proved useful.

BACK AT HQS, the latest scandal involved a pair of OFTPOTs who had been assigned to a remote country. The husband had abused the wife—or at least that's what she'd told the US ambassador when she arrived at his home in the middle of the night, screaming and pounding on the door.

The ambassador hadn't known that the pair were Agency officers. He checked with the State Department and with Agency HQs, which reluctantly acknowledged the truth. Many layers of managers in the organizations were upset and the OFTPOTs got their one-way tickets home. HQs convinced both to resign from the Agency.

This story has a happy ending, though. Those two are still married and are getting along just fine.

THE CHEMICALS COMPANY kept agitating for more money from the Agency. The most recent ploy claimed that they needed more money to avert IRS scrutiny. They produced some gibberish that they'd apparently cut and pasted from an IRS publication. HQs was smart enough to see through the con attempt, and turned down the request.

The company bosses were experts in the chemicals field, but they weren't good at the basics of business. They couldn't control costs. An accident with a batch of dangerous chemicals hit them with unexpected cleanup and legal bills. They'd hired too many people, and many of these employees' days were numbered. To amuse myself, I predicted which ones would be fired. One was constantly making excuses. He didn't appear at the next staff meeting, and, sure enough, he'd been axed.

I accurately predicted several subsequent firings during the next few months.

The company's managers announced that they'd rented out a rooftop bar nearby for a party. They talked it up, telling employees how great it would be, how there would be plenty of exotic food, drinks, and expensive entertainment. On the day of the party, the managers fired about a third of the employees. By evening, those who had been fired had packed their belongings in cardboard boxes and gone home, while the people who remained filed into the party. It seemed the party had been scheduled to help the remaining employees forget their colleagues—the sooner the better.

My secretary never knew that her employment depended on the US government and thus on me, not on the whims of the company. She continued to behave superciliously with me, but when the bosses came by for a visit, her fingers trembled with the stress.

A month later, the chemicals company saga finally came to an end. Business hadn't gone well, and one day the company owners called their Agency contact and said, "We're about to go out of business. You need to send us $100,000 right away, and another $100,000 in a couple months."

This was the most self-defeating thing the company could have said. The only reason they'd been able to fool the Agency was that they claimed to be successful, powerful. The bubble burst when they claimed to be in financial trouble.

HQs called me. "We want to get rid of this company. Is that okay with you?"

★ 11 ★

Hazardous Microbes

> On a bleak island in the Aral Sea,
> one hundred monkeys are tethered
> to posts.... a small metal sphere lifts
> into the sky then hurtles downward,
> rotating, until it shatters. . . . a cloud
> the color of dark mustard begins to
> unfurl, gently dissolving. . . . They pull
> at their chains and begin to cry. . . but
> it is too late: they have already begun
> to die.
>
> *Ken Alibek,* Biohazard

I still hadn't made progress with BW targets, although I'd sent in lots of requests for approval. My contacts at HQs tried to help, but were blocked by the man in charge of the Russian BW targets program. He was nice enough, but he couldn't grasp the necessity of human sources. I wrote to him and met him whenever I could.

I'd found a good target, a top weapons scientist. The target had his own website, which encouraged contact. But our Russian BW man claimed that another case officer had already contacted the scientist and determined that he was unrecruitable.

"That's not possible," I said. "We haven't contacted any of these BW scientists. How do we know?"

The Russian BW man showed me a document written by the other case officer, describing the scientist's refusal to meet with our officer. I read it carefully.

"This document is about a different guy. Their names are somewhat similar, but this isn't the man I'm talking about," I said.

"I'll take another look at it," the man said.

At last I met Grace, a woman at HQs who knew how to approach BW targets. She was with the Agency's analytical department, not part of the clandestine service. She'd prepared a list of Russian BW targets who were supplying the technology to rogue states. I couldn't believe my good fortune in discovering this woman. Her list was excellent and she was a genius for having put it together.

The great thing about the list was that it declared the targets to be valuable, which saved a lot of work. When I found a lead by myself, HQs could delay by arguing that the leads were not valuable. HQs could sit back and play gatekeeper, taking potshots at the leads, forcing me to "sell" them.

Grace could also get me approvals to contact the leads on her list. She was part of a group targeting rogue state BW programs. The people on the list were Russians, but she could argue that they were legitimate targets of her group. If I could categorize the targets as rogue state targets instead of Russian, I wouldn't have to go through the rigmarole of dealing with our Russian BW man.

My Russian was poor, but all of these targets spoke and read English, skills necessary for keeping abreast of advancements in their fields. These targets weren't subject to the "Moscow rules" of the old Soviet Union, and they were easy to locate.

It was a perfect scenario for me. I knew how to approach and recruit human sources. Once the question and answer sessions had begun, it was a simple matter to move to harder and harder questions. These guys weren't open to meeting by playing tennis.[36] I didn't play much tennis and I wouldn't have wanted to play tennis with BW scientists, anyway.

GRACE AT HQs sent me a message. An important biological weapons scientist would be present at a scientific exhibition in Scandinavia. I nicknamed him Stockholm because of the conference's location. I called the conference organizers and got his phone number in Russia. I made an unauthorized call to him and learned that he would not be able to attend the conference. I did, however, give him my "help me solve a problem" speech, and he reacted favorably.

Stockholm was eager to talk and we set a meeting in the US. If he had any ambition whatsoever in his life, the United States would feature in some way, whether as a place to do advanced studies, to educate his children, or to find funding for his commercial ideas.

THE AGENCY HAD persuaded Congress that the reason it wasn't recruiting important sources was that targets were afraid to talk to Americans. The Agency used this smokescreen to get more money from Congress to hire more officers who could "pose" as non-Americans. The Agency always seemed to need "five more years" to get this done. During my many years of overseas service, I never encountered a human target who was afraid to talk to me because I was an American.

Stockholm and I exchanged emails. He was just a guy trying to make a buck. I bought an airplane ticket for him over the telephone, with an alias credit card number. The airline required that someone pick up the ticket at one of their offices in the US, so I asked my father to do it. Whenever I asked him to help with an operational chore, I always knew it would get done right.

I met Stockholm for the first time to discuss scientific projects, so with this businesslike setting, we were able to sit down in my hotel room and get straight to work. Stockholm was a big talker. I let him tell me his life story. HQs liked long descriptions of "biographical/assessment," and Stockholm provided plenty of color. I met him for two hours at a time and wrote up notes and questions during the intervals between meetings.

Midway through the week, he was ready to go into a commercial recruitment: He agreed to provide secrets. He thought that they'd be used by a non-US government entity. It was too fast for HQs to agree to a normal recruitment; HQs liked to absorb things slowly, and they'd go ballistic if I said that I'd just met him and was ready to recruit. The intelligence Stockholm provided wasn't time-sensitive, so I wasn't concerned.

I wrote up each day's meetings separately. By the end of the week, I'd documented five meetings. It would seem to HQs that a lot of meetings had taken place over a long period of time. Some officers would meet a human target five times over two years and then be ready to recruit.

Meetings with Stockholm were arduous. His body odor was typical of Russians, but his breath was congenitally virulent, and seemed to come from the maw of the devil himself. I opened the windows to the frigid cold just to breathe. "It's a bit cold in here, don't you think?" he said, oblivious to his problem.

"No such thing as bad weather only bad clothes," I said, and told him to bundle up.

Being in America was exciting for Stockholm. I encouraged him to order room service meals and to take treats from the minibar.

Each day we met and went into more detail on the connections between his BW facility and the rogue states threatening the United States.

I handed him some money. "You've spent a lot of time with me and taught me about your industry. We have many good ideas to start working on, but we don't know which ones will pay off in the end. I'd like to consider paying you a salary, so that you can feel that your time is being used properly, whether we develop a successful business or not."

FOR THE NEXT SET of meetings with Stockholm, this time in War-saw, the Kid flew in with two sets of alias documents. I'd need the first set for meetings with Stockholm, the second for travel to meetings with another target. The Kid's efficiency was valuable because these alias documents and disguises could easily be misplaced at HQs if he didn't keep an eye on them personally.

The Kid told me that Max's father had died. I was sorry that I could only ask the Kid to relay my condolences. Security concerns meant I couldn't attend the funeral.

My meetings with Stockholm went well, and the level of detail on Soviet BW programs and assistance to rogue state programs increased. I'd allowed Stockholm to talk at length during our early meetings, while I collected the biographical/assessment that HQs liked. Now I had enough of that, and I had to rein him in and force him to focus on intelligence production. Stockholm had created his own agenda for each meeting, so I had to get him back on track with my own.

I left the meetings happy with the material I was getting, and flew off under my other alias to a series of dull meetings with another target in Bratislava. HQs hadn't approved me to pay Stockholm a salary yet, but I'd begun to compensate him anyway. It wasn't much, and it would only cost me a few thousand dollars of my own money before HQs started to pick up the tab.

I LEFT BRATISLAVA, and traveled to Egypt for yet another round of meetings.

I remembered my first visit to Egypt as a child, after the war in 1967 but before the one in 1973. My family had been passengers aboard a cruise ship in Alexandria's harbor. I had a little Kodak Instamatic camera and took pictures. When I snapped a picture of a submarine moored in the harbor, an Egyptian woman standing next to me let out a groan.

I wondered why. I snapped another picture, and she groaned again. I wondered whether pressing the button on my camera was somehow making her groan.

I snapped another picture. She groaned again. *Yes*, I thought, *the picture snapping is making her groan.*

I snapped another picture. She walked away, and returned with the ship's captain and my father. My father took the film from my camera and handed it to the captain.

Now I was back in Egypt again, but this time I'd be taking my photos home.

I'd met an Egyptian diplomat, but HQs told me to back off. They said another case officer had met the guy and spoken to him, and that he hadn't been friendly, so HQs had decided that he was unrecruitable.

"Just because we didn't hit it off with one case officer doesn't mean the guy should be considered unrecruitable."

My arguments cut no ice. I decided to travel to Egypt anyway, visited the pyramids and the museums, and poked around to see what I could find.

In police states, people are arrested and disappear, never to be heard from again. During a visit to Cairo, watching television in my hotel room, I watched an Egyptian version of Candid Camera. Actors pretending to be secret policemen confronted a pedestrian and grasped him by his upper arms.

"We have evidence that you are working for the CIA," the actors said.

Fear caused the unfortunate pedestrian's knees to buckle and he fell to the ground. He wept, hopeless: "No, no, no . . ."

The actors lifted the pedestrian to his feet and pointed at the hidden camera. "You're on Cairo Candid Camera," they said.

The pedestrian collapsed again, this time in relief.

THE EXCUSE OF SECRECY weakened accountability for money. Some officers would spend their HQs funds rapidly and then were unable to account for it properly. An OFTPOT couple from a late 1980s class had bought furniture in Indonesia with the taxpayers' money, then shipped it to Spain to have it re-worked. Then the couple bought two fancy cars. Then the husband quit the Agency and became a computer salesman. The woman stayed on and soon announced that she needed to buy a bunch of computers for operational purposes, which she then bought from her husband. Shortly after the sale, she quit. Pre-9/11, though, the amounts of money missing and wasted seemed to be in the four to six figures; after 9/11, it seemed to vanish by the billions.

Some of my accountings dated back eight years, and HQs made a big push to bring them up to date. When they'd finished, they called me into the office and Flora presented me with a bill for $114,000. "The Agency has overpaid you in this amount. Can you write us a check immediately?" She seemed to be a bit afraid of my reaction. My colleagues would have howled if presented with such a bill, and she was relieved to find me non-confrontational. I could account for every dollar.

I looked over the accountings and it only took a few minutes to see they'd made an error in their bookkeeping. They actually owed $228,000. I showed them the error and they accepted that my calculations were correct. I was keeping up my reputation as the officer with no administrative problems.

Jonah had just returned from ten days in a hotel room in an Eastern European city. Another case officer had approached a target in Eastern Europe and said, "Call this number if you're interested in working for the Agency." He'd given the target Jonah's hotel room and phone number and Jonah sat there waiting. The hotel didn't have room service, but there was a pizza joint downstairs that brought Jonah pizzas every day. The target never called.

I thought to myself: *I'll try to arrange my life so I don't have to sit in a hotel for a week. A watched phone never rings.*

The freedom to control my own time was a great benefit of not working in a government office, and I could control my time when I was in a foreign city to meet intelligence targets. When I was in Washington, D.C. I had a daily schedule set for me by HQs and

I couldn't just pick up and leave. Early on Friday afternoons, the office would grow quiet as employees slipped out for an early weekend. At 1500 it was quiet, but by 1545 it was deserted.

Max didn't mind staying over weekends. He liked to go to a shooting range in Virginia and plug away at targets all day. I didn't have anything to do. I'd seen all the sights in the Washington area, and I'd been to all the museums.

The intelligence I'd produced during my last set of agent meetings had caused the US State Department to issue demarches to some foreign countries, essentially cease-and-desist orders pertaining to WMD development. HQs had carefully vetted the demarches to make certain they wouldn't point to my sources.

I spoke to an HQs mandarin who wasn't impressed with my demarches. "Demarches aren't worth the paper they're printed on," he said. "They'll use them for toilet paper."

MY LOCAL STATION wasn't aggressive about conducting intelligence operations, since they were too concerned about what the local government might think, but they were good guys and they let me do operations in other countries. My family lived happily in Western Europe while I did my work elsewhere.

The few cases I handled locally sounded good and looked good, though they really weren't of much value: a banker to terrorists, a supplier of WMD materials, and a rogue state diplomat.

IT BROKE MY HEART when I learned that Max had left the Agency. He'd done great things and was popular within the organization. We met at the same TGI Friday's restaurant where we'd celebrated our certification as case officers. "Everything's going great," he said, "but I'm tired of waiting for the inevitable one-way ticket home. One false move and I'll be back in an HQs cubicle, my career over, and then I won't have any other skills to fall back on. I've got to get a business career going while I'm still young enough." He tried to stay involved, to help out where he could, and whenever he came across a lead, he told me about it. I followed up with every lead he gave me.

Now only Jonah and I remained from our class.

AT HQS, I stopped to see Grace, the woman who'd used HQs databases to create lists of good BW targets. I'd boasted to her that I could take one of her lists of targets and get intelligence from every source on the list, and I'd done it with one list already. She was a treasure, this woman. If she had created lists for other missions, such as terrorism or Iraqi WMD, and case officers had used her lists, America would be in a very different place today.

I was happy to have figured out a way to get past the HQs gatekeepers on the BW targets. By convincing our Russian BW man that the targets fell under the jurisdiction of Grace's rogue state group—meaning that it wouldn't be his responsibility if something went wrong—I was able to get past him.

I then focused on rogue state scientists we suspected had links to Russian scientists and facilities. I walked over to the area at HQs that handled rogue state BW targets.

"The Russian BW program wants me to target these rogue state scientists," I said. "These targets are connected to the Russian BW program." I wasn't sure there was actually any connection, but it sounded good.

"Has the Russian BW chief approved this?" they asked.

He didn't know a thing about it.

"He sure has," I said.

"Well, go for it, then."

In most rogue states we didn't have a CIA station, so I didn't have to worry about getting past that obstacle—always a formidable and time-consuming one. My formal bosses were in Europe, but because I was conducting operations outside of their geographical turf, they felt sure that they'd have no accountability.

So everyone thought that someone else would be in trouble if anything went wrong. This opened the path clear for me to contact a new range of targets.

I headed home and began contacting the targets. In many cases, my contribution was limited: What I really did to advance these cases was make the call. They were receptive, and I typed up the contents of the telephone conversations in messages to HQs.

Once it was clear how easy it was to contact the targets, HQs jumped on the cases and assigned other officers to pick them up. On the one hand, I'd be cut out of the operations, but, on the other hand, the cases would move forward. That's what mattered.

These targets had been given encrypted names by the Agency, which made them look official and intimidating. Once I showed that the target was a normal man who dressed poorly and wanted to make a buck, case officers were eager to make contact.

THE MARINE CORPS holds a ball each year to celebrate its November 10, 1775 birthday. I wanted to attend, but because many State Department employees would be present, my local station thought it better for my cover if I stayed home.

Through good fortune, I never had any threats to my cover, though there were a few unusual incidents. While in Houston visiting friends, I went to a steakhouse and a psychotic, drunken middle aged woman approached and grabbed at my friend's crotch. He winced, but then she let go, distracted by a new thought.

She looked at me and her expression changed from drunken to contemplative. She said in a normal, conversational voice, "You're a spy, aren't you. I know you're a spy." She gathered her thoughts for a few moments before the drunken, crazy look overcame here again. She shouted and cursed and grabbed at my friend again, and restaurant employees escorted her out of the restaurant.

A cover isn't officially blown unless there is evidence that has come to the Agency's attention. If an officer's entire family, high school class, and all his neighbors know he works for the CIA, his cover isn't officially blown until someone at HQs notices and puts it in writing. Not that this is the best system; it's just the way it is.

My cover remained secure as near as I could tell, and I'd been trained to protect it, but my vulnerability lay within the Agency itself. Hundreds of careless individuals had access to my true name details. Recently there'd been a scare in which someone at the Agency, by mistake, mailed extensive details about my cover to a rogue state. The mail bounced back marked "return to sender." There was no way to know if the rogue state had opened the package, and this uncertainty, combined with the sheer number of management layers involved in the mailing who preferred the matter be ignored, saved me. The matter was swept under the rug, and I lived to serve another day.

Edward Lee Howard had left for Moscow prior to my joining the Agency, but Ames and Nicholson were active after I joined. In February 2001, the FBI agent Robert Hanssen was arrested. Hanssen had been working for the KGB, on and off, since at least 1980, when he had provided the KGB with information on Dmitri Polyakov, a Soviet general working for the Agency. The Soviets executed Polyakov.[37] In addition, because some operations uncovered by the KGB had not been exposed to Howard, Ames, Nicholson, or Hanssen, there were suspicions that there was yet another mole in the Agency.[38] At least one of these people probably had access to my true name details.

Our State Department officers sometimes told their young children that they were spies. Sometimes, as children may be relied upon to do, they told other children. My own returned from school one day and announced, "Billy says his Dad isn't really a diplomat. He works for the CIA."

I knew that a new Agency officer had arrived in the local embassy, transferred from another post, but I wasn't sure which one he was. He had children in the same school as my own, so I asked my son, "The Smith children—do you know what kind of work their father does?"

"He works in the embassy as a diplomat, but really he works for the CIA."

I took a few extra precautions with my children, such as searching their suitcases carefully before traveling. I didn't want any BB guns or pocket knives to attract the attention of an airport screener. A family member once gave us a set of loud, bright red and yellow luggage. It was a thoughtful gift, but the luggage had to stay in the closet.

When my children were older, I told them that I worked for the Agency, but only after careful evaluation of their ability to keep the secret, and only when I decided that they had a need to know. When I was planning to be away traveling for a long time, I thought it was important that they knew that I wasn't going away just to make a buck, but that I had a mission of importance. Also, teenage boys can be rambunctious and disobedient to their mothers, and I wanted to emphasize how crucial it was that they maintain their self-discipline and obey their mother while I was away.

Dozens of times I've heard employees say, "After your first or second tour, everyone pretty much knows that you work for the CIA." Actually, a good foreign intel service will know the identities of CIA people in an embassy before they've even arrived. A persistent line in the Agency held that it was hard to distinguish the real diplomats from Agency employees. Even at Moscow station, the Agency thought some of its officers were unknown to the KGB. This was silly. The Moscow embassy included hundreds of Soviet citizen employees, most of whom were controlled by the KGB.

When the Soviet government was upset with the US government, they'd pull the Soviet citizens out of the embassy, and the American embassy would shut down, unable to function.[39]

Whether true or not, a popular Agency saying was that, "Anyone who wants to know who works for the CIA at the embassy just needs to look at the cars in the parking lot. The cars that are there after five o'clock don't belong to real diplomats."

The saddest bit of self-deception is "dispersed cover," in which Agency officers don't actually work in the CIA area of the embassy, but in an office a few doors down. The chief of my training course, Roger, had been under "dispersed" cover. This surreal practice is predicated on the belief that because you are not located in the same office in the embassy, people will never suspect that you work for the CIA.

A HIGH-RANKING CHIEF retired. Just before he left, he wrote me a note and told me he thought I was "audacious," and I really appreciated that.

My routine ground on, finding human targets, figuring out ways to trick HQs into approving contact with them, the work of meeting them in squalid hotel rooms, spending a lot of time away from my family. My targets weren't as important as I wanted them to be, and I remained deeply frustrated with the bureaucracy; still, I was making a good contribution to national security.

As an intelligence officer operating outside the HQs and State Department systems, I'd never be an HQs mandarin, and I had to accept that. My friends in the private sector were building great fortunes and, while I envied them, I had to accept the choices I'd made. My goal was to serve as an intelligence officer.

 THE HUMAN FACTOR

PART TWO

★ 12 ★

Darkness and Brief Dawn

> Darkness cannot drive out
> darkness; only light can do that.
> *Martin Luther King Jr.*

I woke on September 11, 2001, expecting a routine day. Because of the difference in time zones, it was afternoon when news flashed on my computer that there was a fire at the World Trade Center. Switching on the television set, I watched the second airplane hit.

The kids learned the news when they came home from school. The younger children didn't understand, but they could tell it had affected the adults.

I knew I was watching an intelligence failure unfold, and within seconds of watching that airplane hit the World Trade Center, I thought: This will bring reform and accountability to the CIA. 9/11 was precisely the kind of Pearl Harbor that the CIA had been founded to prevent.

I thought: America will see that it needs a functioning intelligence agency, not a failed bureaucracy.

For a period of nearly three months, all HQs resistance to my operations evaporated. Operational proposals moved swiftly through the many layers of management, with individual bureaucrats afraid to get in the way. For this brief period, the scales had tipped the other way: No bureaucrat wanted to be seen to be fearful or risk-averse. Every operational proposal I sent to HQs was approved. I could go anywhere and do anything.

DURING THOSE MONTHS, the Agency achieved one of its greatest successes. In late October, a small group of Agency case officers flew to Afghanistan and helped arrange for the supply of materiel to the Northern Alliance forces engaged against the Taliban. The case officers introduced US military special forces teams to the allies, and helped pinpoint and direct incredibly accurate air strikes against Taliban targets. The officers contributed to the surrender of enemy units and influenced other enemy units to switch sides.

The Agency officers were successful because they had a clear mission and a clear chain of command. They were unburdened by bureaucracy. There was no CIA station in Afghanistan. The officers had paramilitary and language skills, not HQs staff experience, and few HQs political connections. Some of the officers were recent graduates of the basic case officer course.

These cowboys helped defeat the Taliban government and corner the remaining al Qaeda leadership in the mountainous Tora Bora area of Afghanistan.

On December 15, Agency officers in Tora Bora listened to a radio that they'd picked up from a dead al Qaeda soldier. They heard Bin Laden speaking to his men. They knew he was nearby.[40]

Just as the team closed in on Bin Laden, new managers arrived from HQs to replace the cowboys. The new managers were loyal to DCI Tenet and DDO Pavitt and were veteran HQs staffers.

The new managers did what they knew how to do: They set to work creating a station, with its office spaces, turfs, and layers of management, eager to claim credit for the capture of Bin Laden. Most of the cowboys were withdrawn from the mountains.

By late December, with most of the cowboys gone and replaced by HQs' hand-picked managers, Bin Laden escaped US forces. No progress toward his capture was made during the following years.

AFTER 9/11, Agency employees expected the axe of accountability to fall at any moment. The bureaucracy, a living, breathing creature, was in fear for its life. Employees at HQs expected the Agency's top managers to be fired. Talk at HQs was that the "seventh floor," where the CIA's top mandarins dwelt, would be swept clean.

Nothing happened.

It was a great opportunity for housecleaning and reforms in the Agency. The days turned to weeks, and still nothing happened. Within a few months, the bureaucracy began to sense that it might survive. Its confidence returned, and rather than cowering and waiting for its punishment, it was emboldened. It worked to evade responsibility for the intelligence failure, and blamed the FBI. CIA Director Tenet stated that there had in fact been no intelligence failure.

By late December, at about the same time that Bin Laden escaped US forces in Afghanistan, the flow of HQs approvals for my operations stopped. HQs had returned to normal.

The media began to report, erroneously, that the Agency had produced warnings of the impending attacks, which had been ignored by the President.

By March of 2002, the bureaucracy was certain that no heads would roll. It figured that its methods—avoidance of risk, creation of management layers—had been vindicated. Bolstered by the knowledge that what had worked in the past would always work, the bureaucracy roared back stronger than ever.

THAT'S NOT TO SAY that the Agency didn't have to do a little damage control. It had suffered the worst intelligence failure in its history, and had to answer a few pointed questions from Congress. Reverting to old tricks, the Agency promised to reform the clandestine service by employing more field officers who were not members of the US Department of State.

The Agency told Congress, as it had done since the end of the Cold War, that today's intel targets, especially terrorist targets, don't go to diplomatic cocktail parties.

This idea had pleased Congress in the past. As a top bureaucrat and counterterrorism manager explained to me during a HQs visit, "It's not like Congress even told us to get out of our embassies. They just told us that the way we were operating now wasn't working, and they wanted to know what we were going to do about it. So we proposed to get out of the embassies again, and Congress liked it."

Congress massively increased funding for the Agency and earmarked billions in funding for non-State Department programs.

I was wary because I'd seen so many colleagues sacrificed to the idea that the Agency was going to get out of the embassies. The Agency had been promising to get out of the embassies for decades, had already spent many millions on the task, and had never been able to field more than a few effective case officers. The bureaucracy hated the idea of non-State Department work. The bureaucracy, its very life-blood, its system of offices and layers of management, was served by the embassy system, from which it would remain unwilling to pull away.

DURING MY NEXT VISIT to HQs, I overheard a couple of people talking about the Godfather.

"My secretary said there was an urgent call and handed me the phone," a man said. "It was HQs on the line, and they told me to make sure not to let him into the building and to change the locks on the doors and the combinations of the safes as soon as I could."

"Wow, that's wild," someone said. "That guy has been with us for a long time. I wonder what he did wrong?"

"I don't know, but his badge has been canceled and his security clearances have been revoked."

The news made me sad, almost depressed. I'd learned a lot from the Godfather and had always considered him to be one of the Agency's finest. So few people in the Agency understood what he understood, which was how to make the call. I never saw him again.

The rumor at HQs was that he'd botched some accounting. He'd had a reputation for being careless with his accounting, though most doubted that he'd ever intentionally stolen so much as a penny. Whatever the case, I certainly missed him. He had seemed invulnerable, but at last he'd met his end just like any other officer.

WITH MANIC ENERGY and in the smoke and haze of post-9/11 confusion, the bureaucracy turned its sights on non-State Department officers then serving in the field.

The Agency told Congress it would build up its non-State Department programs, but it actually began to cut the numbers of non-State Department officers in the field. The logic of the Agency's contradictory move is difficult to explain. Maybe it reasoned that it could first make a clean sweep of the non-State Department program, followed by a big build-up. Whatever the reason, pressures on non-State Department officers intensified.

Officers serving overseas used Agency funds to buy laptop computers for use in their cover work. Strict guidelines prevented government employees from using government computers for personal use, but the rule was looser for non-State Department employees. We were permitted to use our government-purchased computers for personal use, reflecting a different work environment.

A clever bureaucrat at HQs realized that non-State Department officers had come to think of the computers as their personal property and had forgotten the items were the property of the US government. Although the officers were allowed to use the computers for personal use, the bureaucrat knew one thing for sure: The officers weren't allowed to use the computers to look at pornographic web sites.

When officers came through Washington, D.C., this fellow asked to see their laptops and then he performed a forensic search of the computers for pornography. Computers retain information on the websites they have visited, for instance, even when the user thinks he has covered his tracks.

About 10 percent of the computers had been used to visit pornographic web sites and HQs used these findings to torpedo the careers and the overseas assignments of about 10 percent of our officers.

Officers disciplined for having pornography on their computers naturally didn't want to talk about it. The genius of the pornography sting was that it was impossible to argue against. No American wants a federal employee viewing pornography on his US government computer. A single officer tried to fight back, and in retaliation the bureaucracy spread a rumor that the material on his computer had been child pornography. This was a transparent lie—he'd have been arrested, not merely fired, had it been true—but it stuck, and he was disgraced.

According to historical sources, a Roman legion which had failed in battle was lined up in ranks and then "decimated" by the execution of one in ten soldiers. I called the effect of the computer sting the "Porno Decimation."

AS THE PORNO DECIMATION wound down and no further culprits were found, rumors circulated that big changes to the non-State Department program were coming. HQs was vague, but the feeling was that "changes" would involve many one-way tickets back to the US for officers serving overseas. It was a surreal time, knowing that Congress had devoted so much money to non-State Department officers serving overseas, but having to worry about when the inevitable cutbacks would be made.

A senior manager was assigned to evaluate the officers serving in the field. She was rumored to be well-connected politically and to have the full backing of top Agency management, which would give her the clout to carry out whatever was coming. During a visit to HQs, I was sent into a conference room to meet her and her assistants for an interview. She took notes as we spoke and was clearly determining whether I would be permitted to remain as a deep cover officer in a foreign assignment.

She seemed like an ordinary HQs manager, as competent as any other. She wore a plain purple dress and she spoke airily about the positive plans she was considering. She seemed to enjoy being surrounded by an entourage of underlings. My position within the Agency was strong and I thought the interview went well.

A couple of weeks later, rumors and talk of change stopped. We'd had a temporary reprieve.

IT TURNED OUT that the senior manager who had interviewed me was married to a man who had come under suspicion of spying for the government of Taiwan. Her husband was a senior diplomat in the State Department. A September 2004 search of their home by the FBI found more than 3,600 classified State Department documents.[41]

The manager had known that her husband was taking classified documents out of a secure area at the US Department of State and bringing them home. The FBI also found classified CIA documents that she had removed from CIA HQs. [42]

She was quietly removed from her position and sent to the staff of the new Director of National Intelligence, John Negroponte. Her husband was charged, however, and he pled guilty to three lesser felonies involving his relationship with Isabelle Cheng, a Taiwanese intelligence officer. He was eventually sentenced and sent to prison, in January 2007.

IN LATE 2004, a new chief was introduced. He set about defining and instituting the changes that were to come. He announced that there would be a "realignment." In other words, some officers would be removed from the program.

The new chief ordered everyone to send in a memorandum

answering a series of questions and prompts, for instance: "Give an example of your most important operational contribution." HQs would evaluate these responses as part of the process of separating the star-bellied Sneetches from the plain-bellied Sneetches, so to speak. Most of my colleagues, desperate not to be realigned, sent in long, groveling replies that we called "Beg for your job" letters.

I sent in a one-line response: "I am currently on my third consecutive, full-length, *successful* overseas assignment, which no non-State Department officer has ever done."

Even before the formal realignments began, HQs started picking off officers here and there. My colleague who wore earrings received his one-way ticket home to a station in Texas. HQs also accused him of being a pathological liar and a fabricator. He objected and filed a lawsuit against the Agency.

In a sort of mini pre-realignment, some officers were given their one-way tickets home and made managers back at HQs. They assisted HQs with the dirty work of "realignment." Martin, my old friend from my first assignment, was one of them.

Once he was settled into his HQs job, I asked, "What's HQs looking for in these 'Beg for your job' letters?"

"HQs doesn't even read them," he said. "HQs already knows who's going to get kicked out of the program. Everyone to be realigned is sick, lazy, or incompetent, with a few good guys thrown in to make it appear otherwise."

HQs gave about half of the existing case officers one-way tickets back to cubicles at HQs. The holding tank at HQs filled right up, just as it had after the Ames and Nicholson purges. After more than a decade of telling Congress that we were working hard to get out of the embassies, and after taking billions of dollars to do so, we had fewer non-State Department officers overseas than before.

"HERE'S HOW IT WORKS, Ishmael," Martin said. "The managers get together in a room at HQs with a list of all the officers. They go through the names one by one and discuss each one. If the officer seems to be doing an adequate job and doesn't have any enemies in the room, the managers go on to the next name."

Once the "realignment" was more or less complete, HQs invited the remainder back to HQs for a conference. Looking around the room at my colleagues, I had to admit that it was a much stronger group than it had been. I was proud to be associated with these people. I also noted the absence of several colleagues who had in the past boasted loudly of their achievements.

The process wasn't quite finished, though, and more heads were to roll. No one was ever reassured that he was completely safe. Cuts would be ongoing, and there was a palpable tension in the room.

At night, the chief of our program, a gregarious man, stayed out very late drinking, surrounded by sycophants seeking to save themselves from the cut. It didn't work. In the weeks that followed, many of the folks who suffered realignment were the very ones who'd stayed up late paying court to the boss.

I was pretty sure I wasn't going to be realigned, but I wanted a little insurance. I saw our chief at the other end of the conference room, talking to one of the yes-men.

"Chief!" I said, projecting my voice across the room. "I'd like to speak to you when you have a moment."

"Sure, Ishmael," he said, and broke off his conversation at once.

We met together in a corner of the room.

"I don't get a chance to meet you top managers very often," I said. "I just want to let you know some of my concerns. I don't think the Agency is aggressive enough in achieving our missions. I know where our targets are. I know who they are. I know that we can use them successfully, but we're afraid to call on them. We need to get out there and meet these people, not make excuses." I described some examples, such as weakness in WMD targeting and the institutional fear of making telephone calls to rogue states.

The chief paused and seemed to consider my words carefully. "I agree with what you're saying. Can you write up your thoughts in a memorandum, send it to me, and I'll see what I can get done. I know a lot of people at HQs and may be able to force progress in some of these areas."

I'd been telling the truth. I believed what I'd told him. I knew he couldn't do anything about it, though, so I wasn't going to get worked up about writing a memo. What I really wanted was to leave him with the impression that I was self-confident, aggressive, maybe even a little mean, so that he'd leave me alone.

Weeks later, after HQs managers convened in a room to go through the list of officers, Martin told me, "I don't know what you did, but the chief likes you. When your name came up, he said, 'That guy's okay,' and we went on to the next name."

The conference continued. At the end of each day, we went outside and did "team building exercises," such as that perennial favorite, the "trust fall." It was as awful as it sounds. Your colleague falls backwards, you catch him, and he learns to trust you.

But we were a nation at war. Once upon a time, everyone who joined the Agency was a military veteran. Today, few were, and after many years of peacetime, our work force was made up almost entirely of civilians. War zones terrified most of our officers. A speaker at the conference who'd recently returned from a conflict told wild and frightening stories, including tales of the water torture interrogation of terrorists.

The 9/11 attacks had been so shocking that for several months afterward there was a definite sense of "anything goes." As time went on, though, memories of the horror of the attacks dimmed, and Americans began to pay more attention to the humanitarian treatment of terrorist prisoners.

These cutbacks and realignments, which took place during the years following 9/11, were a continual distraction. Working to avoid the cuts, and to remain overseas, demanded much of my time and energy. Nevertheless, I kept pushing intelligence operations forward.

ABOUT SIX MONTHS AFTER 9/11, my operations returned to a pre-9/11 tempo as business as usual returned to the Agency. My direct station bosses continued to approve my operations as they always had, but the many layers above often stalled.

I traveled to the US to see an agent, and I stopped at a CIA station in Delaware to pick up my alias package. The person who helped me find my package in the station's safe room was a case officer with a stutter so severe he could barely speak. His body's perspiration control must have been malfunctioning, because he sweated so heavily that his shirt was soaked clean through, though it was cool in the office.

He logged onto a computer to help me print some messages that I needed. He was the only person in the station who was willing to help me find anything, so from my point of view he was the most able-bodied one on hand.

I read the messages, shredded them, and then left the station. My alias package contained disguise pieces and credit cards that I hadn't used before, so I put on the disguise and went to a 7-11 to buy a comb and some pork rinds to make sure the credit cards worked. The clerk seemed uncomfortable. Outside, I looked at my reflection in a rear-view mirror and saw that the hair on my mustache was sticking straight up, as though I'd been electrocuted. HQs later told me their contractor had used a batch of bad hair, which body heat caused to stand on end.

IN WASHINGTON, I had an appointment with a new chief at my hotel room. I disliked any new layer of management. He knocked on the door of my room and I let him in. Without a word of greeting, he walked to my suitcase and unsnapped the nametag, revealing my true name.

"That's not a very good idea, is it?" he said.

"I'm traveling in true name, so there's nothing wrong with having my name written on the luggage tag."

He ignored my response.

"So, what do we need to do to get you productive, to get you moving on some operations? Are you lazy?"

I had to bite my tongue. My operations were better than anyone else's.

"We need to get HQs to *approve* more operations, and then maybe I can get out there and do them."

"You sound disgruntled. Are you going to be a problem?"

"No, I'm not disgruntled. Aldrich Ames is disgruntled. I just think we need to work harder and do a better job."

He left the room without a further word. I sat in silence, wondering what I was going to do about this rude, arrogant, and ignorant man.

TO MY INDESCRIBABLE RELIEF, it turned out my new chief wasn't bad at all; he'd simply made a bad first impression. As soon as he left our meeting, he went straight to HQs and worked with the accounting people, getting me a year's back salary. Then he went to other HQs desks and cleared the way for several of my proposed operations. He turned out to be a heck of a nice guy, committed to the mission and quite capable.

Unfortunately, because he had the tendency to make an awful first impression, he had legions of enemies within the Agency. CIA people often didn't get along, and when meeting a case officer for the first time, it was common for them to list all the people they didn't like in the CIA and why. People paired off into shared hostilities.

I made it a personal mission to tell everyone in the organization that this new chief was a jewel. One officer said, "Bullshit, Ishmael, the guy's an asshole. He's not a nice person—you just intimidated him, that's all." Everyone else listened to me and promised to give him a second chance.

After meeting the new boss, a friend invited me over to the Supreme Court to visit one of the justices, with whom my friend was acquainted. We discussed the justice's concerns about terrorism. The Supreme Court had been evacuated recently on a bomb threat that had been a false alarm. We talked to him for a few minutes, then his secretary led us on a tour of the Supreme Court building.

The next day I ran into Charlton. Charlton was a locus for new money flowing into the Agency after 9/11. Charlton understood and supplied what the Agency wanted; in exchange, the Agency never asked him to provide receipts. Flora the accountings lady would never have been able to verify expenses in those countries, anyway. Charlton created and rented facilities, such as front companies, offices, residential apartments, corporate shell companies, often in out-of-the-way countries where the Agency had limited access. Some of these countries were rogue states; some were merely backwaters.

During Agency briefings to Congress, the Agency could point to a map studded with pins, each representing an Agency presence. Many of these pins were the Potemkin facilities Charlton had created.

One of Charlton's million-dollar offices was located in a Timbuktu-like backwater city. Once, traveling through the city on an unrelated operation, I had time to kill, and out of curiosity I visited Charlton's office. It had a brass plate on the door. I opened the door to a single room containing a single desk. A calendar and a travel poster hung from the wall. A local man sat at the bare desk reading a novel. He looked up and set his novel on the desk when I entered the room. "Sorry, wrong address," I said.

"No problem," he replied, going back to his reading.

★ 13 ★

Trying

> If at first you don't succeed,
> try, try again.
> *Thomas H. Palmer*

The domestic station I'd just visited, in Delaware, was agitating to take over an agent. It was fine by me, because handling the agent had become a mechanical task, limited to the drudgery of producing intel reports and paying his salary. The station sent me a memo describing the officer who would take over the case. He had a sound academic background in the types of weapons systems with which the agent was dealing. Something seemed odd, however, about the turnover scenario—something I couldn't quite articulate.

The case officer in question was the man with the stutter and perspiration problem. I introduced him to the agent. I wanted the new case officer to begin taking notes right away, to get down to business so the momentum of the case would build. He didn't respond to my hints to start collecting the intelligence, so I walked over, handed him a notepad, and put a pen in his hand. He ignored the pen and paper. As the meeting wore on, I realized that the poor guy had such trouble speaking that he avoided it at all costs.

In the future, he brought printed questions for the agent to read. The meetings occurred in the US, so he had no problems traveling and arranging meetings. I watched him for a few days in the Delaware station. I was concerned that when he realized how difficult the process of wringing secrets out of the agent could be, he'd try to drop the case. I wasn't sure his boss in the station knew how bad the officer's communication abilities were. But in the end what mattered was his heart and motivation, and, as it happened, he persevered and did a more than competent job.

ON A VISIT to France, I performed a surveillance run through the neighborhood of St. Denis and the basilica containing the bodies of many of the French kings. Macabre statues of the dead marked their tombs, and relics and shrines filled the many rooms. I continued on my surveillance route in the industrial and Arab neighborhoods, through Porte St. Ouen, and back into the city.

At the end of my route, I held a routine meeting with an agent who had some vague and peripheral information about terrorist money flows. I wasn't sure if the information would ever be valuable, and I wanted to end the case, but HQs seemed to like it. HQs liked cases that presented little risk and kept employees looking busy. I didn't mind, since I enjoyed visiting Paris.

Generally speaking, there aren't many good French targets. France is a free country with a free press, and the newspapers do a better job of divining French government intentions than an intelligence service could hope to do. The real operational value of France is that it's a large and wealthy country: A great number of terrorists and weapons proliferators travel through and conduct business there.

Ending the agent meeting, I continued down to the Seine and crossed over a bridge. The river was running high. Parisians measure it against a statue of a Zouave below the bridge; the water was up to his knee that day. I continued to walk south until I came to a small neighborhood church. I found St. Denis creepy, and Notre Dame was too crowded, but most of the other churches in Paris are nice places for contemplation. I sat in the church asking myself how I could achieve our missions, how I could do a better job—how I could help to protect America.

IN ORDER TO SHOW progress in converting more case officers to non-State Department, the Agency designated all new trainees as non-State Department officers. The Agency hired an enormous number of people following 9/11, who were hired and trained as had always been done, in official training facilities, role-playing as diplomats stationed in an embassy. At the conclusion of training, graduates headed overseas would become embassy officers, but in the meantime, on paper, they'd be listed as non-State Department officers. Just in case Congress asked how many new non-State Department officers there were, the Agency would be able to answer, "Since 9/11, we have *hundreds* more."

Training and deployment to the field could take years, and the Agency was gambling on the hope that in that time Congress would more or less forget the idea of moving away from embassies.

The Agency was given virtually unlimited billions of dollars by Congress, and it had to figure out ways to spend it. It was difficult to deploy case officers overseas, so the Agency began deploying them to assignments within the United States. The Agency raised the pay and benefits for employees assigned to domestic posts almost to the level enjoyed by those serving overseas.

Traditionally, pay and benefits had been higher for overseas service than for service in the United States. The Agency had wanted to encourage employees to work overseas where living conditions were often more difficult. The new pay and benefit packages for domestic service encouraged employees to stay in the US. Domestic stations lost their status as dumping grounds and actually became sought-after assignments. Some offices in the US were reportedly choosy about which employees they'd take.

The quality of new hires had always been high. The Agency had employed many Ivy Leaguers, perhaps because its predecessor, the OSS, was a desirable alternative to the infantry for those with language skills and high IQ scores. The percentage of graduates of prestigious schools remained high; at a conference I attended at HQs, all of the eight colleagues I shared a table with were Ivy Leaguers. No Agency recruiter could go wrong who hired an Ivy Leaguer. The quirkiness in the Ivies' admissions policies meant graduates often had the foreign travel and language skills the Agency prized.

GOOD PEOPLE ENTERED THE CIA, but few would ever do real human source intelligence operations. Most of the people hired during the CIA's expansions would undergo lengthy training only to wind up purged from overseas and sent back either to Langley or to the myriad Stateside offices to do busywork. The treatment of these well-qualified employees could have unintended consequences.

Take the case of Valerie Plame, for instance. She was, it turned out, the pretty blonde woman I'd met during the Ames and Nicholson purges back in the mid-1990s. After having been purged from her overseas assignment in the non-State Department program, she'd been sent back to a desk job at HQs. At a party in Washington, D.C. during her first weekend home, she'd met the man who was to become her husband, Joseph Wilson IV.

In February 2002, the Agency sent her husband—a retired diplomat with experience in Africa—to Niger to determine whether the Iraqi government had purchased uranium from Niger.[43] While "drinking sweet tea," he interviewed officials who assured him that they'd never sold uranium to the Iraqi government.

Plame later denied having recommended her husband for the mission, and although there was evidence that suggested otherwise, I think the Agency would have sent Wilson to Niger whether Plame had worked at the Agency or not. If she recommended him, she probably did so in good faith. That's how HQs did things: The Wilson mission provided the Agency with a risk-free and harmless way to look like it was doing something about the lack of intelligence on Iraqi WMD activities in Niger.

On July 6, 2003, Wilson wrote an article in the *New York Times* criticizing President Bush's decision to invade Iraq because of the threat posed by Iraq's WMDs. Then, in a newspaper article on July 14, 2003, the columnist Robert Novak identified Wilson's wife as the Agency employee who'd recommended Wilson for the mission. The government was rocked by allegations that the Bush administration had blown Plame's cover in retaliation for Wilson's article.

Much later, the source of Novak's information on Plame was revealed to have been Richard Armitage, a State Department appointee and opponent of the war in Iraq.[44]

A colleague who'd worked with Valerie told me that she'd done a good job of getting set up during her brief career as a non-State Department officer. He thought she had talent and would have made a good officer had she not been purged and sent to HQs.

The now-infamous Plame affair affords an excellent insight into a typical Agency career[45]: four years in training, followed by a short tour in a European embassy working on a safe and unimportant target (the Greek government), then more than five years of training, including graduate schools at Agency expense, then two months overseas—all aborted by a purge that probably wasn't necessary. The Agency favored the risk-free, lengthy training tours that kept officers looking busy. Unfortunately, when it came time for HQs managers to select which officers to purge, Plame's record of nearly 12 years without achievement would have put her name near the top of the list.

Newspaper reports suggesting Plame had been involved in intelligence operations overseas as a non-State Department officer are false. Plame spent nearly all of her career in training and HQs desk assignments[46], and trainees and HQs desk officers are not assigned to overseas intelligence missions. CIA censors seem to have approved those portions of her book that were critical of the President, but to have blocked those portions that would have revealed she was not an active intelligence officer. Following the purge, Plame spent the rest of her twenty-year career in an HQs cubicle. Such a career path was not unusual. Had she been properly led, Plame could have been a successful case officer overseas, instead of a pawn in a political battle.

SINCE 9/11, Iraq was playing a bigger role in our operations. HQs got word that an Iraqi nuclear target would be traveling out of Iraq to attend a university seminar. I volunteered to contact him. I knew the Iraqi's destination city well and spoke the language.

I lobbied HQs hard to let me call the Iraqi. The first memo I received in response dangled a vague hint that it might be okay if I contacted him, so I took this as full approval and immediately telephoned him at his office.

"Hello, this is Ishmael Jones," I said, "and I've seen your name on the list of attendees for the upcoming seminar. I plan to be there as well, and look forward to meeting you. When I arrive, I'd like to discuss whether you would have any interest in serving on our board of fuel and energy research."

We exchanged a few emails. It was important to start contact with him immediately so he'd be expecting to see me when he arrived.

HQs didn't like my method, though, and preferred that someone "bump" into him at the seminar. "Bumping" meant trying to create the impression that the meeting had occurred by chance, so he would not think it was a CIA setup.

Some of the layers of management above me favored my approach, but the managers who controlled the turf decided to send someone else to meet the Iraqi. HQs had learned that he liked to play tennis and they sent a tennis-playing officer from halfway around the world to bump into the Iraqi and arrange a match.

I begged HQs to abandon the tennis plan. War was imminent

and the Iraqi would be suspicious. The Iraqi would rely on instinct. We needed to make him feel comfortable. Since I spoke the local language and was familiar with the city, the Iraqi would sense that I was comfortable and self-confident and would in turn feel more at ease meeting me.

"We're worried that the British SIS will see your phone calls to the Iraqi," a HQs manager said. "This would be bad for your cover."

"How can the British see my phone calls, and how would we know?"

"Well," he said, "we send them the transcripts."

HQS SENT the tennis player. He arrived jet-lagged, sweaty, and nervous. The Iraqi smelled him coming from a mile away. The Iraqi had spent a lifetime in a low-trust society, where a wrong step could mean execution, and he could tell when something wasn't right. He didn't rely on an analysis of the firmness of a person's handshake or whether a person looked him in the eyes. His skills were developed far more subtly than we could imagine and our officer didn't even get a chance to ask the Iraqi for a tennis game. It had been a flaccid plan, even by Agency standards. The officer had to spend a week on the operation, which would only have taken me an afternoon. Using the tennis player made the operation more complex, which HQs liked.

HQs wasn't upset about the outcome, because the operation produced a lot of noise and paperwork. An attempt had been made to contact the Iraqi. No one would realize the attempt was passive, weak, and doomed to fail from the beginning.

I returned to working my other operations. My others were small fish, not big fish. I was broken-hearted not to have been able to meet the Iraqi.

The Iraqi target went back home to Iraq and months later the war began. Had we contacted the scientist using common sense, without interference from turf bureaucrats, without seeking to generate noise and paperwork, we may have been able to gather information on Iraqi WMD or lack thereof. This target was only one of many who could have provided us with intelligence on Iraqi WMD.

During the postwar debate, many people accused President Bush of lying about the existence of weapons of mass destruction in Iraq and leading us into a war there based on that lie.

But no one was lying. There weren't any human sources to tell us about the existence of weapons of mass destruction in Iraq. The information sent to President Bush was all guesswork. All the analysts at HQs, all the layers of managers, were making guesses based on exactly zero information from human sources.

AFTER OUR CASE OFFICER blew it with the Iraqi scientist, I argued that I should now be allowed to contact the Iraqi, but HQs refused. Even on the eve of the invasion of Iraq, HQs was afraid: "Iraqi security services are likely monitoring his phone, and your call would certainly look suspicious." Agency special operations people were already inside Iraq on dangerous missions, yet we were afraid to make a phone call.

As the invasion was about to begin, I couldn't bear it any longer. I picked up the phone to contact the Iraqi. Our soldiers were going into Iraq uncertain of what they were going to face.

It was too late. The invasion had begun and the Iraqi's phone was dead.

I FLEW TO HQs hoping that personal meetings with HQs managers would help push operations forward. But the atmosphere at HQs seemed sluggish and unfocused. During my visit, the hotshot HQs manager who had been promoted to the heights of the CIA's clandestine service came to the attention of the Agency's office of security.

As brave American soldiers fought the War on Terror, he sat in his car in the executive parking lot at CIA HQs and engaged in sexual activity with a subordinate Agency employee. Security guards caught this activity on surveillance tapes.[47]

The hotshot was never officially reprimanded or held accountable for his behavior, and he was allowed another couple of years at the heights of the clandestine service before he finally resigned. A Marine Corps officer would have been drummed out of the service at once.

I SAW JONAH at HQs and we went for lunch at a pizza place. I hadn't seen him in a few years.

"It's the end of the line for me, Ishmael," he said. "A special panel will meet at HQs to decide if I should be fired."

Jonah had made his boss angry, apparently very angry. The specifics weren't clear. Jonah's chief had ordered him to travel to a small town far from the capital city to meet him, but there had been a mix-up in communication and Jonah never received the order.

A week later, Jonah met another State Department officer who told him that the chief was upset, and why.

"So in order to make things right," Jonah said, "I sent the chief a bottle of champagne with a note attached: 'Do unto others as you'd have them do unto you.'"

An HQs bureaucrat told me a different story. "Jonah sent the chief a bottle of champagne with a note. It said, 'Do unto others as they do to you,' and Jonah had added a little picture of what appeared to be a burning building."

The chief accused Jonah of making a terrorist threat, and used the note as evidence. Jonah was given a one-way ticket home to HQs, where he would be judged by a special disciplinary panel.

"Get a lawyer," I said.

"No." Jonah shook his head. "I don't want to get a lawyer. That could make the board angry. If I show the board that I'm a team player, they'll rule in my favor."

"Get a lawyer," I repeated. "If you don't, they'll just think you're weak. If you get a lawyer they'll be afraid. Don't get yourself fired. You'll leave me all alone here."

Jonah never got a lawyer. The board was made up of humorless bureaucrats, but he'd spoken with each member and thought he had enough votes to keep his job.

Then HQs replaced one of the board members who favored Jonah with the man who had led the "Porno Decimation." This guy hated case officers. The board studied Jonah's case, deliberated, and voted to fire him.

Burly men from the security department delivered the decision to Jonah and escorted him out of the building. I sought out a member of the board I knew, and pled Jonah's case.

"There were other issues as well," he said. "He had a history of judgment problems."

Now I was, as I'd feared, the last member remaining in the Agency from my training class. It was a lonely place.

ONCE THE POST-9/11 realignment was complete, the bureaucracy revealed that it had plans for us. HQs invented several lengthy training courses. HQs liked courses: They kept everyone busy and out of trouble. The new training courses taught shooting, driving, picking locks, and capture and interrogation. I was able to avoid the driving course because I'd taken the same one years before with my wife. I took the shooting and the lock picking courses, which were fairly straightforward.

The capture and interrogation course didn't look like much fun, so I sought to avoid it. But after several of my evasions, HQs made it clear that it was no longer optional.

This wasn't the usual course, the one taught to new officers at the Agency's main training facility. It was something new, something

Martin had set up with the help of a bunch of rednecks who lived out in the woods.

The first ten days of the course featured instructors' lectures, which took place in a windowless room within a vast corporate training center. We learned that traditional capture and interrogation had afforded opportunities to talk to captors and gain their sympathy. Modern capture likely involved execution within a short period of time. We practiced first aid and rudimentary map and compass work. A stern, crew-cut female psychologist lectured on mental techniques for dealing with pain. She turned out the lights, we stretched out on the floor, and she led us through meditation and self-hypnosis exercises. The man next to me snored lightly. When the psychologist turned on the lights, he awoke and said, "This meditation exercise is the best part of this course."

A retired colleague arrived and told his own tale of capture and interrogation. He'd once been captured by terrorists and beaten. As the beatings increased, his worries increased. Terrorists can be reluctant to free a hostage who has been severely beaten because it doesn't paint them or their cause in an especially charming light. Also, a severely injured hostage looks less human and thus becomes emotionally easier for terrorists to kill. Our colleague had stuck to his cover story just as he'd been trained. If your cover story is that you are visiting a city to sell agricultural implements, stick to it. Don't give up. The terrorists were able to verify parts of the cover story, so they released him.

It was a good lesson, but we'd all heard it before. Whenever there was a conference or training course, HQs wheeled this guy in, regular as clockwork.

At the end of the ten days of lectures, a redneck in a bus drove us out to the woods to hike and camp and to practice navigation and survival techniques. At the end of the trip, we were separated into groups of three and sent along a path through the forest. Each group was then captured by men posing as a militia group. We could hear the popping of the blank rounds fired by the "militia" as it captured the team several hundred yards ahead of us. When our turn came, the instructors put bags over our heads, handcuffed us, and threw us in a pile in the back of a truck.

They put us through calisthenics and bright-light interrogations. Sitting in a chair in my underwear, handcuffed, with a bag over my head, I wondered where I'd made the wrong turn in my life that had led me here. During the lecture portion of the course, I'd discovered that the course was mandatory only for officers in overseas espionage assignments. Management layers at HQs, employees serving in domestic assignments, and employees involved in boondoggles like Charlton—though theoretically all headed overseas eventually—were exempt.

This was meant to be similar to the official Agency course, but because it had been slapped together by Martin and the redneck instructors, it was disorganized and potentially dangerous. The weather made a big difference, and when my group took the course, it was winter and quite cold. The instructors kept me outside in my underwear, occasionally threw buckets of water at me, and forced me to drink lots of ice-cold water.

The instructors had learned how to run the course by trial and error. A clever colleague from the previous session escaped by jumping out a window and making his way back to Washington, D.C. barefoot and in handcuffs. HQs and the instructors were furious, but he insisted that he'd done the right thing, the same thing he'd have done had he truly been captured. He was right, and the fury died down. Thanks to him, though, the rednecks locked us in leg irons so movement was much more difficult, and they kept a watchful eye to make sure there weren't any escapes.

The instructors had told us to bring our true-name identification on the camping trip. I didn't trust them, so I had hidden all of my identification in my rental car. Then I took the keys to the rental car and buried them in a hole in a forest near the corporate training center. I wanted to avoid revealing my true-name identity to anyone. I didn't know the people who would be running the course and I assumed that they were properly cleared Agency personnel; even so, I wanted to restrict the number of people who knew my name. Exposure to people within the Agency itself, such as to Ames and Nicholson, had accounted for most of the blown covers I'd seen.

The instructors searched us and confiscated all of the identification they could find. Later, during interrogations, they spread the cards and papers on the desk in front of them as a basis for their questions. They gave me a hard time because I had no identification, but it was worth the trouble to preserve my anonymity.

About midway through, I thought about how everyone from HQs had avoided this misery. My temper took hold.

"Take off these handcuffs," I said through the black bag on my head. "I've had enough of this bullshit."

They ignored me. "God damn you rednecks," I screamed, "take off these handcuffs."

"Do not take the Lord's name in vain," someone said. They pulled me outside and poured ice water on me. I shivered uncontrollably.

"Not a single HQs bureaucrat is here to take this course. It's time for this bullshit course to end. Get these handcuffs off."

An instructor held my nose and poured water on my face, so I'd have to drink in order to breathe.

He paused, and I said, "All right, asshole, you and your redneck buddies and all of those HQs assholes are going to pay for this."

They just laughed and poured more water. They left me outside in the mud and ignored me while they ministered to my colleagues.

It was the coldest I had ever been, and I wonder today whether it was just very uncomfortable or if my body temperature was actually dropping. The human body seems designed to deal with external cold temperatures by keeping its core warm. The hard part wasn't the wet and the cold but the water drinking. The forced drinking of a couple of quarts of ice-cold water injected the cold directly into the body's core. I'd felt the life force draining out of me. The warmly dressed instructors didn't empathize.

As my body temperature cooled, though, so did my temper. The instructors meant no harm. I realized they were trying to do their jobs as best they could. The problems with the training were microcosms for bigger problems with the Agency. Too much money plus an organizational unwillingness to confront our enemies overseas had led to the creation of these training courses. Right in the middle of the War on Terror, the Agency had pulled officers out of foreign assignments to attend these courses.

When the bag came off my head it was a sunny day and the course was finally over. The instructors had meant well. There were no hard feelings, and we shook hands all around.

I WAS GETTING OLDER, and the bureaucracy was wearing me down. A small consolation was that I was the only one who hadn't given up his true-name identity. Most of the Agency's non-State Department officers went through the course and all of their true-name material was closely examined by the instructors who, in fact, did not have authorized access to this information. It's unlikely that any of the instructors misused or sold it, but I was still pleased that they didn't know who I was.

The military runs similar courses, but theirs are organized, everyone has to take them, and there is plenty of supervision. Soldiers who take such courses have also had physical exams and have been deemed fit to endure the course. By contrast, our course had a few men in their fifties who hadn't had a physical exam in a long time, two of whom had actually been captured by terrorists in the course of their work. A man suffered from a fit or seizure during the next running of the course and nearly died, and HQs quickly cancelled further sessions[48].

The day after the course, I underwent a routine Box exam. The examiner's primary goal was to find another mole like Aldrich Ames. Such a mole would want access to HQs computers, so I pointed out to the examiner that I'd never had access, indeed had actively avoided it. He hooked me up to the Box and asked me his questions. When he announced it was over, I checked my watch: 40 minutes. "That went about as quickly as it could have," I said, "but I know a lot of people who say they're in and out of their polygraph sessions within 25 minutes."

"Oh, those guys are lying," he said, "Forty is as quickly as we can run it."

RELEASED FROM HQS and its training courses and happy to be free again, I flew to Libya with HQs approval. The country had opened up somewhat to westerners. Libya's dictator, the madman Muammar Qaddhafi, was frightened by the US response to the 9/11 attacks, and he'd quickly made it clear to the US government that he'd had nothing to do with the attacks. Rumors circulated that after seeing the airplanes hit the World Trade Center, Qaddhafi had grabbed the nearest phone, called the US government, and said, in effect, "It wasn't me!" Before his terrified call, Libya was high on the list of countries to hit after Afghanistan in the War on Terror.

I enjoyed travel to Libya. It was still a somewhat dangerous environment, in the sense that the Libyan security services were watchful and aggressive. If I were arrested, I'd be in seriously hot water. But the physical danger was light, and there was little street crime to worry about. The Mediterranean weather was hot but dry in the summer and cool in winter. Arriving at the airport, I hailed a rolling wreck of a taxi outside the airport and took a hair-raising drive into town. Billboards and posters depicting the deranged leader and his ludicrous "words of wisdom" lined the roads.

The only hotel in Tripoli considered habitable by pampered western businessmen was the Corinthia. It was spectacular, with beautiful views of the Mediterranean, a great swimming pool, and an excellent Middle Eastern buffet.

I met a series of Libyan contacts. They reassured me of their grasp on reality by pointing out that their leader was unbalanced. "He's mad, you know," they confided to me. "All Libyans realize this."

The first evening I arrived was the anniversary of the madman's rise to power. I walked out of the Corinthia Hotel, and headed east through the old walled city of Tripoli, most of which looks much as it did hundreds of years ago. I passed the former British embassy, a building within the old city, with a plaque commemorating that use. I exited the eastern gate of the old city near the Roman arch. I passed the old fort and entered the square, where I joined the throngs of Libyans waving green flags and celebrating, or at least pretending to celebrate, Qaddhafi's rise to power.

The madman had transformed the once beautiful harbor, filling in much of it with dirt and then paving it over.

During the wars against the Barbary pirates in the early 1800s, the Libyans captured the USS *Philadelphia*, a sister ship of the USS *Constitution*, which is today moored in Boston Harbor. The pirates anchored the captured *Philadelphia* within range of the guns in the old fort. A team of US Navy sailors, led by Stephen Decatur, set the Philadelphia on fire to prevent it from being used by the enemy. It sank. Using old maps from a book I'd brought with me, I tried to guess where the wreck of the *Philadelphia* lies today.

I walked past the old Al Wadan Hotel, once the country's best, run down since being nationalized by the government after the revolution. A few surly-looking men lounged in the seedy lobby.

On the way back to the Corinthia, I passed through the souk of the old city, a warren of alleys unchanged for centuries, the same smells of spices as delivered by caravan down through the ages, gold and silver shops in the same spots they had always occupied.

The houses in Tripoli had a bunkered look. Qaddhafi opened on the topic of land and property that "only those who are living there have a share in it,"[49] which led to the takeover of some homes by squatters. If a family left their house to go on vacation, they worried that it could be stolen in their absence. As a result, Libyans fortified their houses, making it difficult for outsiders to tell whether anyone was home—and difficult to break and enter.

Tripoli had once had a large community of American oil workers. On my way to visit a contact for dinner, I passed a schoolyard that had baseball diamonds in the playing fields, although the sport hadn't been played there for decades.

I visited the American cemetery near the shore in Tripoli, a deserted little plot that contains the bodies of American sailors from the Barbary wars.

During my visits to Libya, one of my contacts preferred to meet in a basement. Everyone has phobias, and this man had unwittingly hit on mine: basements. I don't like to go down into them when I'm involved in an intelligence operation. I dreaded the walk down, imagining that I could get a bullet in my head at any moment.

WORRIES FOR MY OWN SAFETY while traveling in rogue nations were nothing in comparison to my concern over news I received as soon as I returned home. My son fainted at school and the school nurse called an ambulance and rushed him to the hospital. Tests showed that he had a dangerous medical condition, and the doctors moved him to a more advanced, specialized hospital. The doctors gave him many tests, and we discussed and studied the results. Things looked bleak.

At night, my wife slept at the hospital, on the floor next to my son, and during the day I sat in a chair next to him, so one of us was always on hand. He showed some signs of improvement, and after about eight days we were able to take him home.

We worried about my son, and I also worried about the

possibility of receiving my one-way ticket home. With his health problem, my son wasn't qualified for an overseas assignment, and if the Agency had him take a physical, he wouldn't pass and we'd be returned to the US. All that mattered to us then was my son's health, but I also made sure to keep the situation secret from the Agency.

We studied his condition closely, reading all of the literature on the subject.

Meanwhile, HQs summoned me to a conference. I didn't want to leave my wife alone to take care of my son and the rest of the family, but I arranged to attend a medical course given near Washington, D.C. to learn more about my son's problem, during a two-day break in the HQs conference.

DURING THE FIRST EVENING of the HQs conference, I avoided the "team building exercises," and instead went to a rec room in the barracks-style housing block we inhabited during the conference. I practiced shots on a pool table for a couple of hours. Eventually my colleagues returned from their exercises. They'd been constructing rope bridges and then hauling each other over them, shouting encouragement and building unity.

"That 'team-building' stuff is a colossal, ridiculous waste of time," a colleague said, "and I looked around for you to see your reaction. But I couldn't find you. We all laughed when we realized you weren't there!"

The director of the CIA, George Tenet, arrived at our conference along with Suspenders. Tenet was a doughy man who chewed on an unlit cigar like a U-boat captain, in contrast to Suspenders, who was as dynamic, fit, and commanding as ever. Suspenders was by this time nearly at the top of the clandestine service. He gave a speech, and when he finished speaking, some toady raised his hand to ask an obsequious question: "Sir, what will we do to work against risk aversion in the Agency?"

Suspenders paused for effect and fixed the man with his most penetrating gaze. He pointed his fingers at him like a drill instructor and said, "I will tell you this: In all of my years at the Agency, I can honestly say I have never seen a case of risk aversion. I have seen bad ideas, but I have never seen risk aversion."

It reminded me of Tenet's statement that 9/11 had not been an intelligence failure. The Agency's new mantra was, "There *is* no risk aversion."

I'D AVOIDED THE PURGES, but HQs was inventing new ways to draw down our overseas presence. For instance, they were now requiring officers to change assignment every two years. Plenty could go wrong when one swapped assignments, and consecutive successful assignments were rare. Charlton and I were the only officers I'd known who'd had a third consecutive overseas assignment, and I didn't know any who'd made a fourth one. Even officers in the State Department, where transfers were easier to carry out, usually spent three years in the same location. Changing assignments every two years looked like another HQs tactic to reduce our strength overseas.

My wife and I went out to dinner to discuss ways to handle the latest threat from HQs. After brainstorming, we created what we called the "Rogue State Initiative."

I volunteered to move my family to a particularly nasty rogue state. My choice was selfish because I understood how the bureaucracy worked: They'd never approve the move because if arrested there, my family and I could be killed, tortured, or traded for something or someone the rogue state wanted from the United States. HQs would love the concept on paper, though, and it would give HQs a tidbit for briefings to senior managers and Congress. It gave HQs a new pin on their map, in an unusually exotic and dangerous location.

My Rogue State Initiative would work as follows: HQs would

dither for a year or two, during which I could continue to work overseas; if HQs actually called my bluff and approved me to move to the rogue state, I would go. There were a lot of things that could be done there.

When I dangled the Rogue State Initiative in front of HQs, HQs bit, as I'd been almost positive they would. They loved the idea.

THE 2004 ELECTION SEASON rolled around and leaks appeared in the press from "CIA sources." The leaks tended to cast President Bush in a poor light and to support his opponent, John Kerry.

A former chief of my program, a committed Democrat and active fundraiser, seemed to me a likely suspect. He was now a contractor, having retired and created a company that won contracts from his cronies in the Agency. HQs mandarins and his contracting partners asked him to cool it, to lower his political profile until the election was over.

"Why don't we stop these leaks?" I asked a HQs mandarin.

"We'd like to," he said, "but we haven't been able to find the source."

Grifters

<
Corruption is authority plus
monopoly minus transparency.
Anonymous

As the years passed after 9/11 and the numbers of trained case officers built up on the shores of the United States, HQs didn't know what to do with them. HQs couldn't keep these people in training any longer, but didn't want to send them overseas. The problem was "solved" by the creation of more offices within the US, always using funds meant for non-State Department programs overseas. The offices, located in commercial buildings, were certainly not State Department facilities, but they weren't what Congress had had in mind when it granted the funding to the Agency.

Potemkin offices spread throughout the United States, used as holding tanks for newly trained officers. A common feature of such an office was an expensive big-screen television set. Tuned to various news channels, it gave an office the active feel of a newsroom.

I visited one of these new offices, in California, to discuss an operational plan. When I met the chief, I saw that there was a plasma-screen television bolted into the wall behind and above me. As I pitched my operational proposal, the chief's eyes kept wandering to the screen.

The chief wasn't interested. He said that he was busy untangling himself from an operational plan that had gone wrong. He'd given

$5 million to an agent to start a bank and the agent had absconded with the money.

"Did you get any of the money back?" I asked.

"Well, we're still trying."

A colleague of mine was put in charge of setting up one of these domestic offices. "They gave me a budget of forty grand to buy television sets," he said. "I told them I didn't want any, but they said I had no choice."

IN THE EARLY STAGES of my career, I'd done a lot of trolling for leads, attending cocktail parties, diplomatic events, conventions, and trade shows. But I realized HQs already knew the identities of most of our leads, and we just needed to contact them. Reading a cable at HQs, I saw a passing reference to a rogue state biologist who worked in its weapons program.

"Anyone in touch with this guy?" I asked.

"Nope."

"Anyone ever tried to call him?"

"Nope."

"Mind if I call him?"

"Maybe. Write up your request for approval."

I learned the target was circulating a résumé, looking for a job. It would be a perfect way to contact him. I picked up the phone and called the man to set a meeting.

"I've got a copy of your résumé in my hand," I said. "You're an accomplished scientist and I think we might be able to have a profitable collaboration in my area of expertise, the software industry. Would you like to talk more about it? Let's get together."

"It's interesting that you mention the software industry," he said. "I've done some research in that field, and I'd very much enjoy meeting you to discuss it further."

We set a meeting for the next week.

Then I asked HQs for permission to call him. HQs resisted. "How will you tell him you got his name?" HQs asked. "He'll be suspicious if you just 'cold call' him. You need to be able to tell him how you got his name."

I'd been calling lots of people for many years and I'd never had a problem with this. If anyone asked, I'd said that his name had come from the Internet, or that I just didn't recall, or that a colleague had passed it along.

For HQs, I invented a complicated scenario. The scientist had once done part-time contracting work for a company in Hanover, Germany. I set an appointment with the Hanover company to discuss software products. I told HQs that one of the company's employees had mentioned the scientist's name. It took me several pages to convey all this to HQs, and to persuade HQs to like it and believe it would work. By the time HQs approved, I'd already met the scientist three times.

The biologist was from a rogue state with no Agency station. This was always a plus, because it removed layers of managers from the operation. He proved to be open and receptive. We got down to business right away, and he was producing intelligence for me after the second meeting—of marginal value, but a decent start. Since he was looking for scientific projects to do, we could lay our papers on the table and I could take extensive notes about his past and present activities. I began producing intel reports on the rogue state's biological weapons facility.

I'D PLANNED TO MEET an agent at a nuclear materials seminar in Hamburg. He canceled at the last minute, but I went to the seminar anyway and looked around. I found a target from a country with a nascent nuclear program and engaged him in conversation. He gave me some openings for further conversation, and we met later for dinner. He went home to his country and we exchanged an occasional phone call and email message.

The nuclear program was sleepy, but it was a program just the same. I decided that it was worth keeping in touch with this new Hamburg friend.

Time passed and I read in the paper that the man's country was making noises about being interested in nuclear power for commercial purposes. It always went this way. I decided to pick up the pace in my relationship with the Hamburg contact.

I invited him to visit me and paid for his travel and hotel. As usual, I had to tell HQs that he just happened to be passing through my city and would visit me while he was on vacation. We met and were soon involved in discussions deep enough to produce intelligence reports of average quality.

When HQs saw that my Hamburg contact was easygoing, reliable, and produced intelligence reports, they predictably asked to take over the case. I was accustomed to this and expected it, and was prepared to introduce Hamburg to another case officer from their turf.

This case was different, though. HQs didn't want to insert their own man to assert their control and to claim credit: HQs wanted to start the case over again, so that it would go on longer and involve more people.

"This guy's already producing intelligence," I said. "We don't need to start all over."

HQs introduced a "team" approach which involved lots of people where only one would do. The idea was to "swarm" the target, to send lots of people to meet him, each of whom might provide the insights necessary to allow us to recruit him.

"He's already producing intelligence," I insisted. "We don't need 'assessment.'"

I invited him to meet me in the US, and paid for his travel to Boston. We got rooms at the Hilton at Boston airport. I met him in my room for a series of meetings, going through the details of his country's developing nuclear program.

Hamburg was late to our meeting the next day. "Do you mind if we cancel?" he asked. "I've been invited by a couple of colleagues to go on a tour of the laboratories at MIT."

I was disappointed, but I told him to have a good time. I hadn't known that he had any friends in Boston. I sat in the restaurant for lunch, and it had a good view of the lobby. I watched Hamburg waiting in the lobby for a few minutes. To my surprise, the Twins approached. Hamburg shook hands with them and they left for their visit to MIT. *A curse upon the Twins and their masters*, I thought.

The next morning I met Hamburg for breakfast, also at the Hilton. While we sat in the restaurant, a man approached and introduced himself to Hamburg.

"Professor Hamburg," he said. "I am Professor X—, from Tufts University. I had heard you were visiting Boston, and I thought I'd come by to say hello."

Hamburg was happy to see the man. I hadn't seen this professor before but knew he must be one of our access agents. Hamburg was enjoying the attention, starting to feel like a celebrity. He'd been a lonely nuclear scientist when he'd arrived in Boston a couple of days before, and now he had me, the Twins, his new acquaintances at MIT, and Professor X— from Tufts to fawn over him. I excused myself, found a telephone, and called HQs.

"What are you people thinking? Why are you contaminating this operation with all these access agents?"

"Teamwork, Ishmael. We're swarming the target with access agents to get better assessment."

"I don't need assessment. I need you to call off these worthless access agents. They're just getting in the way."

"Think *teamwork*, Ishmael."

I'd had other case officers poach on my cases before, and hadn't minded. As long as the job gets done, it doesn't matter who does it. The difference in the Hamburg case was that HQs was trying to assign it to access agents who weren't qualified to run the case or gather intelligence. It was a way to turn a simple case into a hub of activity.

DIRECTOR GEORGE TENET spoke before the 9/11 Commission in April 2004. Tenet told the 9/11 Commission that it would take "five more years of work to have the kind of clandestine service our country needs." [50]

Democrat Lee Hamilton of Indiana said, "When I hear a statement like, 'It's going to take another five years,' I ask myself, 'Well, where were we for the last ten or fifteen?'"

Republican Thomas Kean of New Jersey said, "Five years to rebuild? I wonder if we have five years."[51]

Like most directors of the CIA, Tenet was a nice guy. He was remarkable for his lack of military, business, leadership, or foreign experience. He'd been a loyal Washington staffer for years, a man who got along well with his superiors. Unfortunately, prior to 9/11, Tenet had devoted his energies not to intelligence collection but to Arab/Israeli peace negotiations. Tenet traveled from capital to capital with a large entourage, including 35 security guards, in a C-141 Starlifter[52]. Tenet's autobiography contains humorous anecdotes about meetings with Yasser Arafat[53].

ON JUNE 3, 2004, Tenet resigned. Porter Goss, a former congressman from Florida, was appointed director in his place.

Goss brought four aggressive staffers from the House Intelligence Committee to serve as his assistants, one of whom he planned to appoint as the Agency's Executive Director. A leaker in the Agency told the press that the candidate had once been caught shoplifting.[54] This caused Goss to withdraw the candidate.

Patrick Murray, one of Goss's new assistants, was angry about the leaks. He confronted senior Agency managers, including Suspenders, and told them he'd hold them responsible for any future leaks. The dispute grew confrontational and led to the resignation of two senior Agency mandarins.[55] Suspenders was caught in the fracas, demoted, and transferred to a powerless job. I was excited about Goss's arrival and hoped he would take further action to reform the Agency.

The position of Executive Director, the number three position in the Agency, remained open. Agency mandarins recommended that Goss appoint Dusty Foggo as Executive Director. Foggo had spent his career in the Agency managing and awarding government contracts. Goss appointed Foggo in October 2004.

WITH PRESSURE from a new director, and growing numbers of fully trained case officers piling up in the United States, the Agency began to explore ways of setting up more offices overseas, designed, like other Agency offices, to employ chiefs, deputy chiefs, and branch chiefs. These offices were indistinguishable from State Department ones, except that they did not enjoy diplomatic immunity.

The layers of interconnected managers within the offices meant that if one member of the office were blown, they'd all be blown. In practice, using good tradecraft, this probably wouldn't happen.

The real threat to cover is not a hostile foreign intelligence service, but the internal politics of the Agency. When I heard that one of these non-State Department offices was going to call itself a station and that its chief would call himself a chief of station, I knew the concept was doomed. Martin agreed with me. There was already a station and a chief of station in the country, and that chief jealously guarded his turf.

Once established, the new office worked hard to find and recruit human sources, and their potential looked strong. Then one of the officers had a minor security incident. Although it took place in another country far away, the rival chief of station amplified the incident and argued that it threatened the security of his station as well. HQs quickly shut the office down. The officers returned to the limbo of HQs cubicles, with their families living in the Oakwood.

IN THE POST-9/11 gold rush, money flowed to the Agency's retirees in vast quantities. Before 9/11, many Agency retirees came back to work as contractors at a reasonable hourly rate. Following the attack, the retirees were re-hired at $150,000 to $200,000 per year, in addition to their pensions of about $75,000 per year.

Agency retirees' incomes put them in the top 1 percent of family incomes for Americans, at a time when the median household income in the US was $43,000 a year. If the retirees were OFTPOTs, their combined take from the Agency could be as high as $600,000 per year. It was great money for eight hours a day of chatting with friends at HQs and drinking coffee. Harry and Roger, my instructors from training, were still working at HQs. I saw them walk by, frail and halting, but still taking $225,000 a year each from the Agency.

The retirees were happy and pleasant to be around. They were unburdened by career goals because they were no longer part of the system of promotions and management layers. Contractors didn't hold management jobs, so the influx of contractors at the bottom of the organization pushed most active-duty employees higher up in the layers of management.

The really big money went not to the ordinary retired case officers, though, but to the retired Agency mandarins who formed contracting companies. The requirement that everyone involved in Agency contracting have a security clearance kept anyone out of the game except former Agency employees. Retired mandarins had good connections to top Agency managers and were able to get Agency contracts.

Some of the contracting companies were "body shops" that supplied retirees to the Agency. The company would get a contract from the Agency to supply a number of retirees, at $250,000 per retiree, for example, and the contracting company would take

$50,000 and disperse $200,000 to the retiree. A former Agency mandarin's contracting company supplying 200 people to the Agency could claim a revenue of $50,000,000 per year with a gross margin of $10,000,000 per year. Conventional wisdom within the CIA was that the payoff to the former mandarins running these companies would come not from gross revenue but from the sale of the company to a larger beltway contractor.

Other companies sought contracts for operational duties. The thinking was that contractors could perform the lower-risk intelligence missions that active-duty case officers were too busy to perform. The companies operated access agents: The Twins, the two most energetic and incompetent access agents I encountered in the course of my work, were now employed at high pay by a former mandarin's contracting company.

Competing with the Twins was getting tougher. Before 9/11, I'd dealt with merely bureaucratic obstacles. Now, I competed against a profit-driven contracting company run by a former Agency mandarin. If I were assigned the operation instead, the mandarin lost money.

Contracting companies run by former Agency mandarins also operated many of the Agency's training courses, and supplied Agency operations in Afghanistan and Iraq. They sold the Agency everything from bottled water to teams of security guards.

Fraud was less of a concern than were waste and influence peddling. The contracts were awarded by active-duty staffers who were close friends and lifelong colleagues of the former bureaucrats now running the contracting companies. The staffers also planned on joining those companies upon retirement. The companies were delivering on their contracts, but the terms of those contracts were perhaps too generous.

The Edwin P. Wilson case gives an insight into the contracting world. Wilson, in cahoots with former and current CIA officers, set himself up as a contractor who set up fake companies for the CIA. Skimming the contracts, he built a fortune in the tens of millions of (1970s) dollars. Wilson didn't deal in human sources—there's no money in that. He took money to set up offices that never appeared, to make shipments designed to give CIA cover companies legitimacy, supplying weapons and materiel as part of his operations. Wilson ultimately went to jail in 1982 not for his corruption in CIA contracts, but for illegally supplying Muammar Qaddhafi with 21 tons of C-4 explosive, supplying the Libyans with weapons that they used to assassinate dissidents and to conspire to murder federal prosecutors and witnesses.[56]

★ 15 ★

The Way of the Weasel

Just say no to cubicles.
Scott Adams, Dilbert and
the Way of the Weasel

Since 9/11, the manager who made bad first impressions and the other managers in my station had remained in place. I'd been blessed to have had fifteen years of good-hearted managers at the local level. HQs was a different story, but I'd always gotten along well with my direct station bosses, and they'd always approved my operations.

The time came for a switch in management. The arrival of Porter Goss had shaken things up at HQs, and some of the mandarins were looking for places to hide.

A new set of managers arrived at the station in my Western European city of assignment. The new managers had been raised at the feet of the hotshot chief and Tenet, rising in the organization through staff jobs at HQs.

Curious about the incoming chief, whose name was Salieri, I asked Martin at HQs for information about him. "He's a pussy," was all Martin had to offer.

I was summoned to a meeting with Salieri and his new crew at a conference room in the HQs area. Like most mandarins, Salieri was well-dressed and better groomed than the middle managers. There were about a dozen people in the room, including the new managers and several of my colleagues.

Salieri introduced himself. "I'll be the new chief," he said in a soft-spoken manner. "I've been in language school for the last few months. I'm very much looking forward to learning about your operations. I'd like to go around the room now and listen to each one of you describe your activities."

So far, so good.

He nodded at me to begin. I said, "I'm handling WMD targets that I've recruited in five countries: Rogue State One, Rogue State Two, Rogue State Three, Threat Country One, and Threat Country Two."

I don't want to embellish the value of these sources: Some were in the early stages and produced intelligence of marginal value. I didn't consider them terrific, but by Agency standards they were extraordinary. They gave access to five different weapons programs in five different countries. No officer bound by State Department protocols could have operated on so many different bureaucratic turfs.

He nodded, impassive and inscrutable.

I said, "By restricting myself to only one target per country, I reduce risk." I wanted to cover myself in case he were risk-averse, in which case his concern wouldn't be with the quality of the cases but the risk involved.

Salieri nodded again and motioned to the man sitting next to me to speak.

During a break in our meetings with the new chief, I said good-bye to the bad first impression manager. He'd worked hard and helped me as best he could. We exchanged compliments.

I also spoke to a colleague who was working on a boondoggle. "You've got to get yourself one of these," he said. "When you're working a boondoggle, you don't get hassled. I never had any trouble during the realignments and purges and I was able to avoid the Interrogation Course, too." His boondoggle involved buying land, building structures, digging holes in the ground. Lots of people were able to look busy. Charlton had built a career working exclusively on boondoggles. He'd never recruited a human source or written an intelligence report.

My colleague was right to say that this kind of work made life easier. No meeting agents in hotel rooms. No cold calling to prospective agents. No risk of a flap. No threat of realignments and purges. But also no chance of doing something for my country, which is what I'd joined up for in the first place.

The meeting adjourned and we headed back to our overseas assignments. Until my assignment to Iraq, this meeting was the last time I saw any of the Agency managers to whom I directly reported.

AS SOON AS Salieri and his new crew were installed, my access to information from HQs ended. All message traffic containing human source leads stopped. Incoming messages dealt exclusively with administrative issues: salary, benefits, federal holidays, administrative reorganizations of HQs desks, and holiday greetings from top bureaucrats.

Salieri created new layers of managers. It wasn't clear who my direct boss was. Different layers of managers wrote to me at different times.

Among the new layers of managers were OFTPOTs who were junior to me in rank. They'd had little operational experience. I'd never met them, and I never would.

Fortunately, though it might be harder to begin new cases, my ongoing operations looked like they'd be allowed to proceed.

Then the new crew introduced a strategy I'd never encountered before: the "do it again." Each time I sent an operational proposal through the OFTPOTs, they bounced it back to me brusquely, marked "do it again." The Agency tends to be collegial in its writing style and such confrontation is rare. Nevertheless, I edited each proposal and sent it back to the OFTPOTs. "Do it again" occurred as many as six times per operational proposal.

I sent a proposal to contact an Iranian nuclear proliferator, a person we suspected of helping Iran obtain equipment that could help them get a little bit closer to making a bomb.

In reply to my proposal, an OFTPOT said, "You need to fix the grammar."

My blood pressure shot up; my vision narrowed. I stood up and paced back and forth in the hallway of my office. I returned to my desk and looked for the grammatical errors in my message, but couldn't find a single one. I showed the message to my wife, but she couldn't see any grammatical errors either. I reworded the proposal to make it look different, and sent it back in.

My daughter's school called. She'd gotten in trouble for giving Ex-Lax to another child and telling the child it was a bar of chocolate. It wasn't a nice thing to do, and a not-so-funny coincidence made it even worse: The other student was the child of the OFTPOTs. They weren't supposed to know my true name, but they did.

A few days later, the OFTPOT responded to my rewording, "You need to answer the question. You didn't answer the question. Do it again."

Again, furious, I stood up and then paced in the hallway. I didn't know the question to which the OFTPOT was referring. Adding to my frustration was the knowledge that my son's medical condition would block transfer to another overseas assignment.

After the third or fourth time, the pacing wasn't enough to cool me down, so I put on my coat and left the building to take a long walk through the city. After I'd walked about an hour and a half, I saw a group of Arab teenagers ahead, loitering on a corner. One of them had a pellet pistol, with which he took potshots at passersby. The pellets were plastic and didn't appear to be causing any injuries.

I walked past the group and felt a few pellets hit my back. I turned and approached the group, saw the shooter hide the pistol behind his back, and pushed him to the ground. His companions didn't intervene. They laughed and told him he had it coming.

When I got back to my office, I rephrased my message about the proliferator.

The OFTPOT replied, "You still didn't answer the question. You need to answer the question."

I was certain that the OFTPOTs were simply delaying my proposal until the Iranian had left the country. I had no choice but to proceed without approval. I called the Iranian nuclear proliferator immediately and set a meeting. I continued to push the case forward until my intelligence operations in the region came to an end.

THE WINTER 2005 OPERATION involving Dr. B—, the man whose scientific paper I'd found tacked to the poster board at the conference in Paris, had had momentum before Salieri and his OFTPOTs arrived at the station. I was able to get approvals through the OFTPOTs with only a few rewrites.

I'd just finished meeting Dr. B— in Warsaw. As usual, my after-action reports made the meetings look as though they'd been risk-free and one-sided—as though he'd called me each time and I'd never called him. I didn't feel the least bit of regret about it; I'd had to do it, after all, for years, just to get anything done at all.

I got him a ticket to Budapest and arranged to meet at the airport. We shared a taxi into the city. I knew that Dr. B— liked to sightsee, so we walked along the river, visiting tourist spots along the way, and then across the river and up to a museum on Castle Hill. Our tourist walks finished, we got down to business. I asked questions and took notes, again dividing our meetings into a series of a couple of hours each. He was eager to continue the relationship. Opportunities were rare in his home country and he saw me as a person who could help him make money and advance in his scientific field.

As with the planned meeting in Warsaw, my approval for the meetings in Budapest didn't arrive until after they'd ended.

Dr. B— and I met elsewhere on a few more occasions. The intelligence reports I produced using his information were becoming better and better. Then, during a meeting in Nicosia, Cyprus, Dr. B—'s demeanor seemed to change slightly.

"I've got to run to another meeting," he said, looking at his watch. He seemed more confident. He was polite, but he had other business, other opportunities. I was no longer his only contact with the west. I asked him whom he planned to see, and he showed me a business card.

It was the Twins.

The next day, Dr. B— and I met for an hour, but again he had to break away early. Just as before, he was polite, but he was getting to be full of himself. I asked him who he was going to see, and he told me the name. It was a colleague, another Agency officer.

The Agency's meetings interfered with mine and hampered my ability to extract intelligence from Dr. B—. Moreover, by paying attention to him, they'd managed to make him less cooperative. The mistaken belief that three different organizations were courting him had only served to make him arrogant.

I knew what had happened. Once I'd started sending in intelligence reports from Dr. B—, I'd made the case look easy. Once it looked easy, it attracted the attention of hordes of HQs people vying for a chance to take it. The first priority was to make as many people as possible look as busy as possible, and their second, predictably enough, was to claim ownership of the intelligence production I'd created.

HQs said, "Multiple approaches to Dr. B— will help us gather assessment."

"I've already gathered the assessment on Dr. B—," I said. "He's already producing intel reports!"

HQs sent the Twins a great deal of money with which they

created a scientific conference specifically designed for Dr. B— to attend. The conference was to be elaborate and expensive, and would involve dozens of Agency people. At the conference, the Twins were to "gather assessment"—that is, to evaluate his willingness to provide intelligence. Again, I emphasized that Dr. B— was already producing intelligence—all this expense and effort would be wasted.

Alas, the bureaucracy needed to be fed. It needed to look busy, and it needed to spend money to do so.

Dozens of Agency people were now involved in the case. Momentum shifted to getting Dr. B— to the United States for meetings.

"He's already available for meetings," I said. "We don't need to invite him to the US. We can get all the intelligence we need right now, if you'll get all these people to back off."

It was no use. HQs arranged a multiple entry, long-term resident visa for Dr. B— and his family. On the question on the visa form that asks if the applicant has ever been involved with WMD, HQs checked "no". With Dr. B— in the safe environment of the United States, there'd be ample opportunity to conduct operations. HQs arranged for the Twins to get him a scholarship to an American university.

Once these arrangements were in place, and Dr. B— was in the US, the Agency sent an officer identifying himself as a US government representative to talk to Dr. B—. Dr. B— refused. With that, the operation ended.

I didn't learn this until much later—HQs hid it from me, and repeatedly told me the operation was moving along well.

As of this writing, Dr. B— continues to travel back and forth from his country to the US. The weapons his nation is believed to be developing are a clear threat to Americans. If his country creates a functioning weapon and uses it, the death toll will dwarf 9/11's. I believe that Dr. B— has used his university connections and scholarship to gather additional scientific information for his country's nuclear program. He's an approachable person—available for contact any time we might want to pick up where I left off.

THE OFTPOTs ASKED ME for a list of all the unusual security incidents I'd witnessed, such as sightings of suspicious people and possible surveillants. I told them I hadn't seen any. They sent me a sample list that they'd compiled and urged me to add incidents to it. They'd gone back in history more than a decade and written down every incident they could find in Western Europe, including the 1995 surveillance of case officers in France, and their subsequent expulsion from the country, when Dick Holm was the chief there.

Most of the incidents on the list were trivial. Over the years, embassy employees who were not CIA employees occasionally stopped by the CIA station to say they had "gut feelings" that someone might be listening to their home phones.

Others reported having seen a suspicious character on the street or subway.

The list was inconsequential, but it was growing.

In recent months, case officers assigned to the embassy had used their home phones to set meetings with agents. When the officers left their apartments to go to the meetings they found suspicious-looking men waiting outside their buildings. Sometimes the men followed them down the street; other times, the officers arrived at their meeting place to find different men observing them.

Many of these security incidents happened to the same person, who happened to be in charge of creating the list of the station's incidents. It was as though he were being rewarded for the number of security incidents he compiled.

An OFTPOT told me to create and run a complex surveillance detection route by walking in the city and driving in the suburbs, trying to see if anyone followed me. I sent them my proposed route.

They didn't like it. "Do it again," they said. I ignored them and never heard anything further about it. Surveillance detection was something I did every time I went outside the house, not just for special occasions.

A VISITING COLLEAGUE helped add to the list of security incidents. He was a surveillance magnet—surveillants seemed to follow him out of idle curiosity. When he left his house or hotel in the morning, there always seemed to be someone lying in wait. When he traveled, he saw suspicious people watching him at the airport and in restaurants. At home, people followed him to the grocery store and the health club.

When this surveillance magnet turned on his personal computer, he could see by the changed settings that someone else had been using it; when he got in his car, he could tell by small adjustments— the mirrors, the radio—that someone else had been inside the car. Following his visit to Salieri's turf, the surveillance magnet documented each incident in detail, adding bulk to the station's growing list of security incidents.

During a visit to HQs, a friend showed me the surveillance reports. They were in a restricted file and he wasn't supposed to show them to me, but he did anyway. The next day I saw the surveillance magnet walking down the hall.

"I'm sorry to hear you've had such a rough time with surveillance lately," I said.

"They said I was under surveillance, but I wasn't."

Magnet, I thought, *don't lie to me.*

HQs had had enough of the man, too, and sentenced him to a hopeless job in a cubicle in the HQs basement. He sought a transfer to any Agency office with a window, but his requests were denied. HQs then put him under a security investigation, a murky and in some cases interminable process then popular at HQs. "Maybe we'll know more in six months," a security officer told him.

WHEN THE LIST of security incidents got long enough, the station declared a stand-down, which meant it would no longer conduct intelligence operations.

It seemed extreme to shut down like that, but I didn't expect HQs to intervene. The mood at HQs was hard to pin down. In a speech on March 2, 2005, our new director, Porter Goss, said, "The jobs I'm being asked to do, the five hats that I wear, are too much for this mortal. I'm a little amazed at the workload." It sounded like the bureaucracy was wearing him down.

The stand-down permitted Salieri to say: "I sure do want to get out there and work on terrorists and proliferators of weapons of mass destruction. But we have a bad security situation here. The locals could shut us down any minute and cause a big flap. We sure don't want that, so we're paying very close attention to our counterintelligence situation."

All of my operations ended. To test the strength of the stand-down, I sent four more operational proposals, all of which were rejected with a curt form letter: "Due to the station's current security stand-down, these proposals cannot be approved."

I sent several proposals for operations in countries half the world away, but received the same reply.

The stand-down wasn't all bad. At least I knew where things stood, and I didn't have to read any more frustrating "do it again" notices. I had plenty of time to spend with my family. Also, the stand-down coincided with great news on the home front: my son's medical tests showed that his condition had improved tremendously and was no longer a threat. He'd been through many tests and hospital visits. His health had been such a serious concern that the improvement in his condition made the bad news about the stand-down seem insignificant.

All the other active officers serving in the region were issued their one-way tickets home. They meekly accepted the decision and moved back to cubicles in the US.

I was lucky to escape the same fate. The Agency was still briefing its mandarins and Congress that I was the officer getting ready for a rogue state assignment.

HQS ORDERED ME to spend a week at a large Agency facility where new case officers were in training. The trainees would be studying non-State Department operations; I would evaluate the course and offer suggestions. I drove a rental car to the facility. I didn't have the proper identification to enter, but I knew the woman who controlled the gate: Sylvia, an old friend from early in my career. "How the flock are you?" she said. We chatted about the past for a while and then she let me in. Driving into the facility, I wondered which building had been used to imprison and interrogate Yuri Nosenko[57], a Soviet KGB defector from the 1960's[58]. Nosenko had been held in solitary confinement for about three years.

Right away, I had a good feeling about the training. The bulk of it still involved role-playing as diplomats at embassies and cocktail parties, but it was well organized. The instructors had lesson plans that had been evaluated carefully by supervisors. When an instructor was teaching a lesson, the others were required to keep quiet: No instructor was permitted to chime in with time-wasting and self-aggrandizing anecdotes. Most of the instructors were dedicated and experienced.

I sat with groups of trainees as they discussed ways to approach human sources. I thought their ideas were creative and often better than mine. Just as my training class had once been "the best we've ever had," these people, unpolluted by the bureaucracy, were now the unparalleled cream of the crop. What if the President of the United States were given the opportunity to pick any ten of these bright young trainees and to order to them to find our top priority human sources? If freed from the restraints of management layers, embassies, and turf squabbles, this group of ten could find any intelligence the President desired. Would the Agency turn these talented people into burnouts?

AT MY CURRENT ASSIGNMENT, no further intelligence operations would occur. By that point, I wanted out just as much as the bureaucrats wanted me out. I wanted to land on a turf where intelligence operations could be conducted efficiently and aggressively.

My Rogue State Initiative had worked well, but when it came time to make the move, the Agency got cold feet and cancelled the assignment. It was as I'd predicted, and I sympathized with them. Imagine the paperwork if I were to be picked up by the security service without any diplomatic immunity.

"Well," I said, "who wants to live in that hellhole anyway?" But with the Rogue State Initiative over, my continued overseas service was in jeopardy.

THE STATION CONTINUED its stand-down and developed a theory that the European Union was acting as a single counterintelligence service, targeting American intelligence officers throughout Europe. The station urged the Agency to shut down operations on the entire continent. I thought it was all hogwash.

All I knew for sure is that they wanted me out of there. They'd gotten rid of the other active officers. My continued presence chafed them.

They began to imagine, or to claim to imagine, that I was blown to all the European intelligence services. The theory was painfully simple: I traveled to countries outside Europe, specifically countries in the former Soviet Union and rogue states in the Middle East and North Africa. It was a catch-22: the mere fact of conducting intelligence operations where they needed to be conducted meant I was blown.

In truth, I'd been operating in the field for a long time, and the CIA was a leaky ship. Maybe Ames, Nicholson, Hanssen, or other, undiscovered, moles had given my name to foreign intelligence services. Maybe one of the 17,000 documents on the personal computer of former DCI Deutch had had my name and identity in it. Maybe my name was in the classified Agency documents found in the home of the State Department officer suspected of spying for Taiwan. Maybe, maybe, maybe—in any case, Salieri and his crew would have said I was blown. They didn't want to do any work.

REPRESENTATIVES OF four layers of management met me in a large room in a handsomely furnished Maryland office. The Agency had expanded so much that it no longer fit inside the HQs building; it had rented dozens of buildings in the Washington area. This one was in an expensive office building with a nice view. The other tenants were law firms and investment banks. The Agency space was cavernous and mostly empty.

"Ishmael," they said, "Salieri sends us messages every day asking when the hell we're going to get you out of there."

"Yeah," I said. "They don't like me. I don't like them either. They won't conduct or allow any operations, and I want off their turf. What's available overseas?"

"Well, unfortunately, as you know, your Rogue State assignment fell through, and we don't have anything else. We want you to come back to HQs. When you get back, we'll work on setting up your next assignment. You shouldn't have to be back at HQs long before you get overseas again."

"I've never seen a colleague return to HQs who *ever* served overseas again," I said. "I won't subject my wife to a year in the Oakwood to find out. Let's think about what the President would want—*fewer* officers overseas bringing him WMD intel?"

The next day a manager approached and offered me a job as the deputy chief at HQs in charge of a group of clandestine spies. He was trying to help out; he figured it was a good job. I thanked him, but declined the offer. My motives weren't pure. I knew I didn't have the stamina to last long in the belly of the bureaucracy, with its endless, deadening meetings.

The next day the same manager approached and offered me a similar job, one layer up from the one he'd offered the day before. "Thanks for the promotion," I said, "but I'm not trying to negotiate. I'm here to serve my country. That won't happen in an HQs assignment.

"Look, let's think about what the President wants. He wants spies bringing him intelligence from overseas, not more managers at HQs. Let's think as if the President were in the room with us now. 'Mr. President, do you want Ishmael bringing you intelligence on WMD or do you want him sitting around at HQs?'"

"Ishmael, I really wish you'd cut out that 'what the President wants' bit."

IN MY NEXT MEETING at HQs, I met three layers of managers in a room.

One said, "We don't want any more singleton officers overseas."

I'd never heard the term. "What's a singleton?"

"A case officer who operates alone. You're a singleton. We need to structure our officers overseas so they work as teams. The singleton concept is outdated. It's over."

"But espionage is a one-on-one activity," I said. "A case officer meets the agent in a hotel room and gets the intelligence. No one else should be present. It's a lonely job. That's what espionage *is*—being a singleton."

"At your grade, Ishmael, you should be a manager. People at HQs are asking why someone at your grade is a singleton."

"I manage human sources. Before Salieri's stand-down, I was managing five of the most deadly threats to Americans in the world today. What else do we need? Congress gave the Agency billions of dollars to fund singletons overseas."

They offered me an assignment to lead a group of case officers overseas who would target human sources in WMD. The officers were newly trained and HQs figured they needed guidance. I'd always enjoyed passing along my tricks of the trade to new case officers, so it sounded like the assignment would be a winner.

IT WAS TRUE that targeting WMD sources worldwide—and teaching other officers how to do it, too—sounded like it had great potential.

But for the same reasons that similar groups had failed, this one was doomed. If one of the officers had a security incident, it would be linked to the others, and all of them would be given their one-way tickets home.

Dave, an old acquaintance of mine, had been involved in setting up the group. He was known to be a CIA officer by at least one hostile foreign intelligence service. If HQs wanted to shut down the unit, they could do it based on Dave's participation alone. He'd rented and furnished an office that looked just like a US government one, so I planned to shut it down and to open another somewhere else.

I planned to de-link the officers, especially from Dave. That way, I'd be able to prevent HQs from arguing that the compromising of one officer would blow the whole station. In fact, I also planned to demote myself by reducing the office to a mere "platform" rather than a formal base or station, in order to avoid the ire of turf bureaucrats.

I met the officers assigned to the platform. They were talented and energetic. A couple of them were inactive, not out of laziness but because no one had taught them how to conduct operations. Others were dynamos, living on airplanes and in hotel rooms, attending a new seminar or summit every few days. HQs loved them, but it was speed dating: lots of activity, but no deals getting closed.

I began to teach basic tradecraft—along with some techniques of my own—to the new trainees. Some officers had already begun to conduct operations, and I instructed them in basic recruitment techniques. Happy that things were proceeding successfully, I traveled to HQs with a list of things I needed to get done.

When I walked into HQs, something smelled wrong. The secretary ushered me past the cubicles and offices to my new boss's corner office. Heads popped up out of the cubicles to take a look at me as I passed.

I shook hands with the boss. "Thanks again for this opportunity," I said. "I'm really excited about the progress we're making already, and I have a list of items to cover."

He squirmed. "Um—you haven't heard the news, have you? We learned last week that your assignment has been cancelled. Someone should have told you. I don't know why. Something having to do with counterintelligence, I think. That's all I can say."

I was disappointed, needless to say. I left his office and prowled around HQs looking for anyone who could tell me why my assignment had been cancelled. No one knew a thing. I wanted a decent explanation, and demanded meetings with progressively higher layers of management.

AFTER A FEW DAYS of sorting through the layers, I met a division's chief of operations, called a COPS. He invited me into his office. "Here's why your assignment was cancelled," he said, and he showed me an email.

It was from Salieri. It said: "Ishmael should be removed from his assignment because he is blown to a sophisticated foreign intelligence service with worldwide reach. Exposing the group of new officers to him would be dangerous."

"Thanks for showing me the email," I said. "Salieri's lying—I'm not blown—but I understand the position you're in." Having received such an email, the COPS had had no choice but to end my assignment.

I WAS ANGRY WITH Salieri and I sent him a message: "That email you sent cancelled my assignment. I'm not blown to any foreign intelligence service. What's going on?"

"I don't know anything about that email," he answered.

Emails are not officially recorded documents. I wasn't supposed to have seen his message, so he figured he could deny its existence.

"That email cancelled my assignment," I replied. "Since it was false, and you say you don't know anything about it, it should be a simple thing for you to retract it and get my assignment going again."

"I don't know anything about it. There will be no further discussion of this issue."

SALIERI WAS A TOP MANDARIN, and he had a lot of pull at HQs. The platform assignment was dead. It had been located in a nearby country, not on Salieri's turf, but much too close for comfort. Rumors that I was blown to a sophisticated intel service helped squash any further assignments.

I kept repeating my line: I'm not blown, and I can be anywhere in the world within 24 hours to conduct important intel operations. But HQs just wanted to give me that one-way ticket home.

I met in a room with four layers of management. We sat at a round imitation wood table in a conference room, with the window shades closed and the lights on. The top-ranking bureaucrat did all the talking, and the others nodded.

"How are your wife's foreign languages?" the bureaucrat asked.

"Pretty good."

"So she can read and converse well, but she doesn't sound like a native?"

"That's right."

"Well, her languages are going to get a lot better, once she's picked up by the police."

I thought I understood, but wanted to make sure. "You mean she'll be able to practice plenty in jail."

"You got it." His three underlings nodded in agreement.

"Come on, you guys, don't do this. You know this is bullshit. Salieri claims he didn't even send the email saying I was blown. But I'm not blown. You know it and I know it."

But I couldn't convince anyone. I was rumored to be blown and I also had powerful enemies, like Salieri. He knew the other bureaucrats would close ranks behind him.

WITH MY SITUATION still in limbo, HQs ordered me to bring my family to the United States for physicals. We were all in fine health.

The phone rang in our hotel room with a call from HQs. "Your family must remain in the United States. You may return overseas alone, but only for the purpose of packing and shipping your household goods. Once you have completed that, you are to proceed directly to an assignment at HQs."

No other assignment possibilities appeared. My contact at HQs told me they'd tried to find me something in the Middle East, but the chief there had asked, "Well, okay, but he wouldn't be doing any actual operations, would he?"

I didn't see any way out. I didn't plan to stumble around the HQs basement, a pariah, stinking of failure, with my family living in the Oakwood.

Had I been in the Marine Corps, I would have obeyed instantly, unthinkingly. The Marine Corps issued orders for the benefit of the United States. CIA orders were issued for the convenience of the bureaucracy.

"It's been a good run," I said, "but it's the end of the line for me. Process me for resignation. Get the paperwork ready and I'll be there next week to sign the papers and leave the Agency."

I TRAVELED BACK to HQs to resign. The lower-level people said they were sorry to see me go, and I appreciated their kind words. I'd known some of them for many years. They were good people, trying to do their jobs as best they understood them.

I had an 0900 meeting in a conference room at HQs. I paced back and forth outside the room. There was a selection of snacks spread out on a counter outside the room, and a fat man swayed back and forth, evaluating his choices.

"Take one of each," I suggested.

The door to the conference room opened and five layers of managers invited me in.

"You need to demonstrate faith in the Agency," they said. "If we tell you we have information indicating that you're blown, you need to trust us."

"There are five layers of managers in this room. You all claim to know the details of my blown cover, but you won't tell me. Yet I'm the only one in here with a 'need to know.' This is just risk aversion. We all know it."

"If you don't have trust in the Agency, then you must leave."

"You're right, and I'm leaving."

They changed their tone and spoke kindly, encouraging me to stay in the Agency. My case was unusual because my career had been spotless. I'd outlasted almost everyone and had a solid reputation as an officer.

★ 16 ★

Headquarters

> You have been in the village a few
> days and already think you know
> everything better than everyone here.
> *Kafka*, The Castle

It's not possible to quit the CIA as one would a normal job. It takes at least a week to check out, especially for someone who's been in the Agency as long as I had.

It was a bittersweet time for me. I hated to leave with the mission incomplete, and I figured that although my career was broken, maybe I could figure out a way to spark reform, to bring improvement to the Agency.

The charges I leveled, with the impunity afforded by my pending resignation, were strong. Our intelligence targets were available, but the Agency was unwilling to contact them. We'd built expensive offices, programs, and layers of management, the only result being the fabrication of stand-downs. I knew the identities of our targets in rogue states, and I knew that we simply weren't doing anything about them.

Also, we'd been given billions of dollars by Congress to put non-State Department officers overseas, and we weren't doing it. The latest I'd heard was that Congress had just given us $3.5 billion, but there wasn't a single overseas assignment available. It wasn't just my problem. There wasn't anyone going out.

I figured that the Inspector General would be a good place to start, so I made a call.

"You can come by at any time tomorrow without an appointment," I was told. "We have a desk officer on duty who can answer your questions. Most of us come in by 0700, but we like to settle in with coffee and donuts. Maybe it would be better if you came in after 0730."

The next day, I drove to the HQs building and made my way through the massive parking lot. A friend had said that his impression on his first day of employment was of pride and excitement, but his impression on his second day was of middle-aged people, heads down, trudging through the dark from their far-off parking spaces.

I found the IG office, buried deep in the interior of the HQs building. The receptionist directed me to take a seat in a padded, soundproof room.

A few minutes later, a woman came in and sat down.

I introduced myself. "I'm here," I said, "to discuss my concern that the Agency is not pursuing human intelligence targets. We're structurally risk-averse, and that translates into an unwillingness or inability to do our duty."

She looked at me closely. "What agency are you from?"

"*The* Agency," I replied.

"Which office?"

I described my office within the clandestine service.

"Are you from the FBI? Are you a law enforcement officer, or a member of the office of security?"

"No."

"So you're not here to conduct a security investigation?"

"No, I'm here to ask what I can do—"

"Well, I was expecting an appointment with a law enforcement officer or someone from our office of security. I don't think you're the person I'm supposed to meet."

She got up and left the room.

Another woman entered the room and introduced herself. She described the IG grievance process, in which an employee can bring up a problem within a certain number of days after the incident in question. She said that the IG then studies the complaint and 60 days later issues an opinion.

My statement, that we didn't have any good human sources of intelligence and that we needed to get some, seemed to confuse the woman. The IG wasn't set up to handle that particular situation.

"I don't think the grievance procedure is the right thing for what I have in mind. Congress might be the right place for me to go. They control the money. Can you tell me the proper way to contact them, so that I can make sure I'm in compliance with the appropriate procedures?"

She seemed relieved to be able to conclude our meeting. She gave me the phone number of an office on the seventh floor of the HQs building, the department responsible for communications between the Agency and the Congress.

A few months later, I determined the reason for this misunderstanding. The IG itself was under investigation. In April of 2006, a CIA employee named Mary O. McCarthy was fired from her job in the Office of the IG. According to a *New York Times* article on April 25, 2006, "A CIA spokeswoman, Jennifer Millerwise Dyck, said: 'The officer was terminated for precisely the reasons we have given: unauthorized contacts with reporters and sharing classified information with reporters. There is no question whatsoever that the officer did both. The officer personally admitted doing both.'"

Other media accounts speculated that McCarthy was the source of information on the Agency's secret interrogation facilities in foreign countries, though the Agency did not confirm the exact nature of the classified information she'd given to reporters. The reporters who wrote the articles on the interrogation facilities won a Pulitzer Prize.

I don't remember the name of the woman I met at the IG's office. She may have been Mary McCarthy; she may have been another IG employee awaiting a meeting with a law enforcement officer as part of the investigation. The IG's office had been expecting someone from the security department that morning for an investigation of their office, and they'd mistaken me for the investigator.

I CALLED THE OFFICE responsible for dealing with Congress. They said they'd give me the information I needed to contact members of Congress and their staffs in a proper fashion. They also offered to help me set up my appointments.

Grace, a former analyst who had helped me find WMD targets, had since moved to a job on the seventh floor of CIA HQs. She heard what I was up to and she mentioned it to CIA director Porter Goss. She told Goss in so many words that I wasn't such a bad guy.

Goss wanted to find out what was going on, so he set an appointment for me to meet him at 1000 the next morning.

After that meeting, I'd go to the security office to turn in my badge and leave HQs for good. My resignation papers were signed and everything was set. After I left HQs, I'd go over to Capitol Hill to see what I could get done.

WHEN I GOT BACK to my hotel room that night, the light on my phone was blinking. Six frantic voicemail messages told me to contact HQs. They'd learned that I was meeting Goss the next day and they were in a panic.

My meeting with Goss would be at 1000. HQs scheduled an earlier (0830) meeting with a deputy director of the CIA.

MEANWHILE, a weird incident occurred back home. My family, unauthorized by the Agency, had continued to live on Salieri's turf in Europe. My children were back in school and one of them had been recommended to receive a community service award. A group of parents gathered at school to review and make the award.

An OFTPOT from the CIA station showed up, badgered my son with inappropriate questions, and argued that my son did not merit the award. Of course, the OFTPOT didn't reveal that his office and I were in the midst of a disagreement, or that it was illegal for him to know my or my family's identity. Fortunately, the other parents overruled him, and the award was granted.

DRIVING EAST on Route 123 in McLean, I turned left in a long line of traffic into CIA headquarters. I held out my badge to the security guard who waved me through the barricades, drove past the machine gun mounted Humvee painted in camouflage, and veered right toward the massive parking lots behind the building. At the northeast entrance I entered my security code, and then walked past a row of a dozen electric carts standing ready to be driven down the corridors by infirm or "plus-sized" employees. Labels with names like "Eunice" on them identified the owners.

An escort took me up to the deputy director's office.

I explained my situation in words that I'd memorized. "I'm a successful case officer with a strong and unblemished record," I said. "A fabricated stand-down and a fraudulent accusation that my cover is blown have ended my ability to do my duty and I'm left with no option but to resign."

He'd studied my case the night before and he knew all the details. "You're not the only person who thinks the Agency can do a better job. There are other US government organizations that would like to take away big chunks of our turf. The Executive Director, Dusty Foggo, is aware of your case and is watching closely. What do we need to do to solve the problem?"

"I need an overseas assignment. I can go to Dulles airport, get on a plane, and within 24 hours be anywhere in the world. All I need is the approval to go. I have a strong record and I've never made an operational mistake."

"I've reviewed your file. What about an assignment to the Middle East. Would that work for you?"

"Thank you," I said. "That would be great."

I LEFT THE MEETING and an escort came to take me to Goss's office. On the walk down the hall, I asked the escort, "What's your job here?"

"I'm the special assistant to Porter Goss," he said.

"That sounds like a fast-track job."

"Actually, I came over from Congress with him. My name is Patrick Murray."

"I've heard of you," I said. Murray was the one who had fired a couple of mandarins when he and Goss had first arrived at the CIA. Murray had a reputation as a tough political infighter. He showed me through the heavy oak door to Goss's office.

"Thank you, sir," I said, "for giving me this opportunity to meet you."

I'd never said "sir" to anyone in the Agency before.

Goss shook my hand and said, "I heard that you're thinking of resigning. I asked to set this appointment. We're building up our clandestine capabilities, and if one of our most experienced non-State Department officers is leaving, I need to know why." He seemed genuinely concerned.

"I've been operating overseas for many years straight, in many different locations, and it's been a good run. The idea of getting out of our embassies is a good one, but the bureaucracy sees it as a threat. All of my colleagues from my training class and from a few of the preceding and following ones are long gone.

"We've been given billions of dollars to build up this non-State Department program. During the last decade, we've spent billions more. With all of these billions, we don't have even one more officer overseas than we did before.

"The bureaucracy has treated me better than most, and it looked like my number was finally up. But just before coming in this morning, I learned that a Middle East assignment is available."

Goss must have been good at dealing with constituents during his long career as a congressman. He listened attentively and I believed that he was an honest man.

"What can we do to solve your particular situation?"

"It looks like it's solved. The deputy director opened an assignment for me to the Middle East. I have a experience in the region and can regenerate old contacts and build new ones immediately."

"Let's get to it, then."

I thanked him and left his office. I headed back to the personnel department and reversed my resignation. Then I went to make arrangements for my travel to the Middle East.

BACK AT THE HOLDING TANK, everyone laughed. "You didn't really solve anything, did you? After all the noise you made, you've wound up in the same pitiful Middle East assignment you had when you started out in the organization."

I called my wife on the phone and she laughed, too, but added, "If you think you can achieve something meaningful there, let's go."

I was smarter and more experienced than I'd been during our past assignment to the region, and with the freedom to travel the world, I knew I could achieve great things. I was starting anew and was full of enthusiasm and momentum.

I roamed the HQs building, meeting desk officers to find new leads and to confirm that I'd be able to restart cases that had been stopped during the stand-down.

Most of the people I visited at HQs desks seemed truly enthusiastic about my new assignment, so I probed them for operational ideas. A couple of desks said, "We're interested in this target, right here, and this is his phone number." Such specific targets are golden and I took notes and planned to get to work on them right away.

A big-bellied guy ran one of the desks.

He leaned back and said, "I don't know who you are. You'll have to tell me about yourself before you can expect to do anything in our region. Send me something." He droned and pontificated. "Sure, we'd like a real case officer—well, er—or an *almost* real case officer, though we haven't had a lot of luck with people like you." He listed some of the failed operations run by "people like me."

I interrupted: "What are your plans? Will you be in this position for a while?"

He sighed. "Well, I was headed out to be the chief in a 'Stan, but I failed my Box. They told me I'll be here until it's all cleared up. They haven't given me a time frame, but it could be a year or two." I was glad I hadn't snapped at this man. His life was in limbo, suspected of a security violation that he probably hadn't committed. The poor slob's career was probably over, and he was going through a rough time. That's why he was acting like a stick in the mud.

The proportion of HQs desks with good ideas, though, was quite high—at least a third of the desks I spoke to had specific targets they wanted me to call. Even the big-bellied guy had a lead or two.

I compiled all of this information and developed several operational proposals: for a rogue state ambassador, a rogue state nuclear scientist, and a rogue state chemical weapons scientist. I sent the proposals to the new base I'd be working for in the Middle East. I had a dozen more at hand to send if and when those were approved. Plus I was regenerating the cases that Salieri had shut down.

When I walked out of HQs that night, I ran into Loman. "Hey, congratulations on your son's community service award," he said. "Say, what's this I hear about the award not being merited?" The OFTPOT who'd been on the panel had telephoned people at HQs and told them that the boy wasn't really qualified. In our supposedly secretive organization, word had traveled to Loman, and Loman had told me, all in the space of about 36 hours. The pettiness was unimaginable—or all too imaginable, I should say.

"Loman, I'm going to hurt that OFTPOT."

I didn't mean it, but I knew my comment would travel right back to the OFTPOT and give him something to worry about.

Starting Over

We shall not cease from exploration
And the end of all our exploring
Will be to arrive where we started
And know the place for the first time.

T.S. Eliot

I got on a plane and went to the Middle East. I found places in school for my kids and made sure I had plenty of cash available. I took a temporary apartment and office and began making tentative arrangements for permanent ones. My residence paperwork and company documents were in order. What ordinarily might take months took a couple of days because I was familiar with the region already.

There had been growth in building construction, but nothing much else had changed. The long-term residents were still there. Everywhere I walked I saw familiar faces. I went to dinner with old friends and I dropped by the clubs to which I'd belonged. I drove by the old house we'd lived in, remembering my young children playing in the front yard.

Nothing had come back yet on my first batch of requests for operational approval. I sent more proposals to regenerate cases on hold since my last post. I was particularly interested in two nuclear scientists with good access. I was proud of my lineup: It represented some of our most important targets throughout several rogue states.

HQs sent me an urgent message: They needed intelligence from one of my targets about his country's weapons program—and they needed it immediately. President Bush was preparing to make a decision and HQs wanted to provide the information he needed to do so. My target wasn't that useful, and he was only in the developmental stage, not yet formally recruited. But he was the best we had. I typed a request to cold pitch the target, and added it to the requests I'd sent to the local base.

The structure of the local Agency office had changed since I'd been there years before. Back then, it was just the chief and me. My chief had been twenty years older than I was and outranked me by three pay grades. Now, the base consisted of a chief, a deputy chief, and a branch chief. It appeared that I'd be at the bottom of the decision-making chain. Also, the chief and his wife were OFT-POTs, which meant that the wife represented yet another boss to get through.

While I awaited responses, HQs contacted me and told me to come back to the US for another seminar.

I MET MY COLLEAGUES at a conference in a US city and we exchanged greetings.

One colleague had been involved in interrogating captured terrorists. There had been no torture involved. The man got the subjects to talk by spending a lot of time with them and speaking kindly to them while asking questions. "Most of the prisoners," he said, "were scared, ignorant kids. We'd bring a terrorist in, get the information, contact foreign governments, and they'd send their police out to capture the guys right away. The information they provided led to dramatic captures worldwide, sometimes of people who were right on the verge of pulling off major attacks."

My colleague had been working on the interrogations for more than two years, and had seen little of his family during that time. The interrogations had provided most of the information that the CIA possessed about ongoing terrorist operations.

An employee at the IG office at HQs, however, had leaked

information on the interrogation centers to the *Washington Post*, which put an end to my colleague's work. Although he'd done some of the Agency's most important work, he found when he returned to HQs that he was "radioactive." No one would talk to him.

Many of the officers at the conference were new to the Agency, having been hired after the major purges. Some of them were still in their on-the-job training assignments in Washington, D.C.

The speakers took the stage. Lining the back and sides of our conference room were administrative support people, all of them enormous. At noon, they ordered out to a fast-food burger joint. Conversations went dead while they fed from elaborate, high-calorie platters. As in the last two decades, the speakers' theme was the coming increase in the Agency's non-State Department programs. One of them told me later, in private, "as soon as HQs gets all the money from Congress, they'll declare failure and move on to something else. We'll never see the numbers overseas that HQs has been promising."

Congress had recently asked the Agency how many new personnel it had hired as non-State Department officers. The Agency created a number by tallying all of the support staff, the officers in training, and the people who were assigned to posts in the United States. The number looked good.

After President Bush gave his "Axis of Evil" speech, the Agency began sending my colleagues on missions to these and other rogue states. They didn't conduct any intelligence operations there—just visited, stayed in hotels, and returned to write detailed after-action reports about their itineraries. HQs briefed Congress about all of them. This became known around HQs as Axis of Evil Tourism.

Each day, I checked to see whether approval had come in to cold pitch the weapons target. Nothing.

At the conference we separated into small groups to brainstorm about obstinate operational problems, for example, how to recruit political leaders in rogue states. I was the moderator for

my group, and I had a hard time getting my colleagues to cooperate. One would come up with an idea and the others would
compete to list the reasons why it couldn't be done. "No one is
allowed to use the word 'can't,'" I said. "No one is allowed to criticize an idea by telling us why it might *not* work." Once they felt
free to offer thoughts without fear of pointless nay saying, they
came up with some good ideas.

Speakers told us that the Agency needed more bodies for
assignments in Iraq, Pakistan, and Afghanistan, and it looked
like we'd have to supply about six people from our group in the
upcoming months. The man sitting next to me whispered, "I have
a solution. We can fill the requirement for people by sending our
six layers of managers: Hilda, Ernie, Bruce, Vic, Elwood, and Gro-
ver will do nicely. Then they'll be doing productive work in Iraq,
and things will run better at HQs, too."

Most of my colleagues were unenthusiastic about going to
Iraq, Afghanistan, or Pakistan. They practiced their excuses. They
were too old, or too new; an officer had a girlfriend he couldn't
leave behind, a gay officer had a partner he couldn't leave
behind.

"What are we, some kind of paramilitary organization?" a colleague asked.

"Well, yes, actually, we are," said another.

The Agency was having a hard time finding people to fill posts
in Iraq. The problem could have been solved by recognizing service there with a commendation or medal, for example, or by
accelerating promotions and giving choice assignments to employees who served there. Instead, service in Iraq was thought to be
for suckers: newly trained people, or those who had no influence or connections within the organization. No mandarins had
considered going to Iraq. The CIA is a civilian organization, and
employees could refuse, especially if they came from divisions
other than the Middle East one.

STILL NO WORD on my request to cold pitch the weapons target. These operational requests crossed a lot of turfs. I needed approval from my local base, despite the fact that it wasn't involved in any way. I needed the go-ahead from Agency elements in charge of the target's home country, those in charge of the European country turf where I planned to meet the target, and those in charge of the nuclear proliferation issue, all of which were large sprawling bureaucracies of their own. So far I couldn't even get past the local base.

In the end, the cold pitch didn't happen—it was too late. The President had to make a decision without the benefit of the information we may have been able to provide, all because the local chief was too frightened to grant approval. It's not certain that I could have provided the necessary intelligence. It's not certain that the decision was a crucial one. But I'm certain we let down President Bush and Condoleezza Rice (who, by the way, would know exactly what decision I mean). I regret having done nothing; I should have gone ahead anyway.

Things didn't look good, and that was business as usual. My proposals terrified the chief. I should have proceeded slowly, but I'd misjudged the momentum I'd built up and acted too quickly. The new spirit I'd felt after meeting Goss had led me to believe that things would be different, but they weren't—not one bit.

The base sent me a copy of the list of their activities for the previous month. They looked busy, but on closer reading the list was heavily padded—a lot of activity, sure, but no targets of any consequence. My heart sank. I began to wonder whether I was getting too old and tired to grapple with the beast any longer.

AFTER A MONTH in the Middle East, responses began to dribble in. The first ones dealt with the possible locations of my permanent office and home. Instead of a yes or no answer, the responses were a vague, "That neighborhood might be okay."

Then came long lists of questions about my operational proposals, as well as reasons why things might go wrong. When I answered the questions, more followed. The time it was taking them to come to a decision was making it impossible to move the operations forward. In one case—I'd already met the target multiple times—the chief asked, "What will you tell him when he asks you where you got his name?"

My colleague Loman had been assigned to a country in North Africa. He reported directly to HQs, cutting a local Agency station out of the loop. Still, he received no replies to his requests for approval.

Finally, he flew to HQs, found a computer terminal, and answered his own requests, approving all of them. He returned to North Africa and carried out his operations. When he needed new approvals, he traveled back to HQs and sent them to himself. He continued to answer his own messages for about six months before he was caught.

HQs managers were livid, and the story spread throughout HQs, making Loman infamous. In the end, incredibly, he escaped with nothing more than a stern warning not to do it again.

I'D NEVER MET my direct boss in this new Middle East assignment, so I asked him to meet me. I thought that, face to face, I might be able to convince him to approve my operational proposals. During my earlier assignment to the Middle East, I'd met colleagues in car pickup meetings in the region. Today, that was considered too risky, so we'd need to meet in the US. I flew back just for the appointment.

At HQs, I walked past the statue of the Agency's illustrious founder, "Wild Bill" Donovan, and portraits of the DCIs from Donovan to the failures and weaklings of the 1990s: William "Mild Bill"

Webster, Bobby Gates, Woolsey, Deutch, and Tired Tenet. I waited in a conference room for the chief to arrive.

He didn't show up. Incredibly, he'd sent his wife in his place. She seemed gray and exhausted, and her breath wheezed from her with considerable effort. Her body language, however, suggested that she thought she was my boss. She probably was.

She explained how she and her husband had come to be employed with the Agency. Either she'd got the job and then brought her husband on board, or vice versa, but I don't recall.

"What sorts of human sources are you handling?" I asked.

"I don't handle cases," she said. "I'm a manager."

She expected deference from me, but she seemed like a nice person, and she was the closest thing to a direct boss I'd met in a long time. As I'd guessed, the office was just scared of my operational proposals. They'd never asked that I be sent to their turf, and then immediately upon my arrival I'd begun peppering them with what they perceived to be very high-risk proposals.

She described the operations they were conducting at the office. It was a full plate, but all of the offerings were trivial. They met with liaison contacts, went to diplomatic parties, and spent a lot of time on the Internet searching résumé and employment databases for leads.

"You should search the Internet for leads," she counseled, nodding sagely.

I RETURNED to the Middle East and sank into a bleak mood. I'd never be able to push intelligence operations through all these timid bureaucrats. I sat and stared at the wall for hours at a time.

I had mastered the psychology of the organization and could have stayed in an overseas assignment forever had I wanted to, but I'd had more than enough. Maybe it really *was* over. I was at a dead end. I'd played my hand. Further attempts to conduct operations—serious ones, at least—would be hopeless. Agency management had been so evasive during the last year and a half that it wasn't even clear for which bureaucrat I was working. Although I'd sunk into a mental swamp, I remembered how many of my colleagues had fallen apart physically, too, and I determined that it wouldn't happen to me. I got up out of my chair and jogged each day through the same desert fields that I had many years ago, along the same paths. I was filled with sorrow, knowing that my chance to do all that I could for my country was fast slipping away.

IN MAY 2006, Porter Goss resigned. He was a good man but the bureaucracy had ground him down.

A week later, Executive Director Dusty Foggo resigned under suspicion of corruption. More than 30 agents from various law enforcement agencies raided Foggo's office and home.[59] On February 13, 2007, Foggo was indicted for corruption in connection with the probe of Randy "Duke" Cunningham, a former congressman now in jail.[60] News articles stated that Goss had appointed Foggo, which was true, but Goss had appointed Foggo on the recommendation of HQs mandarins. Goss had had his own choice for Executive Director.

The first act of the incoming director, Michael Hayden, was to promote Suspenders, who had been pushed aside by Goss. Suspenders was still infamous among my colleagues for his statement, "In my career at the Agency, I have never seen a case of risk aversion." Hayden thought that bringing Suspenders back would be good for Agency morale. But no one I knew had missed Suspenders.

Hayden had been an Air Force general and there were mutterings that the military might be taking over the CIA. The mutterings went away when the bureaucracy realized that Hayden was one of them. He was a military man, but also a Pentagon general. His first messages to the workforce dealt with "diversity as a mission-critical job" and messages of appreciation to his underlings, addressing them by first name, "Chip has done such a wonderful job, but we are happy to see him move on to his new position as chief of . . . ."

During the spring of 2006, American intelligence activities in Europe shut down.

The Agency had been terrified of conducting intel operations in France for a long time. Then the Italian station sent a cable to Agency offices worldwide stating that it did not intend to approve travel by Agency employees for operations in Italy because hotel rooms were difficult to reserve from early spring to late fall.

It sounds unbelievable, but it's a fact.

The station in Switzerland must have thought that this sounded like a good idea; they sent a pan-Agency memo as well, stating that hotel rooms were awfully difficult to get and they didn't want anyone to try to work in Switzerland from early spring to late fall.

The station in Germany was next, stating that due to the upcoming World Cup games in Germany, there would be heightened security in Germany, and of course hotel rooms would be booked up, so there could be no intelligence operations in Germany. Just in case anyone were to try, the station established prohibitively complicated paperwork requirements for any officer seeking work there.

No one seemed to find it unusual that a major part of the Agency's operational territory had just been shut down. America doesn't need to spy on the Germans, French, Italians, or Swiss—they are free people who pose no threat to the United States—but Europe is the world's crossroads, the best place to find and meet human sources involved in WMD and terrorism. Shutting down Europe eliminates at least half of the Agency's ability to target valuable sources.

I drafted my letter of resignation. I had logged enough years with the Agency to qualify for a pension, except for the small detail that I wasn't old enough. I could have lingered for a few more years without doing anything and then collected the pension, but that wasn't the life I'd set out to lead.

JUST AS I WAS ABOUT to submit my second and final letter of resignation, I received an unusual message from HQs: It ordered me—along with seven of my colleagues—to report immediately to Iraq. The war wasn't going well and the Agency needed more bodies. My wife and I discussed the message and agreed that I should go. I was still ready to quit the Agency, but I wanted to leave on a high note; I couldn't leave without doing my part in Iraq. America was in trouble there, and I'd done nothing about it. Perhaps my assignment would open up a more active and aggressive side of the Agency.

I departed for HQs the next day to prepare.

I'd noticed that in the order, HQs had forgotten to inform my local base chief, and I took advantage of that omission. When calls for volunteers had circulated in the past for any operation, including Iraq, I had volunteered, and my local chief had always blocked it. The current chief hadn't wanted me on his turf and didn't want me doing intelligence operations, but to have me taken away was an affront to his turf.

When I was back in HQs and my assignment to Iraq was locked in, I wrote a polite message to the base chief apologizing that I hadn't gotten to him sooner. HQs apologized for not copying him on the message traffic.

He went berserk, responding with a torrent of threats and insults.

To help calm things down, I wrote, "I am going to Iraq as ordered by HQs to work on our nation's most important missions. I've apologized to you, and HQs has apologized to you, for informing you a week late. Begin disciplinary proceedings against me if you wish, but there will be no more apologies. A man going to serve his country in Iraq shouldn't be attacked by bureaucrats who refuse to serve there themselves."

Of the eight of us ordered to Iraq, I'd said yes immediately. One said no. Two said, "Yes, but it will take me a few months before I will be ready to go." Four said, "I most definitely am eager and ready to go immediately, but with the important activities I am currently undertaking, it may take some time before I can break away."

After 9/11, the Agency had few people with military qualifications, and it was jarring for most employees to contemplate going from an office or State Department embassy to a combat zone. Going to a war zone wasn't necessarily good for one's career. One former Agency mandarin had turned down three requests that he report to Vietnam. Instead, he found a pleasant assignment elsewhere. Had he gone to Vietnam, he would have been evacuated along with hundreds of other case officers when Saigon fell. These officers, suddenly unemployed, wandered the halls of HQs looking for assignments. "While they were now searching for jobs, I proceeded to have one of the finest and most productive assignments of my career," he wrote.[61]

★ 18 ★

Remington Raider

> The wave of the future is not
> the conquest of the world by a
> single dogmatic creed but the
> liberation of the diverse energies
> of free nations and free men.
> *John F. Kennedy*

HQs was sleepy when I arrived. It was a Friday before a three-day weekend and the place seemed empty. I prepared for travel by getting the necessary ID cards, as well as extra training in first aid and firearms.

The firearms course took place down in redneck country. The instructors wore goatees and baseball caps pulled on tight. Expensive, flashy cars bought with high disposable incomes—$200,000 to $400,000 to a man—filled the parking lot.

I guessed that these firearms-training rednecks were the same ones who'd run the Interrogation Course. I'd never actually seen those men, having had a bag over my head the entire time, but I was sure that I recognized their voices. Curious, I missed a shot with my pistol and shouted, "God damn it!"

"Hey, don't take the Lord's name in vain," a redneck said.

The firearms course taught combat shooting, which means pulling out one's weapon quickly and shooting lots of bullets at close range. The Marine Corps, by contrast, taught steady, slower rates of fire—marksmanship at longer ranges.

I was lucky to be assigned to this course, because the other option for firearms training was at a large Agency training facility where the students slept in open barracks at night. The snoring was reportedly horrendous. It was never a problem in military boot camp because everyone was young. But with a high proportion of middle-aged, out-of-shape men, it could get deafening.

I was the only case officer taking the shooting course. The other members of my course were support personnel. They were solid but introspective, slow to converse. I'm an introvert myself, but I force myself to be outgoing. They were content in silence.

We shot round after round of ammunition and played paintball as well. The rednecks were happy with our shooting, but unhappy with our paintball performance. I was hit many times and was covered with red welts.

Next was a course to familiarize us, to whatever extent was possible, with Iraq. This course was full of people from support positions, as well. One speaker called an assignment to Iraq a "chance of a lifetime," and I agreed. A man sitting next to me said, "One of the many great things about being an American is that we are a warlike people. Imagine if you were from Luxembourg, where combat will never be a possibility. There was a long drought after the Vietnam War when a fellow couldn't find combat no matter how hard he tried, but an American will always be able to find a war if he is patient and waits long enough." I nodded.

Our first aid course emphasized the most basic skill of all: stopping the bleeding. Excessive bleeding was the primary cause of death for Americans in Iraq, so immediate action had to be taken to stop it. Tourniquets were in all first aid kits, and we practiced applying them. The course began with a slide show of nasty wounds, which made some of us feel queasy.

My family visited me the weekend before my departure, and we had a great time. The kids played in the hotel pool. We went to the new aviation museum near Dulles Airport, and later played catch at a nearby school playground. It was nice to enjoy these moments of normalcy before diving into the uncertain.

FINALLY I WAS all ready; we were just about wheels-up for Iraq. Our instructions dictated that no-one wear military-style clothing or bring military gear such as holsters, but I arrived to see our guys wearing crew cuts and "shoot me first" camo trousers. An incoming plane discharged a group of men and I recognized some friends of mine, returning from Afghanistan.

Airplanes arrived at Baghdad Airport at high altitude, and then slowly fluffed down in tight circles, in order to avoid a low-altitude, easy-target glide into the airport.

The air swirled with dust and the wash of helicopters.

When I arrived at my post, a man gave me a bag of sheets and a key to a trailer. I was elated to be in the war zone, but I'd have to face my greatest fear: living with several other men in a small space. My roommates were unhappy to see another person join their little room, but they were nice people, and we were careful to be polite and to obey unspoken rules of order and hygiene.

I dropped off my bags and went to the office. It was midnight, but there were still plenty of people at work.

It was unusual for someone to show up at the station saying, "Here I am, ready for work." Our people were usually assigned to a specific job, with someone to greet them upon arrival. I found one of the office's managers and we chatted for a while, but then he told me to return in the morning.

I lay awake in bed all night, jetlagged but happy. It was different from the first night I'd spent in a bunk in Marine boot camp. There, after a day of pushups and harassment, I'd asked myself, "What have I gotten myself into?" In Iraq, I was so excited I could hardly sleep. Everything was new—everything surreal. I couldn't wait for morning to come, and I checked my watch every half hour.

I reported to the office in the morning. The managers held a conference. I was neither fish nor fowl; as someone coming in from the field, I wasn't part of their system of management layers and didn't want to be. The only thing I knew how to do was to gather intelligence. The office's managers recognized this and set me to work with a network of Iraqi agents.

I grabbed the keys to an armored car and within hours I had begun my first agent meetings. That night, I found a desk in the office, spread out the notes I had gathered that day, and began producing my first reports. I had a lot to learn about the way the Agency operated in an office setting. I didn't know how to use the telephone system or the office equipment. I spent the first night hammering away at the computer, anxious to get my reports into the proper format so that they'd be useful. During that first week, I slept when I could, a few hours here and a few hours there.

CIA people in Iraq were a different breed. Some were brilliant, many were fluent Arabic speakers, and all of them were brave. At daily office meetings, I was impressed by my colleagues' grasp of the situation. They were the sharpest people in the Agency. The pace was fast, and it wasn't unusual to hear, "We killed these guys last night. We'll kill these other guys tonight."

The hardest thing to understand, as always, was the bureaucracy. For example, for one of the reports I was writing, I wanted to know more about a certain area near Fallujah. I went to the trailer office of an Army representative, and he gave me a lesson on the environment in that neighborhood of Fallujah. But I'd somehow crossed a bureaucrat's turf—I should have gotten permission from the Agency bureaucrat before speaking to the soldier, and then I should have visited the bureaucrat again to debrief him on my meeting. My first week was hectic because I didn't understand these bureaucratic rules. I had to learn all of the key players and their turfs.

It was a beautiful assignment, nevertheless; by and large, I had the freedom to be out of the office getting things done. The station had as many as eight layers of management whose chains of command looped around and around like tentacles. By being outside the office, working directly with agents, my work was more efficient and better for my mental well-being. Having to kowtow to so many managers would have been difficult.

OUR HUMAN SOURCES represented a potentially huge flow of information. The office's managers recognized this: They had sent me to tap it, after all. The next step was getting it into the system so that it could be put to some use.

The intelligence report formats changed often and I had to keep up. It reminded me of Mark Twain's description of piloting the Mississippi. He wrote that riverboat pilots had to memorize the river—an intricate task, and even more so because the river changed all the time. So pilots first memorized the river, and then spoke to the pilots of passing boats to learn about changes to the stretch ahead. Necessary phrases in intel reports changed, were added or subtracted; spellings changed; everything changed, and all of these changes had to be learned and kept up to date.

The first week I scrambled to help destroy a suicide bomber cell, to find missing US soldiers, to identify improvised explosive devices (IEDs), and to identify the locations of important al Qaeda members. Global positioning system (GPS) coordinates helped pinpoint locations of terrorists and IEDs. The reports were simple and blunt: The IED is located behind the middle post of the guardrail on the south side of the road. The terrorist lives at this address at these coordinates.

I traveled by helicopter to a meeting site, and we landed at the same time as another helicopter. The landings raised dust, and later, the pilot told me he'd been blinded by the dust and had nearly crashed into the other helicopter.

AS THINGS SETTLED DOWN, the phone rang with a call from a friend at HQs. "Hey, that chief from your Middle Eastern assignment is really after you, man. He's back here at HQs, telling anyone who will listen about it." The OFTPOT chief was still angry that I had gone to Iraq without coordinating the assignment with him first. He sought to charge me with a disciplinary offense, as I'd suggested he do, but he hadn't found anyone at HQs willing to take it up.

In fairness, the OFTPOT chief was genuinely hurt by what I'd done and thought I needed to be punished. The Agency had taught him to defend his turf and to demand respect for his role as a manager. He felt as strongly about it as I felt about the Agency's mission.

In the Marine Corps, I'd have been equally unsympathetic to anyone who disobeyed the system. Punishment would have been swift. But then the Marine Corps didn't demand that Marines obey malingerers. The Marine Corps didn't obfuscate when it came time to accomplish the mission. The Marine Corps would never have put a lower-ranking officer and his wife in charge of a higher-ranking officer.

A COLLEAGUE AND I put on our body armor, Kevlar vests with thick metal plates on the chest and back. We loaded our weapons and ammunition into an armored vehicle and went to meet a man with information on a suicide bomber ring.

We picked him up in our armored vehicle and found a shady spot to park.

The cell was composed of young Sunni Muslims in their late teens and early twenties, both men and women. They were targeting groups of American soldiers. The idea was that American soldiers on patrol would be on alert and ready to defend themselves against the approach of young men, but would consider women to be harmless. Thus a female suicide bomber would be able to walk more closely to American positions.

Sunni terrorists tended to follow a stricter brand of Islam that forbade contact between males and females, but the boys and girls needed to communicate in order to plan the attacks. As my colleague and I delved into the details with our source, we realized that the gang's main activity was flirting. The boys and girls spent hours chatting on the phone, ostensibly planning suicide attacks, but really just talking. They hadn't carried out any attacks.

Eventually, though, they'd get around to doing something evil. The leaders of the gang were connected to al Qaeda, and using information provided by our source, the US Army captured the gang's leaders.

ARABS HAVE a powerful sense of hospitality, refined over thousands of years. With human sources, and especially Arab ones, I tried to be as polite, soft-spoken, and well-mannered as possible. As I came to know them, we greeted each other in the traditional style, touching our chests over the heart. Our Arab allies fought in the streets, took incredible risks, and frequently lost their lives.

I worked closely with a case officer named Fuego, a naturalized American of Argentinean origin. He claimed to be descended from both Spanish settlers and the native Fuegians of Tierra del Fuego. He'd been an airport policeman when he was recruited as a CIA agent. The Agency sought foreign-born case officers for their native foreign language abilities. Fuego, with his strong record of reliability as an agent, eventually became a case officer. His English wasn't very good and he didn't speak Arabic. He slipped into Spanish when under stress, and when he sought to be understood, he enunciated Spanish words clearly and loudly. Fuego handled the administrative matters for the agents I met; he paid death benefits to the families of human sources who had been murdered, for example, and kept track of vehicles and firearms.

Fuego had a direct, blunt personality. Questioning a salary and expense payment for an Arab agent, he said, "Damn you, I say, you give me the proper receipt! Are you lying? Are you trying to cheat me?"

To another Arab man, who arrived late for a meeting because of a security road block, he said, "You damn guy, don't be late when you meet me. I'm sick of your bullshit."

Another Arab man, who failed to bring information I'd requested, said he had been unable to get the information because of his obligation to attend family events during Ramadan. I was about to tell him not to worry about it and to get the information when he could, when Fuego interrupted: "I don't care about your Muslim bullshit. You bring information, not excuses."

Despite all this—or perhaps because of it—the Arabs loved him. They recognized that he was a genuine person who cared about them. They understood his personality and weren't offended by it. Indeed, they responded in kind. "Damn you, Fuego," said an Arab agent. "Now you have made me angry for the last time. I am going to give you a nice beating." Everyone laughed.

Fuego liked to arrange dinners and lunches. We ate tasty local food, usually lamb and chicken kabobs. Sometimes we had a fish dish for lunch—big groupers cooked whole, one for each person at the table.

The Iraqis amused themselves during dinners by mocking Fuego in a good-natured way. They encouraged him to tell stories, generally those that brought his cultural difference into sharper relief:

"When I met my wife," Fuego said, "I knew immediately she was the one for me. But first, I needed to give her a test to see for sure that she was the right one."

While his girlfriend was at work, Fuego went to her apartment in suburban Loudoun County, Virginia. He bludgeoned his way through the door, leaving it hanging from one hinge, and ransacked the apartment, pulling out drawers and scattering their contents about the apartment. Then he drove to her workplace and, not telling her what he had done, gave her a ride home.

The Arabs howled with laughter. What with the pandemonium, laughter, shouting, and cursing, not to mention the confusion of English, Arabic, and Spanish, it took a half hour for everyone to settle down so Fuego could explain the point of his test.

He'd been advised to invade his girlfriend's home by one of his village elders in southern Argentina. The point of the test was to assess her ability to handle stress. She reacted calmly to the vandalism of her apartment. She didn't lose her head. She passed. Fuego told her he loved her and proposed, and she joyfully accepted.

But the testing wasn't over. The village elder had also counseled him to test the strength of her love.

He did this by abruptly ending the engagement: "It's over. I have spoken. I will not provide a reason."

Heartbroken and distraught, she stopped eating and drinking. Her family feared for her life and took her to the hospital for treatment.

Her hunger strike convinced Fuego that she'd passed the test of love. He résuméd the engagement and they were married soon thereafter. The story ended, and everyone clapped.

(Later, I wondered whether Fuego's tests might have had unintended consequences. He wondered whether he should extend his assignment in Iraq. His wife thought he should: "Stay there as long as you like, dear. The children and I are doing just fine at home.")

"I have honored you by telling you my deepest, most personal secrets," he said. "But everyone has laughed at me. Now it is time for Ishmael to tell us how he met his wife."

Everyone thought this was a good idea. I didn't need much encouragement, because I considered my story an enchanting tale of love and destiny.

"I enjoyed my time in the Marine Corps," I said, "but I knew that something was missing from my life. One day, while assigned to a lonely post on an island in the Pacific, I had a vision in my mind of a woman and I knew she was the one I would marry.

"When I left the Marine Corps, I went to graduate school. The school held a cocktail party for the new students. I looked across the room and I saw the woman I had seen in my vision and I knew she was to be my wife.

"I approached her and said, 'Hello, my name is Ishmael and I intend to marry you.' She assumed I was joking and she laughed uncomfortably.

"I called her on the telephone in an attempt to arrange a date, but she said, 'Ishmael, I think you have the wrong idea. Please don't call me any more.'

"But I persisted, and eventually we were married, and we have lived happily ever after."

My listeners were bored. "Fuego's story was much better," one said.

"It sounds like you stalked her," said another.

"There's something missing from this story," said a third listener.

THE AGENCY DIDN'T HAVE many case officers in Iraq. In the training courses I'd taken before leaving the US, I noticed there were only a few officers present, and the same was true in Iraq. Less than 15 percent of the employees we had in Iraq were case officers, meaning that less than 15 percent were qualified to gather intelligence. The rest were support: the chow hall workers, the personnel department, clerks, secretaries, security guards, and operations support people such as analysts, information technology specialists, reports officers, and people who handled technical intelligence gathering systems. Everyone worked hard and their tasks were important, but most didn't need to be in Iraq. They could have contributed to the mission just as well from their offices at HQs.

The Agency didn't see it that way, though. The number of employees in Iraq was greater than the number of people the Agency had stationed in Vietnam at the height of the war, and the large numbers gave the impression that the Agency was working hard. The Agency didn't want anyone hurt, and the support personnel were restricted

to military bases where they could be kept safe. The Agency, reporting its number to the President and Congress, always neglected to
mention that most of its employees in Iraq were support.

In the maelstrom that was Iraq, could the Agency possibly have
been accused of risk aversion? In a European station, Agency employees were afraid of simple telephone calls to potential human sources.
In Iraq, there was no fear about calling anyone, and the general operational aggressiveness went beyond anything I'd seen elsewhere. The
Agency's risk aversion in Iraq was limited to assigning very few case
officers to the country. By assigning so many support people who'd
never be in a position to recruit human sources, the Agency had
found a way to limit its activities and potential for risk.

In addition, those case officers who were directly involved in
gathering intelligence were new to the Agency, having recently graduated from the basic operations course. I was one of few experienced
case officers directly involved in these operations. Because case officers run the Agency, experienced ones wound up being turned into
managers overseeing support people, which was not a good use of
their skills or experience.

Many of our people in Iraq were contractors. Some were retired
Agency employees, but many were young people with the same skills
and training as ordinary, staff Agency employees. Contractors are
sometimes perceived as mercenaries who are in Iraq just to make
money, so when a contractor is killed the loss seems small compared
to the loss of a soldier or a staff CIA officer. It was a shame, because
these contractors were patriotic Americans, people who found they
could serve their country only through the hiring path provided by
the Agency's contracting companies. The only reason I could see for
these people to be contractors was that the former Agency mandarins
who ran the contracting companies would profit.

The creation of additional bases and offices within the country
added complex new layers of bureaucrats and made room for countless new managerial positions. Each new base had a chief and a

deputy chief, and each base had its own turf.

The top chief in Iraq knew that there was a shortage of case officers on the ground. It was for this reason that he'd put out the request
for more case officers that led to my assignment there. But apart from
persuasion, he had no control over personnel assignments. HQs dictated the office's structure.

The reward system encouraged people from HQs to serve in Iraq
by providing bonuses and overtime. Service in Iraq could effectively
double one's salary. But a case officer already overseas—for example,
in Geneva or Paris—had so many perks and benefits in his overseas
packages that there was no larger financial incentive to serve in a
dangerous war zone like Iraq.

Many of the people we had in Iraq were eligible by job category
for employment only at HQs, so for many this would be their first
and last overseas assignment. They squirreled away their pay, had no
expenses, and thought about all the luxuries that they'd buy when
they returned to the US.

The majority of top Agency managers avoided service in war
zones, which meant that they became the people at HQs responsible for awarding promotions. Thus, as most employees saw it, a war
zone assignment wasn't a great career move. But many of the newly
trained officers were serving in the war zones. Some day they'd lead
the Agency. "One of these days, all of us junior case officers who have
served in a war zone will revolt against the old guys," a new case officer told me.

The Agency was organized by geographical division. Most of the
young case officers in the war zones were members of either the
Counterterrorism division or the Middle East division. The Counterterrorism division, unlike the Middle East Division, had no geographical turf, so its members tended to find themselves restricted to
hardship locations. An assignment to these divisions could mean a
career shuttling between Afghanistan, Iraq, and HQs. More than half
of the assignments in the Middle East division, including Pakistan

and Saudi Arabia, were unaccompanied, meaning that an officer's family had to remain in the United States. Thus a career in either of these divisions would occur mostly in dangerous areas, and away from the family—a career in backward countries with limited opportunities for family life.

By contrast, an assignment to the European division could mean a cushy career of assignments to Geneva and Paris. All of the European locations were pleasant; most of the assignments in the Middle East were not. If a case officer in the Middle East division pulled some strings, he might get Riyadh. He wouldn't have to live in a trailer, but he'd still be separated from his family. If he were unusually lucky he might get Rabat, a dream assignment by Middle East standards, less so by European ones. Newly trained case officers who wanted to serve their country, and who volunteered for hardship assignments, were treated like suckers. Their reward at the end of a hardship tour was usually another hardship tour.

Real State Department diplomats did it differently, with a long tradition of alternating hardship posts with cushier ones. A diplomat in Brussels may have come from an assignment in Bujumbura, for example, or was headed to Bujumbura at the conclusion of his easy Brussels assignment. A real State Department diplomat in Iraq told me he was excited to be in Iraq because he looked forward to his choice of Geneva or Paris upon the conclusion of his assignment.

As the Agency increased salary and benefits for its employees serving in its many offices in the United States, they were in turn less willing to come to Iraq.

And since the Agency had begun paying rent for people assigned to domestic posts, one didn't even need to leave Fresno to earn nearly the same amount of money as an officer in a war zone. We probably had more case officers in California than we did in Iraq.

THE DAILY ROUTINE of a case officer serving in California differed somewhat from that of a case officer serving in Iraq, where violence was everywhere. One day, as I was standing in a dusty road in an ordinary neighborhood of one- and two-storey homes, one of our people was shot. He collapsed, clutching his abdomen. Fuego and I rushed him to a hospital. He'd been hit in the lower abdomen; Fuego held his hand to the wound to prevent loss of blood, just as we'd been taught in our first aid training. No one had heard the shot, and there was no exit wound, so we guessed that it must have been a ricochet or a bullet from far away. There was so much metal flying around Baghdad that we couldn't be certain what had happened. The man still lost a lot of blood, but Fuego's quick thinking had almost certainly saved the man's life.

The bullet turned out to have burrowed deeper than we thought. The doctors had a difficult time, but were able to stabilize the man. Afterwards, the doctors told us that the man had been in great danger. Fuego and I stayed at the hospital with him. I took a break and went outside, found some water, and cleaned the blood out of the armored car.

FUEGO POINTED OUT A WOMAN in the office: "There's the one who was having sex with a security guard, caught on tape by a security camera. How embarrassing."

He pointed again. "That's the one who was having sex with a senior manager in the HQs parking lot." The incident was infamous within the Agency. It was odd, the way some people managed to remain oblivious to the ubiquitous cameras.

Due to the high proportion of support personnel in Iraq, and the greater representation of women in support jobs, the Agency had a fairly large proportion of women in Iraq. Whether romantic liaisons were more common because of the stress of working in a war zone, or whether I was just seeing the ordinary shenanigans of a normal Agency office, I couldn't really say.

In either case, Fuego was a wild gossip, and knew all of the dirt on everyone at the office. He told me that one married man had taken up with a young woman, and then had gone home to the US for a couple of weeks in order to divorce his wife. When he completed the paperwork, he returned to Iraq, only to find that his girlfriend had forgotten him and taken up with someone else.

A colleague in Iraq knew an OFTPOT chief with whom I'd had a run-in. "I'm surprised that guy got an overseas assignment," he said. "He and his wife had an 'open marriage,' and their liaisons caused all sorts of trouble. The two of them were always on the make with other people in the office. It was ugly. The wife had her eye on a case officer in the office, and she drove to his house one night. He wouldn't let her in, and she stood outside screaming."

Although the proportion of women within the office itself was high, there were far fewer women in the surrounding American military environment. This problem was a source of great angst. "Desert hot" or "desert beauty" suggested that a woman was beautiful in this environment but would be plain upon her return to the US. On Thursday evenings, a distorted dating scene could be observed in a recreational area at the US embassy. The ratio of women to men did not favor the shy; I once saw a colleague get cut out of his conversation with a young woman—literally shouldered aside by a more aggressive man.

Legend had it that one of Saddam's sons had been drunk and, laughing, had shot a bodyguard on the patio where the recreational area is located today. Another (still more macabre) legend claimed that, somewhere nearby, another of Saddam's sons had kept a wood chipper with which he disposed of his enemies' bodies.

An internal political battle broke out in the office between a couple of women and their boss. The friction intensified, and the boss removed the women from their positions and ordered them back to HQs. It was a shame, because all of the participants in the dispute were competent, dedicated people. They just weren't getting along.

The two women packed their bags and were scheduled to leave the next day. That night, they had a going-away party for themselves at which they distributed the cases of alcohol they'd brought with them. They'd planned to stay in the country for a long time and had been allowed to bring a small shipment of personal "supplies" with them. The small party attracted many other people, growing rapidly.

The two women were in a rebellious mood, and it influenced the tone of the party. Flowing liquor quickened the pace of events. Men tested their strength in wrestling matches. An Agency contractor got in an argument with an off-duty security guard, and the security guard drew his pistol and waved it about, threatening the unarmed contractor. There was dancing. Women removed articles of clothing. In the early morning hours, a woman engaged in simultaneous sexual acts with two security guards. I'd met her just the week before. She worked in the accounting department, and had seemed so quiet.

I'd been asleep in my trailer the entire time. I know the details because the party, like so many indiscretions, had taken place under the watchful eye of a security camera. Rank has its privileges, and senior employees got to watch the video the next day. "That wasn't sex, that was bestiality," a colleague commented. Station managers were appalled. Everyone assigned to Iraq had gone through such extensive security screening—how could such lapses in self-discipline occur? All of the culprits were identified and sent home.

The Agency's security guards, handsome, dashing, young ex-Special Forces soldiers, were provided to the Agency at great expense by a company run by a former Agency mandarin. The security guards were the usual suspects when parties and sexual relationships went awry.

"You know," the chief of the security guards said, "in reality, I think this is unfair to the security guards. They're no guiltier of sexual transgressions than anyone else."

"Bullshit," the top chief said. "I drive around with those guys all the time and I know them. That's all they talk about." The top chief banned the guards from drinking alcohol and prohibited officers from fraternizing with them.

The chief, who, a few years before, had handled the "realign-ments" of my colleagues in non-State Department programs, had subsequently been sent to Iraq. "I hate that guy," an officer said. "I needed an armored car to go meet an agent, and I asked if I could use his car. He said I couldn't because he had an urgent meeting. Then a while later I saw his car pull up, and the doors opened and out jumped a couple of his girlfriends, carrying some stuff they'd just bought at the PX." The chief later became embroiled in charges of sexual harassment, and he was realigned and sent back to HQs. A successor of his, another top chief, was also sent home and charged with sexual harassment. The power of our top chief in Iraq was immense, but fleeting.

Women could find a lot of boyfriends in Iraq, but I had to wonder whether those relationships would last back in the US. The security guards were popular, but in Iraq, everyone lives in a trailer. Would living in a trailer with one of these men back in West Virginia be quite the same thing?

I missed my wife and children—so much so that I felt a powerful sense of loneliness and isolation.

THE OFFICE WAS always open and people worked at any and all hours. During emergencies, it was common for people to work all night and into the next day. On a normal day, the office got a late start and worked late at night in order to communicate with people on the HQs time zones. The US military, however, began its day early, so an officer who worked closely with the military but also needed to speak to HQs could be found in the office at any time of day or night. There were no weekends. A lazy guy could get away with coming in at 1030, and then headed off to lunch at 1145 for an hour and a half, taking a two-hour break in the heat of the after-noon, followed by dinner, so that working until midnight wouldn't be too difficult. I didn't see any lazy people there, though; these were the hardest workers in the Agency.

I sat in the office as little as possible, only to attend meetings or to type intelligence reports. Everyone spent at least twelve hours there each day, with no days off, but of course the production of each individual varied greatly depending on his energy and competence. The computers kept a database of outgoing message traffic which was a useful indicator of a person's output. Some people had enormous output; a few, though they sat at their desks for twelve hours, had none. One person's productivity might be 100 times another's, yet they were all paid the same. Sending emails to friends throughout the organization was a common time-waster. If anyone giggled while sitting at his desk, it was a safe bet that he was "instant messaging" with a friend in the Agency. If two people in the office giggled alternately, it usually meant that they were sending messages to each other.

I had learned the system and how to produce within the system. I started at a rate of zero intelligence reports per month, which grew to twelve in the first month, then thirty the next month, sixty after that—after that, growth stabilized. Technically, I was America's number one producer of intelligence reports on terrorism, but in fact, hundreds of brave people had put this program together and I was just filling a hole in that system.

The number of intelligence reports—and the grades they received once disseminated—was the best measure we had of productivity. Having gone from zero to sixty, we'd dramatically improved the reporting, mostly on tactical matters like locating al Qaeda leaders and IEDs, and learning about ambushes prepared for American soldiers.

In addition to gathering intelligence, I helped with emergencies as they came up—for instance, the rescue of several kidnapped Russian diplomats. The Russians had come to us for help. We were the people to see in Iraq. Unfortunately, as was common for Russians, they gave us less information than they probably possessed. It became a source of serious tension, because we needed everything they could give us, and fast.

THE AMERICAN MILITARY in Iraq was single-minded in its mission to capture or kill high-profile terrorists. By contrast, the Agency wanted to use some of these terrorists as human sources leading it to other, more valuable targets. Sometimes compromises were necessary. If the military captured or killed every terrorist we at the Agency knew about, we wouldn't have any intelligence sources. The rotation of American military units added an additional problem, because as a unit got ready to leave Iraq, it preferred to clean up its area of operation as best it could as a professional courtesy to the unit replacing it. In practice, this meant they'd go to extra lengths to capture or kill all the terrorists they could find as their departure date approached.

A military representative at one of our meetings said the army had taken down several of our potential sources the night before. Everyone was stunned.

Then he said, "Joke, joke, I'm only kidding," and everyone laughed. It was gallows humor in the strictest sense.

AT A DINNER MEETING with Iraqi friends, we encouraged each other to tell amusing anecdotes.

A former officer with the Iraqi Republican Guard had one. "Back in Saddam's day," he began, "we were stationed near the Iranian border up north, near Sulaymaniyah, and we learned that there were Kurdish infiltrators in the area. They were dressed in civilian clothes. We began to hunt for them and we soon saw three men walking by who looked suspicious. When we yelled at them to stop they began to run, so we knew they were the Kurds. We began shooting and we killed one of them right away.

"We kept shooting and another Kurd fell down, wounded. We captured the wounded man and ran after the third man, shooting at him.

"Unfortunately, though, I was the fastest runner, and I was running far ahead of my fellow soldiers."

The other diners guessed where the story might be heading and smiled in anticipation.

"I was well ahead of the other shooters, so while they were shooting at the Kurd, the bullets were also flying by me." The diners had guessed correctly and raucous laughter broke out.

"I could feel the air of the bullets passing me," he said. "Fortunately, I was not hit, and of course at last we were able to kill the Kurd." The slapstick of it all, the man running after a Kurd as bullets from his friends' guns zipped past, was too much, and the guests laughed uproariously.

On the way back from the dinner, one of my colleagues commented, "You know, these are some nice guys, but in other circumstances they'd be pulling our fingernails off."

BACK AT THE OFFICE, we learned that the Russian diplomats had been murdered and decapitated. If only the Russians had been more open and communicative, things might have turned out otherwise. Their approach to hostage rescue had been to guard information, to quibble over turf, and to analyze each step from the perspective of what they could get in trouble for if something went wrong. In other words, they behaved just like the Agency tended to elsewhere in the world. In Iraq, however, the Agency was flexible and responsive. We had even found several likely locations for the Russian hostages, but the whole thing had moved too slowly to keep up with the more nimble terrorists.

THE MAN WHO'D BEEN SHOT through the lower abdomen was doing better. Fuego and I visited him in the hospital; he was eager to get home. A nurse asked me if I had $10 I could spare so she could give it to an Iraqi patient trying to get home. She said that the hospital gave the wounded Iraqis money for taxi fare, but that it often wasn't quite enough, so she usually tried her best to supply the difference. Today, she didn't have any money. We gave her a few hundred dollars—all the money we had in our pockets—to contribute to her taxi fund.

Another one of our people was grabbed by terrorists as he strolled down the street. They stuffed him into the back of a car. Another of our people saw it happen, and called Fuego.

Fuego alerted the military, which activated a Special Forces team. A car matching the description he'd given was spotted and the team descended upon it. Unfortunately, it was the wrong vehicle, and the team released the driver after a brief interrogation.

A few hours later, the body of our man, his throat cut, was found in a vacant lot. I conducted the investigation of his death and found nothing indicating that he'd been killed because of his association with the Agency. He was a Sunni Muslim living in a dangerous Shi'a neighborhood; I concluded that his death was a random act of savagery. The bodies of murder victims, many showing signs of torture—such as drill holes—piled up in the Baghdad mortuary, at the rate of 100 a day. The massacres of Sunni by Shi'a and Shi'a by Sunni became routine as Iraq collapsed into sectarian violence.

MANAGEMENT POSTS were always filled, but intelligence-collector posts were mostly empty. When a manager left unexpectedly because of a health problem, a newly trained case officer took his place. When intelligence reports went through this new fellow for his review, they invariably slowed down because he was overly cautious and afraid to make even small mistakes. He made each report sound nice by changing "happy" to "glad"; "said" to "stated"; and "advised" to "instructed."

Some of the intelligence reports went through the system too slowly to be of any use; often the meaning of a cable was altered slightly but significantly as it moved through the editing layers.

I could run emergency reports, such as the locations of ambushes set to attack US soldiers, to a military representative, who'd convey it to the appropriate unit. If a threat involved a US citizen, it included a "duty to warn," effectively requiring the office to disseminate the information quickly. Thanks to this procedure, I was able to warn a US citizen of Iraqi origin in time to avoid a plotted kidnapping. But for most reports, I needed to go through the proper channels. I needed more speed.

There was a sinister aspect to the sluggishness of intelligence reporting. Even if reports get old, stale, even *useless*, the Agency takes credit for producing them. It looks busy. Also, if information is out of date when it's received, no one can be held accountable for inaccuracies. This creates an incentive for foot-dragging.

I cut the new manager and a few others out of the chain of people who would review my intelligence reports. This helped a lot, and no one confronted me about it.

But it wasn't enough. Once the reports got through the layers of managers, they went to the reports officers.

According to Agency lore, case officers once upon a time had been able to return from their meetings with hastily written scraps; reports officers had been brilliant minds who could form full intelligence reports from these disparate bits of information. In my day, reports officers had mutated into Collection Management Officers (CMOs) who no longer took part in the creation of reports, but merely acted as gatekeepers who reviewed them. Today's CMOs tell case officers to rewrite their reports in finished form; their job is limited to reading, making modest line edits, and forwarding along the result.

For their part, the CMOs had ossified themselves into layers, each with its chief, an underling, and a representative from the relevant turf within the country—three layers of CMOs to push through after one had received a report through his own layers of lower-level managers.

In the course of my first few days in Iraq, before I'd absorbed the office's preferences, I'd written an intelligence report replete with errors in style and formatting. A CMO spotted it and thought its author needed to be punished. He must have figured that I was a low-ranking guy—after all, I was a mere intelligence producer. He found Fuego and said, "Who is this Ishmael? Who's his supervisor? *Look* at these mistakes."

"He's out at a meeting right now," Fuego said, "but maybe you can talk to him when he gets back."

"No, these errors are too serious for that. I want to talk to his supervisor."

Fuego thought about this for a moment and said, "I'd be careful, if I were you. You might want to avoid talking to his supervisor. Ishmael is a senior case officer and personal friend of the top chief. That's why he was assigned here—he and the top chief go way back."

The CMO walked away and said no more about my poorly-written document.

The top chief and I weren't really old friends, though our paths had crossed over the years. I admired him because he was probably the best case officer I'd met in the Agency. But we were only acquaintances. Rumors that the top chief and I were good buddies spread throughout the office.

These rumors were a great help. I spoke to the CMOs and asked them to speed up the processing of my intelligence reports. They were only too eager to oblige.

They also agreed to my sourcing of intelligence. Normally, when an agent produces information, he needs to specify where it came from. "I overheard it at the barber shop" isn't good enough. Often, Iraqis told me that they'd received a piece of information because "everyone in the neighborhood knows it." Initially, this was insufficient. Later, I learned that it *was*, in fact, good enough—because it kept turning out to be true. Local al Qaeda leaders made themselves visible in order to control neighborhoods, so their identities were often an open secret within a given neighborhood. Terrorists set up a roadblock in a Baghdad suburb, captured several passing motorists, and then murdered them in front of a crowd assembled in the courtyard of a mosque. We were later able to identify the murderers and pass this information to the military, which then captured or killed the terrorists.

My work in Iraq was in tactical reporting on topics such as IEDs and the location of terrorists—information American soldiers can use in the here and now. The Agency preferred strategic intelligence reporting on the opinions and intentions of political leaders. it could give the "big picture" and was useful in creating briefings for ambassadors and congressmen.

It's not fun to produce intelligence reports within the Agency, so a smart guy will quit producing as soon as he can and become a manager, where he can sit back, edit cables, and attend meetings with other Agency managers. I knew that this would be my final assignment in the Agency, though, and I wanted to achieve as much as I could. My production technically made me the Agency's top counterterrorism producer—yet it was a dead-end job, a job no one was interested in doing.

EVEN THOUGH I LOVED the pace of work, felt great, slept great, enjoyed meeting the daily challenges, and was happy to be there, I missed my family deeply. Sometimes, in the late evening, I grabbed a can of beer, went to the recreation area, sat under the security camera, and listened to an iPod. After that raucous porno going-away party, a new regulation had been imposed, banning alcohol entirely from the area.

Fuego walked by. "What the hell you think you're doing, Ishmael? No beer allowed in the recreational area."

"I'm breaking the letter of the law, but not the spirit, Fuego. The rule wasn't meant to keep a lonely guy from listening to music and having a single beer."

A helicopter passed overhead, kicking out flares in case of incoming missiles. The noise drowned Fuego's response. I didn't care, anyway.

A crusty old geezer joined me. He'd been with the Agency since the Vietnam war. He complained that we had more people in Iraq than we'd ever had in Vietnam, but too few case officers. He was uncomfortable with women in a combat zone, too, and he didn't like them wearing pistols. (In the safe areas of Iraq, most of the men didn't wear their pistols.)

Another man joined our conversation and pointed out that there had been safe areas in Vietnam, whereas a person could walk up and shoot you virtually anywhere in Iraq. I'd been to Iraq as a child, as a tourist with my family, but things were very different now. Strolling down the street and visiting tourist attractions unarmed and unwary was completely out of the question.

Gender issues continue to create tension. "They dress provocatively," whined the old man. Homely "desert beauties" walked by, each accompanied by several men.

PARAMILITARY CLOTHING was popular. I had brought a few outfits, but I put them away and wore normal clothes. I usually had a pistol, but I kept it in a briefcase instead of holstered on my belt. This would slow me down in a quick-draw, but it made me less intimidating to the Iraqis that I met.

Our pistols had sophisticated safety mechanisms, so it was safe to keep a round in the chamber. I noticed that the person at the desk next to mine had put his pistol on a shelf with the muzzle pointing at my forehead. People didn't seem particularly concerned about which direction their pistols pointed, because tests had shown that the pistols would never go off unless the trigger was pulled. Even so, I made a point of moving that gun. Tests are only so reliable, after all.

Mortar and rocket rounds landed frequently, and everyone

seemed to have a fatalistic attitude: Either it hits you or it doesn't, but there's not much to be done about it in any case. I didn't carry a trauma kit, but there was always one in the vehicles. On my way to a meeting, I stepped out of my vehicle and felt the slap of a spent bullet on my body armor. I bent over to pick up the mangled bullet, which must have come from a great distance and ricocheted at least once before it came to me.

I was getting tired of running to a bunker when the mortar rounds landed, especially if I was sleeping. I stopped getting out of bed when it happened. I decided that if I didn't get my shut-eye, the terrorists would win. When my roommates headed for shelter, I asked them to lock the door behind them so that busybodies couldn't let themselves in and insist that I duck and cover.

A new roommate had arrived a few days before, a man who suffered from sleep apnea and snored raucously in the bunk beneath mine. I bought a small fan and attached bits of metal and plastic to the fan blades, in order to create a white noise machine which would drown out the snores.

SUPPORT SERVICES at the base were provided by companies owned by former Agency mandarins. If we needed weapons and training, for example, we'd contact a mandarin's company. The mandarins raking in the dough with these contracts were the same ones who had presided over the Agency's failure to gather intelligence in the 1990s. Things were going badly then in Iraq, and real companies with real contracts were leaving because of the tremendous physical danger. But Agency contracting companies had more US military protection, so they made out like bandits.

At one point, we needed approval from HQs to buy weapons. HQs turned us down, and I wondered why.

Fuego said, "The guy at HQs knows I'm involved, and he doesn't like me. We had a big disagreement when we were serving together in Pakistan." I knew the man; he was one of the men who'd been purged and sent to HQs during the Ames and Nicholson purges.

I dialed the man at HQs on a secure telephone: "Hi, this is Ishmael calling from Iraq. I think we may have crossed paths years ago at an Agency seminar."

He remembered me and we chatted for a while. Then I said, "Hey, listen, how about approving our weapons request? I know you don't like Fuego; he can be a pain in the ass sometimes, but our guys need this hardware to defend themselves. Let's not get people killed just because you have a beef with Fuego."

He said he'd see what he could do, and he approved the request the next day.

OUR CASE OFFICERS in Iraq were almost uniformly aggressive, unafraid to conduct even risky intelligence operations. The wild violence of the environment precluded typical risk aversion. Paperwork that was required anywhere else in the world was simply ignored. Crises that would have shut down an ordinary station didn't even attract comment in Iraq.

While this attitude was refreshing, crossing the line into Syria meant entering another bureaucrat's turf, and business as usual.

Terrorists crossed back and forth into Iraq from Syria, where their training camps were based. When we needed to conduct an operation that crossed over into Syria, we faced Agency gatekeepers there who responded to our requests for operational approval with the usual terrified replies—the same excruciating excuses I'd heard so many tedious times.

Our operations were designed to procure intelligence to save the lives of American soldiers, but the turf bureaucrats in Syria saw them merely as threats to the sanctity of their turf. Even in a war zone, bureaucratic frustrations were impossible to escape.

As we study the Iraq war, we naturally look for parallels to the war in Vietnam. In Vietnam, enemy troops used Laos and

Cambodia as safe havens. Diplomatic and strategic considerations prevented US attacks on those countries. Many Americans disagreed with those considerations, but they were, nevertheless, largely legitimate.

The US has no formal restrictions on espionage activity in Syria, but the Agency's turf bureaucrats do, so Syria is a *de facto* safe haven from the Agency's scrutiny. Agency operations from Iraq into Syria were blocked not by strategic or diplomatic considerations, but for the entirely inexcusable reason that Agency turf bureaucrats in Syria chose not to approve those operations.

A CASE OFFICER on his first assignment seemed unhappy. I could tell that he missed his wife and newborn son, and I wanted to cheer him up. "A career in this organization is tough sometimes," I said, "but my wife and I have still been able to raise a family."

"Oh yeah," he said, "Then why has every man here either been divorced, getting divorced, or cheating on his wife?"

He had a point. I'd worked far from the Agency's offices, so my marriage never felt the strain that it would have had I worked within its dysfunctional core. My guess is that it is expensive and harmful to production for the Agency to have a work force with such a high rate of domestic disorder.

OUR WOUNDED MAN got an infection, so Fuego and I returned him to the hospital. It was in the Green Zone in central Baghdad, and we drove around the Green Zone like tourists, the top-heavy armored car swaying back and forth. All the money in Iraq must have been going into security, because the Green Zone was trashed, utterly run down.

From Saddam's "crossed swords" monument there hung cargo nets full of helmets belonging to Iranian soldiers captured or killed during Saddam's war with Iran. The helmets were painted green. There were many types of helmets, mostly of British and Russian design, which Iran must have accumulated over the years. The cargo nets had been ripped open and some of the helmets spilled on the ground. Fuego had an eye for value, and he picked out a World War II-era British paratrooper's helmet that he could sell on eBay. After visiting the crossed swords, we drove over to the fire station where Fuego bought some Baghdad Fire Department tee shirts.

We went to the American embassy for lunch, seating ourselves at the "Flag Officers Only" table. Fuego said, "I always sit at this table when I come to lunch at the embassy because I like the white tablecloth." Later we visited the barbershop and got military-style haircuts, the only type available, in fact, from a barber with horribly mangled hands. "I've heard the guy with the hands does the best haircuts," Fuego told me.

GENERAL CASEY, then the commander of US forces in Iraq, stopped by for a visit and posed for pictures with some of our employees. I cringed and hid behind a palm tree, avoiding the flashing cameras. Photography didn't seem to bother the support employees. I looked over to the tree next to mine and saw an Army Special Forces soldier taking cover. He didn't like being photographed, either.

"What is it with you people and cameras?" he asked.

President Bush had visited the American embassy a few months before. I'd avoided the embassy because there were television cameras everywhere. A colleague got as close to the President as he could, shaking his hand with great warmth, and he was on the world's screens for several days.

I watched a CNN news report featuring the takedown of a terrorist that my agents had helped track. I was excited about the upswing in intelligence production and fascinated by how often the television news told of events in which I'd had a hand.

I SENT AN "INSTANT MESSAGE" to Martin, to whom I hadn't spoken in years. All I wrote was, "Hello, my friend," all that he could tell from the message was that it had come from Iraq. Yet he instantly replied, "Hi, is that you, Ishmael?"

"How'd you know it was me?"

"Just got out of a meeting discussing you. Your chief from the Middle East has really been raising hell about you. It doesn't look good. I told them they're crazy to mess with you: You're the best we've got."

Maybe Martin had told them that I was the best they'd got. Maybe he hadn't. It was hard to tell with HQs folks.

I'd expected this chief to let go, but I shouldn't have. His turf and his position were all he had, and I'd shown disrespect for both.

A thoughtful and diplomatic mandarin at HQs came up with a solution. I was to go to Baghdad airport and fly back to HQs in Washington, D.C., where I'd apologize to another chief. Not the one I'd upset—a different one from the same division. In my apology, I was to make it clear that I understood what I'd done wrong in coming to Iraq without proper coordination, and to make it clear I wouldn't do it again. If the fellow were satisfied with my apology, then that would be the end of it.

I had a few days to answer. I thought about it—and I decided that I wouldn't be making any apologies. I told HQs to process my paperwork for resignation from the Agency at the conclusion of my assignment in Iraq. The top chief called me in to his office and said that he was sorry that I'd decided to leave, but that he figured I knew what I was doing.

HQs wasn't asking me to do much. Agency people tend to be pleasant and non-confrontational. I'd heard the chief that I was supposed to apologize to was a nice guy. But it would have been cowardly to apologize for coming to Iraq without the say-so of a petty bureaucrat, and even weaker to fly home at taxpayer expense. Plus, I'd determined that I'd never be able to get any of my own intelligence operations of any significance rolling at my post in the Middle East, and so I decided Iraq would be my last assignment. The requirement that I apologize just gave me a convenient time to depart.

THE MILITARY'S NEED for good intelligence had led to competition in the intelligence field. Military case officers, who'd received the same training as Agency case officers, tended to get out more, to take greater risks in the streets of Iraq. It wasn't easy to quantify whether those risks paid off. Moving about in Baghdad, for example, wasn't just a matter of looking like an Arab and speaking Arabic: It was the ability to be known and trusted by the people at the road block. The accent would have to be precise to an area of a few kilometers, and a person would have to be Shi'a for a Shi'a roadblock and Sunni for a Sunni roadblock. So no one could roam at will. Fuego often tried, and he'd been in vehicles that had been hit numerous times by small arms fire. The armor stops the bullets, but the impact can send a shock wave that, for a moment, makes the passenger think he has been hit. Fuego had received so many of these shock waves that he believed he could determine the type of bullet and the direction it had come from based on the feel of the shock wave.

Too much wandering could lead to dangerous consequences for innocent bystanders. If an officer were spooked, he might panic and open fire on, or drive into, onlookers. Careful planning was important before traveling. Visiting congressmen asked questions about the Agency's appetite for risk—the question was risk versus reward. What would be gained from additional risk? What is the acceptable number of people we are prepared to lose each year? No one knows the answer, of course. No one has a hard and fast number.

Iraq was a unique environment, and both Agency and military intelligence officers were doing a fine job. In the rest of the world, I thought the military officers were much more capable and less risk-averse. The military can place 30 trained case officers in non-State Department positions nearly anywhere in the world within a matter of days. The Agency, with billions of dollars at its disposal, couldn't do this in a decade. The military's abilities intimidated the Agency; Agency gatekeepers worldwide felt intensely threatened by the military's tendency to carry out operations without seeking their approval or assistance.

A ROCKET PUNCHED THROUGH a bunch of trailers, right through several three-foot dirt barriers, but didn't explode. The holes in the trailers were clean and round. The rocket hit the top of my trailer first, and then continued on, leaving cantaloupe-sized holes.

CIA Director Michael Hayden dropped in for a visit. He was proud to have promoted Suspenders, and certain that the Agency's employees would be excited about it. We assembled to listen to his talk. He was a business-as-usual person, actively appointing new committees and inventing new words for old things. He seemed to think that the work force had been ruffled by Goss's leadership and needed to be reassured, rather than fixed. His favorite word was "corporate": We have to look at corporate issues, do corporate decision-making, view things from a corporate *standpoint*, and of course assess corporate risk.

Hayden discussed his new initiative, to build more Agency facilities throughout the United States so that its offices would be off the Northeastern power grid. In other words, if an enemy attack takes out the electricity in the Northeastern US, we'll have a web of HQs offices operating elsewhere in the country. But we already had dozens of offices spread throughout the United States.

WE HAD A GREAT LUNCH with our Iraqi colleagues. "Where does the fish come from?" I asked.

"Don't ask," Fuego said. They were river fish, and human bodies frequently floated down the Tigris and Euphrates.

An Iraqi friend had lost several cousins the day before, murdered by a street gang. He shrugged it off, expecting no sympathy. Later, I wandered outside to the parking lot and made a telephone call. Most of the cars I saw were heavily perforated by bullet holes. Our Iraqi colleagues were brave. As in Vietnam, we Americans came for short periods of time—John Kerry was in Vietnam less than four months—and then we went home, while they stayed for their whole lives. A month doesn't go by without losing an Iraqi colleague or one of his relatives.

AT THE END of my assignment, I arranged for a flight. I was sad to leave our work in Iraq undone, but happy to go home. It was the chance of a lifetime to have been able to come to Iraq. On my last night, my friends gave me a going away dinner and I ate the delicacy, a lamb's head. The assembled Iraqis and Americans spoke kindly of me and I thanked them. They were the best and the bravest people I'd met in the Agency. That dinner meant a lot to me, and was a fitting send-off both from this assignment and from my career.

In the end, I was the only one of my group of eight officers who ever made it to Iraq. Of the seven others, one of them got close, but he failed the required firearms course. The unanimous opinion at HQs was that he'd failed on purpose so that he wouldn't have to go. I knew that the rednecks who taught the course would have worked with an officer all night, if necessary, to help him pass.

The Agency office in Iraq gave me a nice award and I hope the citation remains as the first thing anyone sees when they open my file at HQs. I turned in my weapons and body armor and went home.

Epilogue

After I resigned for the final time, HQs gave me a few weeks to finish up a final operation. Over the past several years I'd been traveling to my old East African home country to meet a target. When I was preparing to leave the Agency, I went to one last meeting to give the target information about who might be contacting him next.

My meetings with the target had taken place in the downtown area of the city, and I hadn't seen my old neighborhood in more than 35 years. The street crime in the city had worsened since I'd lived there as a boy. The city had been safe then, and I'd roamed everywhere on my bicycle. Today, that would have been suicide. I hadn't had a practical reason to visit the neighborhood during my previous visits, and I figured that this would be my last, so I took a taxi out to see it one last time.

I directed the driver to the neighborhood and asked him to stop. I got out of the taxi and smelled that old mixture of tropical sweetness and open sewers. I looked up to where the house had been. It wasn't there any longer—a different building stood in its place. I walked a half block up and down the street, trying to confirm my sense of direction, and stood again looking at the position where I was convinced the house had been. Suddenly, my old house seemed to appear from within the building. It had been heavily modified, that was all, with a new storey and new rooms connecting it to other buildings on each side. It was still there.

The friendly greetings in Swahili and English had begun once the taxi entered the neighborhood, and the cries continued to increase in number and intensity. A wild-looking, red-eyed man approached and asked me what I was doing. I remembered enough of the local dialect to understand him, and I replied, pointing at the house, "I lived in that house 30 years ago, when I was a boy." The red-eyed man seemed momentarily satisfied and wandered away. I got back in the taxi and directed the driver to go up a block to the Marine House. The Marine House had long since been relocated to the bunkered US embassy compound.

The old Marine House was still there, and looked just as I'd expected it would, lasting for decades without maintenance in a tropical climate.

Rising above the courtyard, the old House's flagpole was still there.

THE END

*   *

*

APPENDIX

ACKNOWLEDGMENTS

BIBLIOGRAPHY

NOTES

INDEX

Appendix

Solutions for reform of the clandestine service

Solutions for reform of the clandestine service within the current system:

1 *Define the mission.* Create a clear, one-line mission statement. Current CIA mission statements are multi-page documents, written by committees, which nobody ever reads. A clear statement, such as, "Provide foreign intelligence that will defend the United States," would help employees measure and direct their efforts.

2 *Focus on the mission.* Recruit and handle high-quality human sources; avoid trivial, easy targets.

3 *Cut layers of management ruthlessly* to speed operations and to put more spies on the street. (See further comments below.)

4 *Get rid of the gatekeepers.* Abandon the geographical station system. Station chiefs are not captains of ships; they are employees located within fortress embassies, seeking to ensure that no flaps occur on their turf. Terrorists and nuclear proliferators don't have geographical boundaries.

5 *Get the CIA out of the United States.* Most CIA employees live and work in the United States. Get the CIA spying on and in foreign countries, where it belongs.

6 *Clarify the chain of command.* Every employee should know his or her direct supervisor, and each employee should have only one supervisor. Supervisors should be senior in grade to their employees. Spouses of supervisors should never be inserted

into the chain of command. An employee's annual evaluation should be written by a single supervisor.

7   *Account for the money.* Make certain that the taxpayers' money
is spent properly. Don't let secrecy get in the way. Don't be
afraid of verifying receipts written in foreign languages in
faraway places.

8   *Create a one-line cultural statement:* Do not lie, cheat, or steal unless
required to do so in an intelligence operation. Spies need to
lie, but only when necessary for operational success. The
organization's efficiency and reliability will improve when
employees can trust one another to speak the truth.

*Recent reforms demonstrate what happens when change is attempted at the
CIA. Congressionally-mandated reforms, following the intelligence failures
of 9/11, did the three worst things possible, by:*

1   *Adding extra layers of management.* They created a new office of
the Director of National Intelligence. No successful organizations have as many layers of management as the CIA.

2   *Accepting the CIA's ploy that it just needs a few more years to hire the
right people.* The CIA has used this ploy for decades. The CIA
has all the qualified people it needs. The problem is that they
are poorly led.

3   *Showering the CIA with billions of dollars* in additional funding
without transparency or a system of accountability, leading
to fraud, waste, and mismanagement.

*The CIA is a failed organization that has proven resistant to reform.
Therefore, the CIA should be broken up into its constituent parts, and
those parts assigned to organizations that already have clear missions and
defined chains of command, as follows:*

1   *Transfer CIA offices and personnel operating within the United States
to the FBI.* The CIA was never intended to be a domestic spy
agency. The FBI is designed to handle domestic intelligence

operations. The FBI is measured and held accountable by its ability to catch criminals, and this accountability provides the motivation for the FBI to perform.

2   *Transfer all CIA embassy activities overseas to the US Department of State.* The State Department is designed to handle diplomacy. Much of what the CIA now does in its embassies involves diplomacy, such as handling relationships with liaison services. State Department officers are able to make contacts with other foreign government representatives in diplomatic venues. The State Department handled these functions prior to the creation of the CIA in 1947.

3   *Transfer overseas human intelligence collection efforts to the US military.* Focus case officers exclusively on the gathering of human intelligence. The fundamental motivation of the American military—to win wars and to protect the lives of its soldiers—will provide the motivation to ensure that its case officers provide the necessary intelligence and do not become distracted by soft targets or by designing programs meant to look busy and spend money. The US military already has a large corps of trained case officers, graduates of the CIA's own training course. The US military already has a better ability to place case officers overseas in non-State Department positions. The military's command structure is clearly defined and much flatter than the Agency's.

We should recognize the scope of the problem:

The lack of human sources of intelligence has haunted American Presidents since the foundation of the CIA in 1947. The lack of human sources has been the greatest threat to the presidencies and the historical legacies of American Presidents, and to the American people.

1   The Chinese invasion of North Korea in 1950 was a complete

surprise[62] and the subsequent handling of the war by President Truman led him to cancel his re-election campaign.

2   The handling of the U-2 incident was President Eisenhower's greatest regret as President.[63].

3   Lack of Cuban human sources contributed to the Bay of Pigs fiasco, which was President Kennedy's greatest failure.

4   The lack of human sources in Vietnam[64] haunted President Johnson in the conduct of the Vietnam War.

5   The Vietnam War was one of President Nixon's greatest challenges as well. The outbreak of the 1973 Arab/Israeli war also took the Agency by surprise.

6   Throughout the Cold War, the Agency's top program, recruitment of Soviet human sources, was a shambles. Lack of intelligence on Soviet intentions nearly led to war on several occasions.

7   President Carter's humiliation and the destruction of his presidency were caused by the Iran hostage crisis and the subsequent failed rescue attempt, both of which featured a lack of human sources.

8   President Reagan's humiliation involved hostages and the ensuing Iran-Contra scandal, both featuring a lack of human sources.

9   President Clinton's legacy was tarnished by the lack of human sources, who could have transmitted information that might have prevented the 9/11 terrorist attacks. Lack of human sources led to a nuclear arms race in the Asian sub-continent.

10 Lack of human sources on Iraqi WMD and on the Iraq war poisoned the George W. Bush presidency.

The greatest vulnerability to the President elected in 2008 and future Presidents will be the lack of human sources of intelligence. Terrorists armed with nuclear weapons will kill hundreds of thousands of

Americans if we do not improve our human intelligence capability.

Comments on mission drift:

1 Recruiting human sources isn't easy or fun. For the case officer, rejection, humiliation, and loneliness are the byproducts of human intelligence operations. Sitting in a hotel room meeting a man with bad breath for hours at a stretch is hard work.

2 Recruiting human sources does not appear to lead to career advancement. It is the lowest form of work within the Agency, and few top managers have ever recruited a good human source. To have recruited human sources in al Qaeda and in Iraqi WMD, a case officer would have had to be in the field for years, away from Agency stations and HQs. He'd have returned to a dead career, with no management experience and with none of the connections at HQs necessary for personal advancement. A person who wants to advance in the organization does so through lengthy service at HQs, with rare assignments overseas.

3 This leads to mission drift: officers prefer fun things that lead to promotion, such as creating layers of managers, handling liaison operations, building boondoggles, Potemkin offices and elaborate cover mechanisms, and elaborate covert action schemes.

4 The Agency's successes tend to be in areas outside the fundamental mission of gathering intelligence. Success in Afghanistan was a military operation, for example. Convincing Libya to end its WMD programs was a diplomatic success.

5 Mission drift causes the Agency to go after little fish, not big fish. Operations involving little fish then cause bigger flaps when something goes wrong, because the American people don't support espionage operations aimed at seemingly unimportant topics.

6   Human intelligence operations are relatively cheap. Mission drift into more expensive non-human source missions provides openings for corruption.

Comments on the destructiveness of excessive layers of management:

Excessive layers cause delays in the dissemination of intelligence reports, often making those reports worthless. Intelligence collection is peculiar in that it is a one-on-one activity: there is no need for the layers. Management consultant Tom Peters discusses the problem of layers by pointing out that, in a chain of six layers, if each layer makes the correct decision 80 percent of the time, this will result in a correct decision by the six layers 26 percent of the time. (.8 to the 6th power = 26 percent).[65]

Excessive layers increase risk when it becomes difficult to determine who is in charge.

Excessive layers increase the number of people who know secrets, making leaks easier and making it harder to find moles such as Ames.

Excessive layers encourage rule-breaking. I rarely conducted an intelligence operation where I didn't have to break an Agency rule. Had I not broken rules, I would never have completed an operation. Promote case officers by giving them more freedom and responsibility in conducting operations, rather than by making them gatekeepers.

I've never come across the suggestion that the Agency reduce its layers. Yet that is one of the first things a businessman or management consultant seeks to do in improving the operations of an organization.

Comments on motivation:

American businesses are driven by profit, which serves as the motivation to keep their organizations functioning efficiently.

It can be argued that the FBI and the US military are bureaucratic, but they too have clear missions—to catch criminals and to win wars—and this helps give them focus. It is less likely that an FBI agent, for example, can rise within the FBI without ever having been involved in catching a criminal. The US military is motivated to win wars. These motivations drive the FBI and the US military just as the motivation to earn profits drives American businesses.

The US military's effectiveness is in part due to "civilian audit, dissent, and self-critique," which are part of the "larger Western tradition of personal freedom, consensual government, and individualism."[66]

Where there is no civilian audit, dissent, self-critique, transparency or accountability, a bureaucracy will thrive, grow, and morph into a monster, such as the CIA is today.

We must acknowledge what drives humans and what motivates an organization.

If the FBI did not need to catch criminals, if the US military did not need to win wars, and if American businesses did not need to earn profits, they would fall into the same rudderless disarray as the CIA. The CIA has no driving motivation and so should be split up and attached to organizations that do have driving motivations.

Acknowledgments

Thanks to my CIA colleagues. It was an honor to serve with you, and I regret I cannot name you here.

Thanks to Lynn Chu and Glen Hartley from Writers' Representatives for taking on the book so decisively and bringing it to the attention of Roger Kimball at Encounter Books.

Thanks also to Stefan Beck and to Dara Mandle for their thoughtful editing of the manuscript. Thanks to Heather Ohle, Lauren Powers, Sam Schneider, Nola Tully, and Lauren Miklos of Encounter.

Thanks to Max Boot, an expert on intelligence issues and one of America's great commentators. Lindsay Moran, former CIA officer and author of Blowing My Cover, is the most talented writer to have written about the CIA. Michael Ross is the author of *The Volunteer*, the best book written about the Israeli Mossad.

I hope readers recognize throughout the book how grateful I am to my wife and family for putting up with these many years of risk and uncertainty.

Thanks to all who become convinced of the necessity for reform of our American intelligence services, which will lead to greater security for all free nations.

Notes

1   Waters, T.J. *Class 11: Inside the CIA's First Post-9/11 Spy Class*. New York: Dutton, 2006.

2   Devlin, Larry. *Chief of Station, Congo: Fighting the Cold War in a Hot Zone*. New York: PublicAffairs, 2007. pp. 55-59.

3   Kessler, Ronald. *The CIA at War: Inside the Secret Campaign Against Terror*. New York: St. Martin's Press, 2003, p. 89.

4   "Dewey Clarridge, who served in the CIA for 30 years, holding increasingly responsible positions in the Directorate of Operations, and Robert M. Gates, who became director of central intelligence in the administration of the first President Bush, both acknowledged that they knew of no significant recruitments of Soviet spies during their long careers. The spies were all walk-ins, or volunteers." Hitz, Frederick P. *The Great Game: The Myth and Reality of Espionage*. New York: Knopf, 2004. p.21.

5   Ibid, p.21.

6   Ibid, p. 58.

7   Kessler, p. 132.

8   Hitz p. 144; Andrew, Christopher, and Gordievsky, Oleg. *KGB: The Inside Story of Its Foreign Operations from Lenin to Gorbachev*. New York: HarperCollins, 1990. p. 5.

9   Mahle, Melissa Boyle. *Denial and Deception: An Insider's View of the CIA from Iran-Contra to 9/11*. New York: Nation Books, 2005. p. 127.

10 Kessler, p. 21.

11 The name Waldo Dubberstein resurfaces in CIA history years later when

Dubberstein supplied American military secrets to the Libyan government of Muammar Qaddafi via the Edwin P. Wilson organization. Dubberstein died on the morning he was scheduled for a grand jury indictment, an apparent suicide.

12 Smith, Russell Jack. *The Unknown CIA: My Three Decades with the Agency*. Washington, D.C.: Pergamon-Brassey's, 1989.

13 A former chief of the CIA's domestic division seems unaware that the FBI *is* our domestic intelligence agency when he recommends the US construct a domestic intelligence corps under the direction of "intelligence leadership," presumably the CIA. (Sims and Gerber, p. 210.)

14 Hitz, p. 71, discusses twenty Middle Eastern agents blown through a common accommodation address.

15 Sullivan, John F.: *Gatekeeper: Memoirs of a CIA Polygraph Examiner*. Dulles, Virginia: Potomac Books, 2007, p. 35.

16 Clarridge, Duane R. and Diehl, Digby. *A Spy for All Seasons: My Life in the CIA*. New York: Scribner, 1997. p. 328.

17 Gup, Ted. *The Book of Honor: Covert Lives & Classified Deaths at the CIA*. New York: Doubleday, 2000, p. 308.

18 Coll, Steve. *Ghost Wars: The Secret History of the CIA, Afghanistan, and Bin Laden, from the Soviet Invasion to September 10, 2001*. New York: Penguin, 2004, p. 374.

19 Alibek, Ken, with Handelman, Stephen. *Biohazard: The Chilling True Story of the Largest Covert Biological Weapons Program in the World—Told from Inside by the Man Who Ran It*. New York: Random House, 1999.

20 Bearden, Milton, and Risen, James. *The Main Enemy: The Inside Story of the CIA's Final Showdown with the KGB*. New York: Random House, 2003. p. 412.

21 Ames's extravagant lifestyle—the Jaguar, the house paid for in cash, the wife with 500 pairs of shoes, $18,000 in annual credit card finance charges—would no longer attract attention after the post-9/11 money influx. If Ames had just held on until after 9/11, he'd have been able to bring home more money than the KGB ever paid him.

22 Wise, David. *Nightmover: How Aldrich Ames Sold the CIA to the KGB for $4.6 Million*. New York: HarperCollins, 1995. p. 5.

23 Bearden and Risen, p. 526.

24 Bearden and Risen, p. 301.

25 Hitz, p. 61.

26 Hitz, p. 58.

27 Doyle, David W. *True Men and Traitors: From the OSS to the CIA, My Life in the Shadows.* New York: John Wiley & Sons, 2001.

28 Andrew and Gordievsky, p. 610.

29 *Time* magazine, February 4, 1991.

30 Sims, Jennifer E. and Gerber, Burton, eds. *Transforming US Intelligence.* Washington, D.C.: Georgetown University Press, 2005.

31 Gup, p. 49.

32 Kessler, p. 36.

33 Drumheller, Tyler. *On the Brink: An Insider's Account of How the White House Compromised American Intelligence.* New York: Carroll & Graf, 2006, p. 20.

34 Hitz, p.99.

35 Holm, Richard L. *The American Agent: My Life in the CIA.* London: St. Ermin's Press, 2003.

36 Paseman, Floyd L. *A Spy's Journey: A CIA Memoir.* St. Paul: Zenith Press, 2004. This book contains good descriptions of the use of tennis in Agency operations.

37 Vise, David A. *The Bureau and the Mole: The Unmasking of Robert Philip Hanssen, the Most Dangerous Double Agent in FBI History.* New York: Atlantic Monthly Press, 2002. p. 42.

38 Bearden and Risen, p. 527.

39 Ibid, p. 300.

40 Berntsen, Gary and Pezzullo, Ralph. *Jawbreaker: The Attack on Bin Laden and Al-Qaeda: A Personal Account by the CIA's Key Field Commander.* New York: Crown, 2005. p. 307.

41 *Taiwan Times*, July 19, 2006.

42 *Time* magazine, July 15, 2006.

43 *Washington Post*, July 10, 2004, based on the Senate intelligence committee report of July 9, 2004.

44 *Washington Post*, September 1, 2006.

45 Wilson, Valerie Plame. *Fair Game: My Life as a Spy, My Betrayal by the White House*. New York: Simon & Schuster, 2007.

46 The Afterword of Plame's book provides some dates for Plame's career. The Afterword was written separately by Laura Rozen, who was not a former CIA employee and thus not subject to censorship. Rozen dates Plame's initial training from 1985-1989, assignment to Athens 1989-1992, more training 1992-1996, assignment as a non-State Department officer overseas 1996-1997, and assignment to HQs 1997-2006. A couple of these dates may have been fudged to suggest that Plame had more of an overseas intelligence role than she really did. Her tour in Athens may have been for two years instead of three; first tours for embassy officers in those days were for two years. Rozen suggests Plame spent a year in her assignment as a non-State Department officer overseas, but the real length of her assignment was two months or less, and she did not participate in any intelligence operations during that time.

47 Moran, Lindsay. *Blowing My Cover: My Life as a CIA Spy*. New York: Penguin, 2005. p. 139.

48 The value of interrogation courses is hard to measure. Compartmentation is the answer because torture can probably extract anything from anyone. "Terrorist outfits and rogue nations such as Iran have sadists on their payroll who can extract information from the most stoic combatant with ease." Ross, Michael, and Kay, Jonathan. *The Volunteer: A Canadian's Secret Life in the Mossad*. Toronto: McClelland & Stewart, 2007. Pages 95-96 describe the Mossad's view of interrogation under torture.

49 Qaddhafi, Muammar. (variants: Gathafi, Qaddafi, Gaddafi). *The Green Book: The Solution to the Problem of Democracy, The Solutions to the Economic Problem, The Social Basis of the Third Universal Theory*. Tripoli: Libyan government press, 1975. Part II, Chapter 3.

50 As early as 1952, the Agency's director, General Walter Bedell Smith, complained of "inferior personnel" and planned to build a corps of highly trained officers in the years ahead. Gup, p. 50.

51 MSNBC, April 15, 2004; Sims and Gerber, p. 7.

52 The Israeli Mossad's code name for Tenet was "Greaseball" because "he seemed to fit the part of stereotypical Mafia don, complete with big cigar and sycophantic entourage." Ross, p. 181.

53 Tenet, George, with Harlow, Bill. *At the Center of the Storm: My Years at the CIA.* New York: HarperCollins, 2007. p. 87–96.

54 "A $2.13 packet of bacon from a supermarket in Langley in 1981" according to Drumheller, p. 174.

55 Steve Kappes and Michael Sulick resigned. By all accounts Kappes and Sulick were among the best of the CIA's mandarins. The CIA's problems are structural and not the fault of individuals. Nevertheless, I would have been happy to see all of the CIA's mandarins cleaned out of HQs with a fire hose.

56 Maas, Peter. *Manhunt: The Dramatic Pursuit of a CIA Agent Turned Terrorist.* New York: Simon & Schuster, 1986.

57 Bagley, Tennent H. *Spy Wars: Moles, Mysteries, and Deadly Games.* New Haven: Yale University Press, 2007, p. 191.

58 The debate continues today about whether Nosenko was a true defector or a dangle sent by the KGB to spread disinformation—possibly even sent to avert suspicion of Soviet involvement in the Kennedy assassination. Both sides present strong arguments. However, the real issue in evaluating the Nosenko case may not have been the question of whether or not he was a true defector, but of his usefulness to the CIA bureaucracy. Dozens of Agency officers spent years handling his imprisonment and interrogation, looking busy, earning promotions, capturing new turf at HQs, and avoiding difficult and risky foreign service. Nosenko may not have been a pawn in the battle between CIA and KGB, but a pawn of bureaucracy, a man used to help create a boondoggle and the illusion of activity.

59 *Washington Post*, May 13, 2006.

60 CNN, February 13, 2007.

61 Paseman, p. 43.

62 Smith, Russell Jack. *The Unknown CIA: My Three Decades with the Agency.* Washington, D.C.: Pergamon-Brassey's, 1989.

63   Weiner, Tim. *Legacy of Ashes: The History of the CIA*. New York: Doubleday, 2007, p. 160.

64   "Within the Agency, our failure to penetrate the North Vietnamese government was the single most frustrating aspect of those years." Helms, Richard M., and Hood, William. *A Look Over My Shoulder: A Life in the Central Intelligence Agency*. New York: Random House, 2003, p. 318.

65   tompeters.com, March 26, 2006.

66   Hanson, Victor Davis. *Carnage and Culture: Landmark Battles in the Rise of Western Power*. New York: Doubleday, 2001, p. 433.

Bibliography

Agee, Philip. *Inside the Company: CIA Diary*. New York: Stonehill Publishing, 1975.

Alibek, Ken, with Handelman, Stephen. *Biohazard: The Chilling True Story of the Largest Covert Biological Weapons Program in the World—Told from Inside by the Man Who Ran It*. New York: Dell, 1999.

Andrew, Christopher, and Gordievsky, Oleg. *KGB: The Inside Story of Its Foreign Operations from Lenin to Gorbachev*. New York: HarperCollins, 1990.

Baer, Robert. *See No Evil: The True Story of a Ground Soldier in the CIA's War on Terrorism*. New York: Crown, 2002.

Bagley, Tennent H. *Spy Wars: Moles, Mysteries, and Deadly Games*. New Haven: Yale University Press, 2007.

Bearden, Milton, and Risen, James. *The Main Enemy: The Inside Story of the CIA's Final Showdown with the KGB*. New York: Random House, 2003.

Berntsen, Gary and Pezzullo, Ralph. *Jawbreaker: The Attack on Bin Laden and Al-Qaeda: A Personal Account by the CIA's Key Field Commander*. New York: Crown, 2005.

Boot, Max. *The Savage Wars of Peace: Small Wars and the Rise of American Power*. New York: Basic Books, 2002.

Boot, Max. *War Made New: Technology, Warfare, and the Course of History: 1500 to Today*. New York: Gotham Books, 2006.

Borovik, Artyom. *The Hidden War: A Russian Journalist's Account of the Soviet War in Afghanistan*. New York: Atlantic Monthly Press, 1990.

Bowden, Mark. *Black Hawk Down: A Story of Modern War.* New York: Atlantic Monthly Press, 1999.

Brookner, Janine M. *Piercing the Veil of Secrecy: Litigation against U.S. Intelligence.* Durham, NC: Carolina Academic Press, 2003.

Brown, Anthony Cave. *Treason in the Blood: H. St. John Philby, Kim Philby, and the Spy Case of the Century.* New York: Houghton Mifflin, 1994.

Budiansky, Stephen. *Battle of Wits: The Complete Story of Codebreaking in World War II.* New York: Free Press, 2000.

Clarridge, Duane R. and Diehl, Digby. *A Spy for All Seasons: My Life in the CIA.* New York: Scribner, 1997.

Cockburn, Andrew and Cockburn, Leslie. *Dangerous Liaison: the Inside Story of the U.S.-Israeli Covert Relationship.* New York: HarperCollins, 1991.

Colby, William. *Honorable Men: My Life in the CIA.* New York: Simon & Schuster, 1978.

Coll, Steve. *Ghost Wars: The Secret History of the CIA, Afghanistan, and Bin Laden, from the Soviet Invasion to September 10, 2001.* New York: Penguin, 2004.

Corn, David. *Blond Ghost: Ted Shackley and the CIA's Crusades.* New York: Simon & Schuster, 1994.

Crile, George. *Charlie Wilson's War: The Extraordinary Story of the Largest Covert Operation in History.* New York: Atlantic Monthly Press, 2003.

Devlin, Larry. *Chief of Station, Congo: Fighting the Cold Way in a Hot Zone.* New York: PublicAffairs, 2007.

Doyle, David W. *True Men and Traitors: From the OSS to the CIA, My Life in the Shadows.* New York: John Wiley & Sons, 2001.

Drumheller, Tyler. *On the Brink: An Insider's Account of How the White House Compromised American Intelligence.* New York: Carroll & Graf, 2006.

Earley, Pete. *Family of Spies: Inside the Walker Spy Ring.* New York: Bantam Books, 1988.

Epstein, Edward Jay. *Deception: The Invisible War between the KGB and the CIA.* New York: Simon & Schuster, 1989.

Franks, Tommy with McConnell, Malcolm. *American Soldier*. New York: Harper Collins, 2004.

Gates, Robert M. *From the Shadows: The Ultimate Insider's Story of Five Presidents and How They Won the Cold War*. New York: Simon & Schuster, 1996.

Glees, Anthony. *The Secrets of the Service: A Story of Soviet Subversion of Western Intelligence*. New York: Carroll & Graf Publishers, 1987.

Greene, Graham. *The Human Factor*. London: Book Club Associates, 1978.

Graham, Bob, with Nussbaum, Jeff. *Intelligence Matters: The CIA, the FBI, Saudi Arabia, and the Failure of America's War on Terror*. New York: Random House, 2004.

Gup, Ted. *The Book of Honor: Covert Lives and Classified Deaths at the CIA*. New York: Doubleday, 2000.

Hanson, Victor Davis. *Carnage and Culture: Landmark Battles in the Rise of Western Power*. New York: Doubleday, 2001.

Hart, John Limond. *The CIA's Russians*. Annapolis, Maryland: US Naval Institute Press, 2003.

Helms, Richard M., and Hood, William. *A Look Over My Shoulder: A Life in the Central Intelligence Agency*. New York: Random House, 2003.

Hitz, Frederick P. *The Great Game: The Myth and Reality of Espionage*. New York: Knopf, 2004.

Holm, Richard L. *The American Agent: My Life in the CIA*. London: St. Ermin's Press, 2003.

Hopkirk, Peter. *The Great Game: The Struggle for Empire in Central Asia*. New York: Kodansha International, 1992.

Howard, Edward Lee. *Safe House: The Compelling Memoirs of the only CIA Spy to Seek Asylum in Russia*. Bethesda: National Press Books, 1995.

Kessler, Ronald. *The CIA at War: Inside the Secret Campaign Against Terror*. New York: St. Martin's Press, 2003.

Kolb, Larry J. *Overworld: The Life and Times of a Reluctant Spy*. New York: Riverhead, 2004.

Lindsey, Robert. *The Falcon and the Snowman: A True Story of Friendship and Espionage*. New York: Simon & Schuster, 1979.

Maas, Peter. *Manhunt: The Dramatic Pursuit of a CIA Agent Turned Terrorist*. New York: Simon & Schuster, 1986.

Mahle, Melissa Boyle. *Denial and Deception: An Insider's View of the CIA from Iran-Contra to 9/11*. New York: Nation Books, 2005.

Marchetti, Victor and Marks, John D. *The CIA and the Cult of Intelligence*. New York: Knopf, 1974.

Martin, David C. *Wilderness of Mirrors*. New York: Harper, 1980.

Masters, Anthony. *The Man Who Was M: The Life of Maxwell Knight*. New York: Basil Blackwell, 1984.

McGehee, Ralph W. *Deadly Deceits: My 25 Years in the CIA*. New York: Sheridan Square Publications, 1983.

Mendez, Antonio J. *The Master of Disguise: My Secret Life in the CIA*. New York: William Morrow and Co., 1999.

Moran, Lindsay. *Blowing My Cover: My Life as a CIA Spy*. New York: Penguin, 2005.

National Commission on Terrorist Attacks. *The 9/11 Commission Report: final Report of the National Commission on Terrorist Attacks upon the United States*. New York: W.W. Norton, 2004.

Ostrovsky, Victor, and Hoy, Claire. *By Way of Deception: The Making and Unmaking of a Mossad Officer*. New York: St. Martin's Press, 1990.

Ostrovsky, Victor. *The Other Side of Deception: A Rogue Agent Exposes the Mossad's Secret Agenda*. New York: HarperCollins, 1994.

Paseman, Floyd L. *A Spy's Journey: A CIA Memoir*. St. Paul: Zenith Press, 2004.

Prados, John. *Lost Crusader: The Secret Wars of CIA Director William Colby*. New York: Oxford University Press, 2003.

Qaddhafi, Muammar. (variants: Gathafi, Qaddafi, Gaddafi). *The Green Book: The Solution to the Problem of Democracy, The Solutions to the Economic Problem, The Social Basis of the Third Universal Theory*. Tripoli: Libyan government press, 1975.

Raviv, Dan, and Melman, Yossi. *Every Spy a Prince: The Complete History of Israel's Intelligence Community.* Boston: Houghton Mifflin, 1990.

Riebling, Mark. *Wedge: The Secret War between the FBI and CIA.* New York: Alfred A. Knopf, 1994.

Ross, Michael, and Kay, Jonathan. *The Volunteer: A Canadian's Secret Life in the Mossad.* Toronto: McClelland & Stewart, 2007.

Scahill, Jeremy. *Blackwater: The Rise of the World's Most Powerful Mercenary Army.* New York: Nation Books, 2007.

Scarborough, Rowan. *Sabotage: America's Enemies Within the CIA.* Washington, DC: Regnery, 2007.

Scheuer, Michael. *Imperial Hubris: Why the West is Losing the War on Terror.* Dulles, Virginia: Potomac Books, 2004.

Schroen, Gary C. *First In: An Insider's Account of How the CIA Spearheaded the War on Terror in Afghanistan.* New York: Presidio Press, 2005.

Secord, Richard, with Wurts, Jay. *Honored and Betrayed: Irangate, Covert Affairs, and the Secret War in Laos.* New York: John Wiley, 1992.

Sims, Jennifer E. and Gerber, Burton eds. *Transforming US Intelligence.* Washington, D.C.: Georgetown University Press, 2005.

Singh, Simon. *The Code Book: The Evolution of Secrecy from Mary, Queen of Scots to Quantum Cryptography.* New York: Doubleday, 1999.

Smith, Joseph Burkholder. *Portrait of a Cold Warrior.* New York: G.P. Putnam's Sons, 1976.

Smith, Russell Jack. *The Unknown CIA: My Three Decades with the Agency.* Washington, D.C.: Pergamon-Brassey's, 1989.

Snepp, Frank. *Decent Interval: An Insider's Account of Saigon's Indecent End, Told by the CIA's Chief Strategy Analyst in Vietnam.* New York: Random House, 1977.

Snepp, Frank. *Irreparable Harm: A Firsthand Account of How One Agent Took On the CIA in an Epic Battle Over Secrecy and Free Speech.* New York: Random House, 1999.

Stockwell, John. *In Search of Enemies: A CIA Story.* New York: W.W. Norton, 1978.

Sullivan, John F.: *Gatekeeper: Memoirs of a CIA Polygraph Examiner*. Dulles, Virginia: Potomac Books, 2007.

Tenet, George, with Harlow, Bill. *At the Center of the Storm: My Years at the CIA*. New York: HarperCollins, 2007.

Turner, Stansfield. *Burn Before Reading: Presidents, CIA Directors, and Secret Intelligence*. New York: Hyperion, 2005.

Turner, Stansfield. *Secrecy and Democracy: the CIA in Transition*. New York: Houghton Mifflin, 1985.

Vise, David A. *The Bureau and the Mole: The Unmasking of Robert Philip Hanssen, the Most Dangerous Double Agent in FBI History*. New York: Atlantic Monthly Press, 2002.

Waters, T.J. *Class 11: Inside the CIA's First Post-9/11 Spy Class*. New York: Dutton, 2006.

Weber, Ralph ed. *Spymasters: Ten CIA Officers in Their Own Words*. Wilmington, Delaware: SR Books, 1998.

Weiner, Tim. *Legacy of Ashes: the History of the CIA*. New York: Doubleday, 2007.

Wilson, Valerie Plame. *Fair Game: My Life as a Spy, My Betrayal by the White House*. New York: Simon & Schuster, 2007.

Wise, David. *The Spy Who Got Away: The Inside Story of Edward Lee Howard, the CIA Agent Who Betrayed His Country's Secrets and Escaped to Moscow*. New York: Random House, 1988.

Wise, David. *Molehunt: The Secret Search for Traitors That Shattered the CIA*. New York: Random House, 1992.

Wise, David. *Nightmover: How Aldrich Ames Sold the CIA to the KGB for $4.6 Million*. New York: HarperCollins, 1995.

Wolf, Markus. *The Man Without a Face: The Autobiography of Communism's Greatest Spymaster*. New York: Crown, 1997.

Woodward, Bob. *Veil: The Secret Wars of the CIA 1981 – 1987*. New York: Simon & Schuster, 1987.

Woodward, Bob. *Bush at War*. New York: Simon & Schuster, 2002.

Index